Automatic Perimetry in Glaucoma
A Practical Guide

Automatic Perimetry in Glaucoma
A Practical Guide

Edited by

Stephen M. Drance, M.D.

Professor and Head
Department of Ophthalmology
University of British Columbia
Vancouver, British Columbia

Douglas R. Anderson, M.D.

Professor
Department of Ophthalmology
Bascom Palmer Eye Institute
University of Miami School of Medicine
Miami, Florida

Grune & Stratton, Inc.
(Harcourt Brace Jovanovich, Publishers)

Orlando   San Diego   New York
London   Toronto   Montreal   Sydney   Tokyo

Library of Congress Cataloging in Publication Data
Main entry under title:

Automatic perimetry in glaucoma.

  Based on a symposium held in Vancouver on May 11, 1984.
  Includes index.
  1. Perimetry—Congresses.   2. Glaucoma—Diagnosis—
Congresses.   I. Drance, Stephen M.   II. Anderson,
Douglas R., 1938–   . [DNLM: 1. Glaucoma—congresses.
2. Perimetry—congresses.   3. Visual Fields—congresses.
WW 290 A939 1984]
RE79.P4A98   1985   617.7'41   85-8069
ISBN 0-8089-1705-6

Grune & Stratton, Inc.
Orlando, FL 32887

Distributed in the United Kingdom by
Grune & Stratton, Ltd.
24/28 Oval Road, London NW 1

Library of Congress Catalog Number 85-8069
International Standard Book Number 0-8089-1705-6
Printed in the United States of America
85 86 87 88   10 9 8 7 6 5 4 3 2 1

Contents

Preface

The explosion of computer technology and the advent of static perimetry resulted in the development of automatic computerized perimetry. Perimetry has always been an important diagnostic tool for the glaucomas and is essential for monitoring the progression of the established disease. Good perimetry is an art that requires skilled professional or paraprofessional personnel. The shortage of time and appropriate technical help has resulted in relatively poor standards of manual perimetry throughout the world. Automatic perimetry has changed that because once software was created to measure thresholds both screening and quantitation became available. It is now possible to obtain high quality visual fields without having highly trained technicians.

The International Perimetric Society organized a symposium on automatic perimetry at the International Congress of Ophthalmology in San Francisco in 1982. With some notable additions the group of participants was reassembled in Vancouver on the 11th of May, 1984 for the purposes of presenting a symposium on the current state of the art of automatic perimetry in the management of glaucoma. It seemed desirable to bring together in a book the theoretical principles, a description of existing instruments and their software, as well as guidelines for their appropriate use in the management and detection of the glaucomas.

We wish to thank the participants for the promptness with which they presented their written material and hope that the collation of this material will be interesting to ophthalmologists interested in automatic perimetry and in the management of patients with glaucoma. We want to acknowledge the great help provided by Reva Hurtes, the librarian at the Bascom Palmer Eye Institute in verifying all the references. We also want to thank Cilco Canada, Inc. for financial support in defraying some of the expenses of the symposium on which this book is based.

Douglas R. Anderson, M.D.

Stephen M. Drance, M.D.

Contributors

Douglas R. Anderson, M.D.
Professor
Department of Ophthalmology
Bascom Palmer Eye Institute
University of Miami Medical School
Miami, Florida

Hans Bebie, Ph.D.
Professor
Institute for Theoretical Physics
University of Bern
Bern, Switzerland

Stephen M. Drance, M.D.
Professor and Head
Department of Ophthalmology
Eye Care Center
University of British Columbia
Vancouver, British Columbia

Josef Flammer, M.D.
University Eye Clinic
Inselspital
Bern, Switzerland

Erik L. Greve, M.D.
Glaucoma and Visual Field Department
Eye Clinic of the University of Amsterdam
Amsterdam, The Netherlands

Anders Heijl, M.D.
Department of Ophthalmology
University of Lund
Malmo, Sweden

Chris A. Johnson, M.D.
Department of Ophthalmology
University of California, Davis
Davis, California

John Keltner, M.D.
Chairman, Department of Ophthalmology
Professor of Opthalmology, Neurology, and
Neurological Surgery
University of California, Davis
Davis, California

Ray LeBlanc, M.D.
Professor and Head
Department of Ophthalmology
Delhousie University
Halifax, Nova Scotia

Richard P. Mills, M.D.
Associate Professor
Department of Ophthalmology
University of Washington
Seattle, Washington

Charles D. Phelps, M.D.
Professor and Head
Department of Ophthalmology
University Hospital
Iowa City, Iowa

George W. Tate, Jr., M.D.
Carolina Eye Associates
Southern Pines, North Carolina

Automatic Perimetry in Glaucoma
A Practical Guide

The Physiological Basis for Perimetry

George W. Tate, Jr.

Schliesslich, möchte Ich betonen, dass Perimetrie, besonders kinetische Perimetrie, eine Kunst ist. Hans Goldmann, 1969.[1]

Since its inception, perimetry has shared much in common with medicine in general. Both are considered to be an art by their greatest practitioners, an art that demands its disciple make a never ending series of judgments based on scientific knowledge on one hand and empiricism based upon experience on the other. Like medicine, perimetry has benefited in recent years from an increasing amount of investigation that strengthens its scientific basis, and of increasing computerization, which serves to transport the skills of the great perimetrists into even the most humble clinic. Unfortunately, an understanding of perimetry does not travel so easily, which all too frequently means the true significance of the results is misunderstood. Indeed, it does very little good for a practitioner to know that two sets of visual fields are indeed significantly different statistically if he is unaware that he himself has artifactitiously created that difference. This chapter gives the reader insight into the basic physiology underlying the decisions that are necessary in day to day perimetry, whether by manual or automatic means. We will also spend a very small amount of time discussing the physics of light, and the anatomy of the visual system to better understand the physiology of how they interact to produce the visual field.

LIGHT

Light is simply radiant energy with the unique property of perception by the human eye. Other than its physiologic impact, it is very much like other portions of the electromagnetic spectrum and can be handled mathematically much as energy in the far infrared or ultraviolet regions of the spectrum that is not visible. This simple and obvious fact, that light can be seen, has unfortunately led to a number of confusing conventions when it comes to the measurement of light. The physicist may simply consider light to be energy and apply the same units of measurement to light as he would to any other type of radiant energy, that is, a radiance-based system. The power output from a light bulb could thus be measured in watts, the energy falling on a surface in watts per square meter, and so on. Other measurement systems have been developed based on the visible properties of light and the conviction that what should be measured is the ability of the light to be seen, a very practical point of view for those involved in disciplines such as illumination engineering or perimetry. These luminance-based schemes are founded on the varying sensitivity of the eye to different colors (wavelengths) of light. The normal light-adapted eye is most sensitive to green light with a wavelength of 555 nm, and the eye's sensitivity falls to zero as wavelength shifts toward either the infrared or ultraviolet ends of the spectrum. A conversion between luminance and radiance measurements can be made simply by multiplying the radiant energy at a given wavelength by the relative efficiency of the eye to that wavelength, resulting in the luminous flux for that particular light.

Unfortunately, there have developed over the years a number of different measurement systems that have led to a confusion in terminology seldom achieved

AUTOMATIC PERIMETRY IN GLAUCOMA
ISBN 0–8089–1705–6

Table 1-1
Interconversion of Units of Luminance

From To . . .	Nit	Apostilb	Milli-lambert	Lambert	Ft-Lambert	Candela/ Ft²	Candela/ in.²	Stilb
(Candela/m²) NIT	1	3,142	0.3142	0.0003142	0.2919	0.0929	0.000645	0.0001
Apostilb (Blondel, equivalent lux)	.3183	1	0.1	0.0001	0.09291	0.02957	0.0002054	0.00003183
Millilambert	3.183	10	1	0.001	0.9291	0.2957	0.002054	0.0003183
Lambert (Equivalent phot)	3183	10000	1000	1	929.1	295.7	2.054	0.3183
Foot-Lambert (Equivalent ft-candle)	3.426	10.76	1.076	0.001076	1	0.3183	0.00221	0.0003426
Candela/ft²	10.764	33.82	3.382	0.00338	3.142	1	0.00694	0.001076
Candela/in.²	1550	4870	487	0.487	452.4	144	1	0.155
Stilb (Candela/cm²)	10000	31420	3142	3.142	2919	929	6.45	1

since the attempt to construct the Tower of Babel. Fortunately, most of these terms are being discarded in favor of the Commission Internationale de L'Eclairage (CIE) standard, where the basic unit of luminance is the Candela per meter squared (or the Nit). The American literature may still contain the term millilambert, whereas the European literature occasionally uses the apostilb as units of measurement for luminance. The table of conversion between the various units of luminance and illumination may be seen in Tables 1-1 and 1-2, respectively. Radiometric units, however, are also used in perimetry. Many workers in the field of color perimetry, especially where narrow bandwidth light is used, feel that making a luminance conversion is inappropriate since that is, in essence, what is being measured by the experiment. These workers still use the radiometric units when reporting their results. The term corresponding to brightness (luminance) is radiance, whereas illuminance corresponds to irradiance. Despite the difference in concept, however, the two groups of units may be treated very much the same.

Two related terms that may cause some confusion are the log unit (Lu) and the decibel (db). A log unit is simply the logarithm base 10 of the chosen unit (e.g., asb., ml, Troland, etc.). Each log unit thus corresponds to a power of 10 of the base unit (e.g., 2 log units = 100,

base units). Moreover, since units may be converted by multiplication of a constant, log units may be interconverted by the addition of a constant. The magnitude of a change in luminance expressed in log units is thus independent of the base unit. A decibel is simply 0.1 Lu.

From the physiologists' point of view, however, even though most perimetrists measure the brightness of both the background and the test spots at the bowl, what is of real interest is the brightness of the image of the retina, since this is what determines retinal function. Attempts have been made in the past to quantitate this by the unit of brightness measurement called the Troland, which is essentially nothing more than the product of the target luminance by the pupillary area. This was first proposed by Troland in 1922 and was defined as the luminance of 1 candela per square meter seen through a pupil of 1 square millimeter in area.[2] Unfortunately, the Troland suffers from at least two problems, that of hazy media and the Stiles-Crawford effect, the former being far more pertinent for the clinical perimetrist. The Stiles-Crawford effect can be predicted and corrected (at least to some small extent) by a variety of mathematical manipulations, but the problem of cloudy media does not lend itself to mathematical attack because of the irregularity and unpredictability of the cloudiness induced by cataract, vitreous opacities, or corneal problems. Moreover, these effects have a very nonlinear effect as a function of pupil size. Most clinical perimetrists have abandoned the attempt to calculate retinal illuminance in the patient population. However, the fact that this cannot be done accurately does not mean that the perimetrist should not always remember that the important variable is the actual retinal illumination. Items such as media turbidity and pupil size must be noted and recorded when performing and interpreting perimetric tests or in comparing the results of perimeters one to another that use differing values for background illumination. (Table 1-3).

Table 1-2
Interconversion of Units of Illumination

From To . . .	Lux	Phot	Milliphot	Ft-Candle
Lux (Meter/Candle, Lumen/m²)	1	0.0001	0.1	0.0929
Phot (Lumen/cm²)	10000	1	1000	929
Milliphot	10	0.001	1	.929
Foot-Candle (Lumen/ft²)	10.764	0.0010764	1.0764	1

Those workers who choose to use color perimetry have additional variables with which to contend. Light of different wavelengths produces the sensation of different colors. Light with a wavelength of 430 nm is violet, 460 nm thus corresponds to blue, and so on up through 650 nm, which is red. Light that is monochromatic appears to be undiluted and the addition of white light makes the color appear desaturated. Colored light is thus traditionally described in terms of three variables: hue (or wavelength), saturation (or purity), and brightness (or radiance). To make matters more difficult, the hue of any color may be matched by a mixture of two or more colors. Because of this the light radiating from two test objects that appear identical in hue and saturation may have a very different spectral composition and thus conceivably could have different stimulus values. Workers in the field have recently recognized this fact and now use interference filters or lasers to provide a monochromatic light source.[3–5]

ANATOMY AND PHYSIOLOGY OF THE RETINA

Anatomy and physiology of the retina has been studied in detail in recent years by a number of authors.[6–11] This section is necessarily brief, but more detailed reviews are available.[12,13]

The retina is classically divided into ten layers, only five of which are pertinent to this discussion. The cell bodies of the retinal neurons are found in three layers, the outer nuclei, the inner nuclei, and the ganglion cell layer, whereas most synapses occur within two layers, the inner and the outer plexiform layers. In the outer plexiform layer, where the first information transfer occurs, receptor cells synapse with bipolar and horizontal cells. The horizontal cells are a horizontal association cell that transmits information sideways along the retina. These three cell types do not exhibit spike potentials but rather transmit analogue potentials across their synapses proportional to the intensity of the light falling upon the retina.[6] The function of the receptor cell is to receive light and generate a potential that is in turn transmitted to the bipolar cell, thence to the ganglion cell. However, the horizontal cells serve to inhibit this transfer taking place between receptor and the bipolar cells, which are some distance away from its point of origin. It is felt that this organization is responsible for simple receptive field organization, which will be discussed later. In the inner plexiform layer, synaptic contact occurs between the bipolar, ganglion, and amacrine cells. Amacrine cells are also horizontal association cells, loosely analogous to horizontal cells. Unlike the bipolar and horizontal cells, the electrical activity of the amacrine and ganglion cells is not a constant potential, but rather a series of spike potentials of graded frequency.[6,9,11,14] The amacrine cells are considered inhibitory and are responsible for motion-sensitive cells and complex receptive fields that respond only to the movement of the stimulus. This information is summarized in Fig. 1-1.

THE CENTER-SURROUND AND THE RECEPTIVE FIELD

With all the rich lateral interconnections anatomically available in the retina, a ganglion cell not only will be influenced by light falling near it, but by light a short distance away as well. The area over which light has some effect is called the cells' receptive field. Different cells may be affected differently. Indeed, ganglion cells can be divided in three types on the basis of their response to a small spot of light that explores the retina and various differences from the cell body. The first type of these is called the "on-cell", which increases its rate discharge when the retina in the vicinity of the cell itself is illuminated by a spot of light. The second type is called an "off-cell"[15] and ceases activity when the retina near the cell is illuminated (Fig. 1-2). In the case of these two cell types, when the illuminating spot of light is applied at distances slightly further away, that is to the surround, the effect elicited is opposite from that seen when the spot lies over the center of the cell's receptive field.[16,17] On-cells are thus turned off by illumination in the surround and conversely for off-cells. This arrangement is generally referred to as the "center-surround" organization of the receptive fields, and the above two types are called on-centered and off-centered fields, respectively. This receptive field behavior has been examined in humans by Westheimer[18–20], Teller,[21–25] and Enoch et al.[26–31]

The third type of receptive field described by a number of workers,[32–34] can only be mapped with moving spots of light. The ganglion cells in this field are called on-off ganglion cells, which respond best although not exclusively to spots or edges of light that are moving in a specific direction.[35,36] A shadow moving through the field may be just as effective as a spot of light itself. The activity of these types of cells is mediated by the amacrine cells and, indeed, the infor-

Table 1-3
Background Luminance of Standard Perimeters

	Apostilb	cd/m²
Goldmann	31.5	10
Tuebinger	10	3.18
Competer	3.14, .315, 3.15, 31.5	0.1, 1.0, 10
Octopus	4	1.27
Squid	settable, 1–120	0 to 38.2
Humphrey	31.5	10
Peritest/Perimat	3.15	1.0
Dicon	0, 10, 31.5, 45	0, 3.18, 10, 14.3

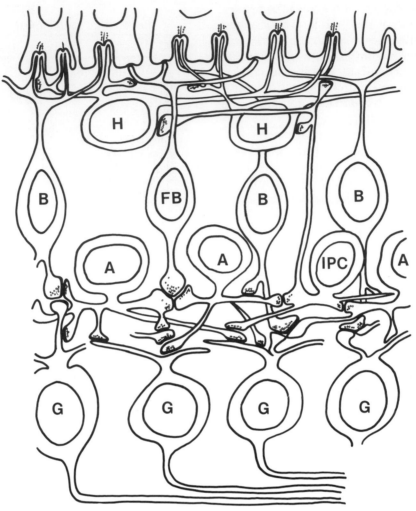

Fig. 1-1. A summary of the interconnections described in the vertebrate retina. In the outer plexiform layer, bipolar cells (B) and horizontal cells (H) send processes into invagonations in the receptor terminals, while flat bipolar cells (FB) make superficial contact with receptor terminals. The interplexiform cell (IPC) makes synaptic connection with the perikarya of horizontal cells or bipolar dendrites, but never with receptors. In the inner plexiform layer bipolar cells synapse with amacrine cells (A) and ganglion cells (G) in any combination. Amacrine cells may synapse with other amacrine cells, ganglion cells, or the interplexiform cell. The IPC may in turn synapse back onto amacrine cells, but never ganglion cells. (*Modified from Dowling, Ref. 6*)

mation flow to these cells is not the simple receptor-bipolar-ganglion cell pathway previously described, but rather receptor-bipolar-amacrine-ganglion cell.

Regional differences in the distribution of the rods and cones as well as the pattern of the interconnections provide another dimension to the psychophysics of the retina. Osterberg[37] has plotted the number of rods and cones in the average retina as a function of perimetric angle (Fig. 3-3). The cones are found in greatest numbers in the fovea where they are connected in a 1 cone to 1 bipolar to 1 ganglion cell pattern. There are no rods in the fovea but the number of rods increases quite rapidly up to about 20 degrees eccentricity, after which the number falls off gradually. In the peripheral retina, several receptors converge upon fewer bipolar and even fewer ganglion cells arranged into a singular

functional unit. There are 135,000 rods per square millimeter, 19 degrees from fixation, and only a total of perhaps as many as 1,000,000 ganglion cells in the entire eye. An intermediate number of bipolar cells suggests a 10:1 ratio between sensory elements and interconnecting cells and a similar 10:1 ratio between bipolar cells and the ganglion cells. This average system, however, only exists in a small part of the retina. As has been stated, there is a 1:1 ratio in the fovea of sensory and transmitting cells, whereas in the far periphery the ratio goes as high as 100:1 or perhaps even greater.[38] Of course, this variable organization of the retina is reflected in many aspects of retinal function, such as a rather good visual acuity at the fovea, which falls precipitously in the periphery (Fig. 1-4), the variation in perimetric thresholds (Fig. 1-5), the variation in the size of the receptive field across the retina, and the marked difference in the light and dark adaptation behavior of the retina between the center and the periphery. It is of interest that if the variation in receptive field size with eccentricity is compensated by dividing the perimetric threshold of a given locus by the visual acuity at that point, much of the variation in threshold disappears (Fig. 1-6).

DARK ADAPTATION IN THE VISUAL FIELD

Varying the state of dark adaptation of the subject varies the result of the perimetric exam in a variety of ways, none of which is necessarily desirable and all of which are important if reproducability is to be maintained. In the first and most obvious case, it changes the overall sensitivity of the retina. This is not, however, done in a simple linear fashion at each spot. The cones and rods dark adapt to different degrees with a different time course (Fig. 1-7). This introduces a change not only in the height of the static profile across the retina, but in the loss of the central peak and the development of a small central scotoma with increasing amounts of dark adaptation.[39,40] Moreover, this introduces a time function into the perimetric equation that is not present to the same extent if one chooses a photopic test. For example, the cones are completely dark adapted in 5–10 minutes. However, the more peripheral portions of the retina can require as long as 30 min or even longer if the subject has been preadapted to extremely bright light.[41] If testing is done during this period, a variety of perimetric artifacts such as spiraling fields in the case of kinetic perimetry or increased scatter in the case of static perimetry will result.[13] Moreover, the basic operating curve of the retina shifts (Fig. 1-8) as one goes from the photopic into the scotopic range.[40] In the photopic range, the Weber-Fechner law ($\Delta I/I =$ constant) holds. In the far reaches of scotopic range, the relationship becomes simply $I =$ constant. The relationship describing this transition is, according to Barlow,[42] $\Delta I/(I + ID) =$ constant, where ID is the "dark light" or "Eigengrau," the photon and neuron noise of the eye. If all were simple, at very low light levels, $\Delta I =$ constant would be approximated by the formula, which at higher levels, the Weber-Fechner law would apply with a transitional zone in between. Unfortunately, things are not that simple. It is frequently stated that the Rose-deVries law ($\Delta I/\sqrt{I} =$ constant) holds in the low photopic or mesopic regions,[42] but, as Barlow points out[42] the Weber-Fechner law may hold well into the scotopic regions, while the Rose-deVries law may hold well into the photopic region. It seems that an equation of the form $\Delta I/(I)^K = C$ is appropriate, with K ranging between 0.5 and 1, depending on variables such as background brightness, stimulus size, color, and duration. Frankhauser points out that under the conditions

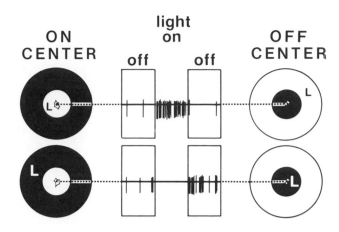

Fig. 1-2. Center-surround organization. Two possible organizations were illustrated, the "on-center" (left) and the "off-center" (right) are illustrated. In the top illustration, a light (L) in the center of an on-center field or the surround of an off-center field causes the cell to discharge. In the bottom illustration, when the light is changed to the surround with the on-center field or the center of the off-center field, the discharge from the cell ceases.

of clinical static perimetry, the Rose-deVries law holds for the currently available perimeters, both manual and automatic.[43] In any event, as long as one operates in a linear region of retinal response, all shifts in background brightness result in no shift in the threshold provided the stimulus and background illumination come from the same light source. This is found in any clinical perimeters such as the Goldmann perimeter or even the tangent screen devices that use reflective targets. It seems that the more one departs from the photopic range, the more stringently background and test brightness must be controlled.

The degree of light or dark adaptation depends on how much light reaches the retina. This is influenced not only by the background illuminance, but also by the pupil size and the amount of light that might be absorbed by ocular media, such as a nuclear cataract. A given level of background intensity may thus be in the photopic range for a normal sized or dilated pupil, but may come to be in the mesopic range for a constricted pupil in the presence of cataract. If the bowl illuminance is made low to increase the dynamic range for testing, one runs the risk that $\Delta I/I$ does not remain constant and that the threshold values obtained (ΔI) during perimetry will be affected by a change in pupil size from one occasion to another.

Chromatic stimuli are also greatly affected by dark adaptation as is shown in Figs. 1-9, 1-10, 1-11, and 1-12. It can be seen that sensitivity to red stimuli increases only slightly and no central scotoma develops to red test, whereas the magnitude of dark adaptation as well as the depth and the width of the central scotoma steadily increases as the wavelength of the test object shortens. This effect is of importance not only in the interpretation of the form of isopters of static

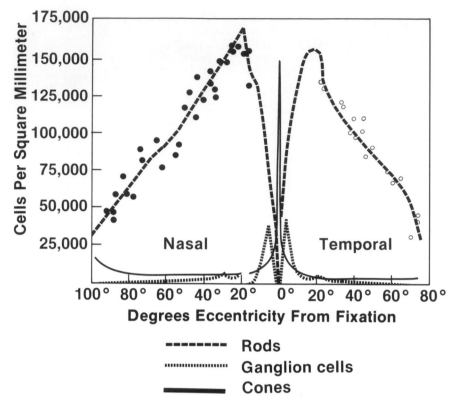

Fig. 1-3. Osterberg's curves for the horizontal meridian through the fovea. The abscissa is in perimetric degrees, while the ordinate gives the density of each cell type in cells per square millimeter.

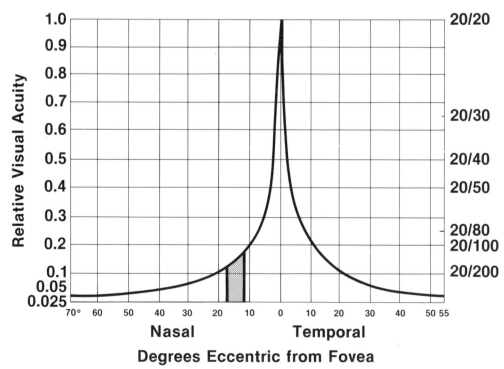

Fig. 1-4. Visual acuity as a functional or retinal location. The terms nasal and temporal refer to the retinal position being stimulated. The right ordinate gives visual acuity in Snellen notation, while the left ordinate gives the same data in decimal notations.

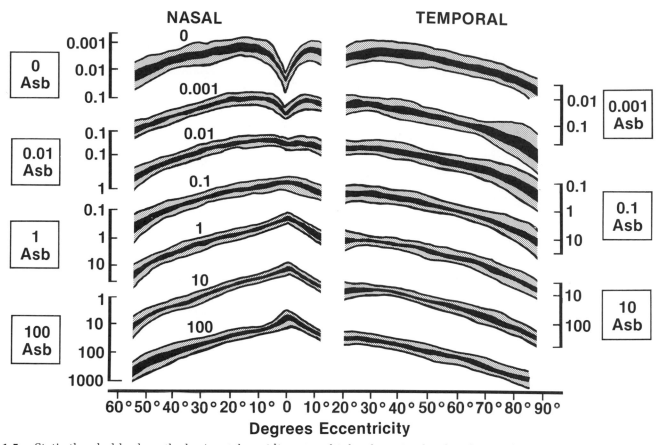

Fig. 1-5. Static thresholds along the horizontal meridian at multiple adaptation levels. The numbers above each curve give the adaptation level for each curve in Asb. Each ordinate gives the threshold brightness in Asb for a single static profile identified by the box beside it containing the background brightness in Asb. (*Redrawn from data kindly provided by Prof. Dr. E. Aulhorn.*)

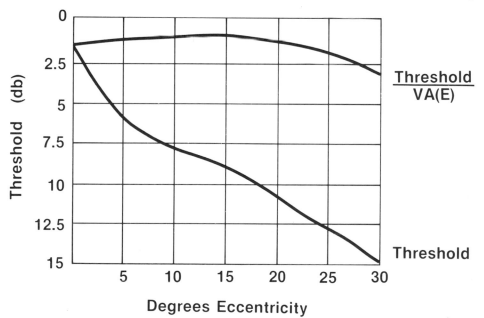

Fig. 1-6. A comparison of a static threshold curve (lower curve) and this same threshold data divided by the visual acuity at each point (upper curve). The threshold data was taken from Greve (Ref 55) while the visual acuity data was taken from Fig. 1-4. These curves represent pooled data.

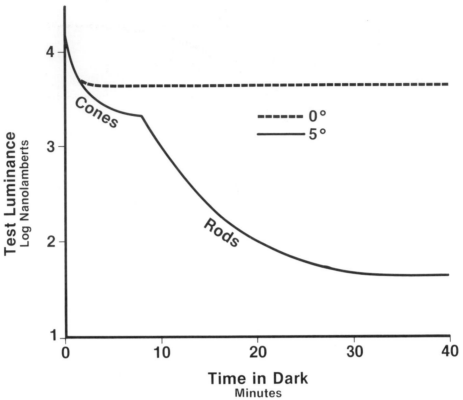

Fig. 1-7. Dark adaptation curves for the human at 0° and 5° eccentricity. Centrally, dark adaptation is virtually complete by 3 to 5 minutes, whereas at 5° the process continues for over 30 minutes. The form that these curves follow varies with retinal location. (*From Tate GW Jr, Lynn JR: Principles of Quantitative Perimetry: Testing and Interpreting the Visual Field. New York, Grune & Stratton, 1977. With permission.*)

meridia through these areas, but also in such mundane things such as the choice of color for fixation targets in the perimeter, with red the obvious choice since otherwise eccentric fixation is encouraged.

It is interesting that dark adaptation studies have been carried out by F. Dannheim[44] using test spots darker than background. The results are similar to those using lighter test objects, but the time course for the dark-point studies is a bit longer and larger test objects must be used.

The selection of an adaptation level and thus a background luminance also influences the dynamic range over which the perimeter can test. Fankhauser and Haeberlin[45] have pointed out that range of permissible test luminances is limited in brightness and that attempts to exceed this limit result in the scotoma under test being "filled in" by scattered light that exceeds the threshold of the surrounding healthy retina. The limit is determined by the product areas of the test spot and the luminance. It is roughly independent of background illumination. With small test objects, (such as Goldmann 0 and I) the test luminance required to reach this value is beyond the range of most, if not all, perimeters.

The lower end of the dynamic range of the perimeter is essentially the usual threshold of the normal retina, which itself is limited by photon and neuronal "noise," at least according to some models.[42,45,46] Since threshold test object brightness is lessened by using lower background luminance, the dynamic range of the perimeter may be maximized by choosing a low photopic (or perhaps even high mesopic) background, a test spot large enough to take full advantage of spatial summation, yet small enough to just barely reach the limit imposed by light scattering at maximal test spot brightness.[43]

LOCAL ADAPTATION

When an illuminated test spot is presented at various eccentricities from fixation to a perfectly fixating observer, the spot disappears after a few seconds. This phenomenon was first described by Troxler in 1804[47] and is therefore called the Troxler effect or local adaptation. It has been studied in detail by Cibis.[48,49] It occurs most rapidly at greater eccentricities from fixation and least rapidly near the fovea, with the center of fovea apparently never adapting at all. Curves of this phenomenon may be seen in Fig. 1-13. It is seen that for virtually the entire retina, the local adaptation phenomenon is complete within 2 min and that for the

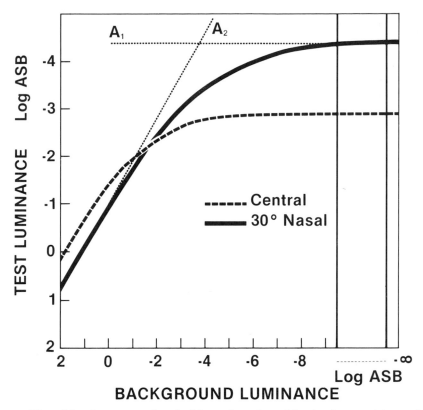

Fig. 1-8. Plot of log increment threshold as a function of log background intensity. At very low background luminances, the curves tend to parallel the abscissa (asymptote A1), while at high background luminances, the curves approach the abscissa with a slope of one (asymptote A2). This may be restated by saying that the curve in the photopic region approaches a state where contrast sensitivity ($\Delta L/L$) remains constant, whereas in the scotopic state, increment sensitivity (ΔL) remains constant. Note also that this transition occurs at higher background luminances centrally than peripherally. Thus, if a perimetric device is to be made maximally resistant to small changes in background luminance, testing should be confined to the linear regions of the curve. (*After Aulhorn and Harms, Ref. 40. With permission.*)

retina outside approximately five degrees, the local adaptation phenomenon is complete within 20 seconds. The phenomenon occurs during stimulation with white or colored stimuli, and will occur even if the colored stimulus has the same brightness as the background. Thus, it occurs not only with differences in brightness, but with differences in hue. Exactly what this phenomenon represents is not known, although it apparently does not involve the same mechanisms as adaptation of the retina by photochemical means.

The phenomenon was also investigated by Yarbus[50] who used miniature projectors fixed to contact lenses to provide absolutely stable retinal images. Yarbus reported that the entire field disappeared within 3 seconds, and that the center was not spared as reported by Cibis. It seems plausible that Cibis' results may thus be explained by the fact that peripherally, the receptive fields are large enough to keep the spot within them during the small movements that occur with even the best free fixation, whereas foveally this is not true.

From the standpoint of the perimetrist, the phenomenon of local adaptation is responsible for an increase in the threshold found in static perimetry if a test spot is gradually brightened as opposed to presenting multiple, interrupted stimuli of increasing brightnesses. The difference in the thresholds obtained by these two techniques varies depending on a number of factors but is on the order of 3 db.

FIXATION AND EYE MOVEMENT

To understand fully how some of the foregoing physiological information relates to the performance of visual field testing, it is necessary that we consider how eye movements interact with the anatomy and physiology of the retina and their effect upon the clinical visual field. It is thought that eye movements play a role in the phenomenon of local adaptation to prevent fading of the foveal image. They enhance the effect of borders within the visual field upon the horizontal association elements of the retina. Finally, although it should go without saying, the accuracy of the visual field test is limited by eye movement.

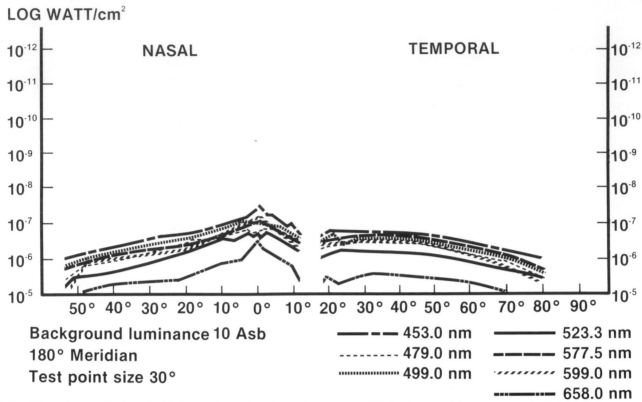

Fig. 1-9. Monochromatic threshold data, photopic adaptation range with background luminance of 10 Asb. Tests were with monochromatic light against a white background. Ordinate is test spot radiance in log W/cm². (*From Nolte W: Bestimmung achromatischer Schwellen für verschiedene Spektrallichter. Inaugural-Dissertation. Universität Tübingen, 1962. With permission.*)

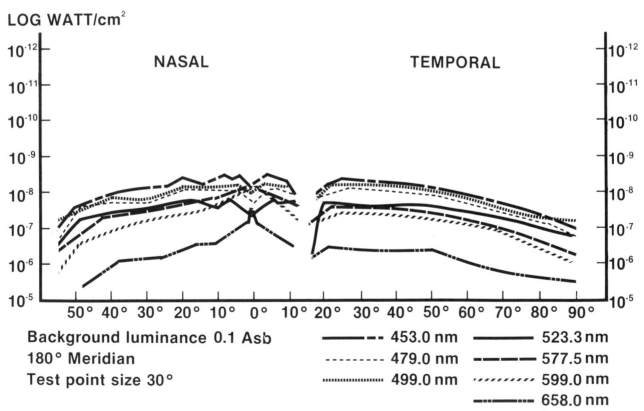

Fig. 1-10. Monochromatic threshold data, background luminance 0.1 Asb. All other data same as Fig. 1-8. (*From Nolte W: Bestimmung achromatischer Schwellen für verschiedene Spektrallichter. Inaugural-Dissertation. Universität Tübingen, 1962. With permission.*)

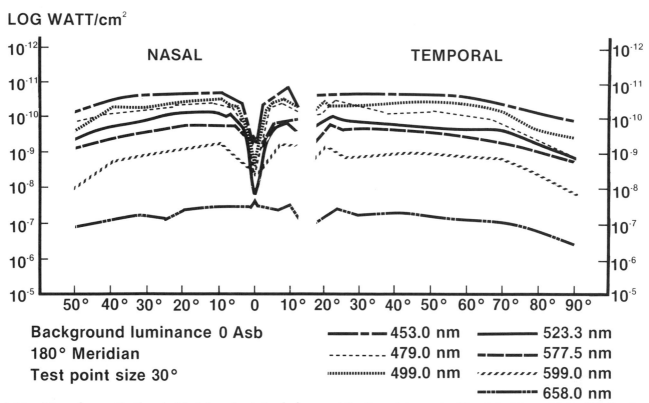

Fig. 1-11. Monochromatic threshold data, absolute darkness. All other data as in Fig. 1-8. (*From Nolte W: Bestimmung achromatischer Schwellen für verschiedene Spektrallichter. Inaugural-Dissertation. Universität Tübingen, 1962. With permission.*)

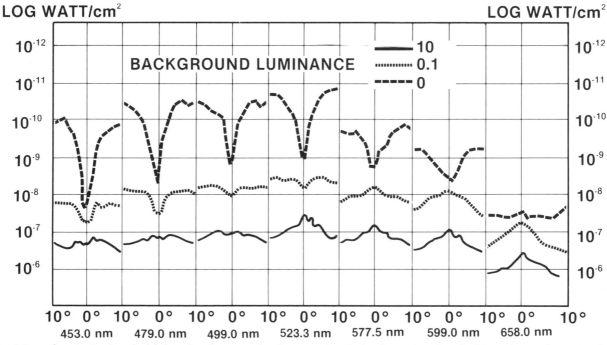

Fig. 1-12. Monochromatic threshold data for the central 10° comparing dark adaptation thresholds at three adaptation levels and seven wavelengths. Note that red (658.0 nm) does not develop a central scotoma with dark adaptation. (*From Nolte W: Bestimmung achromatischer Schwellen für verschiedene Spektrallichter. Inaugural-Dissertation. Universität Tübingen, 1962. With permission.*)

HORIZONTAL MERIDIAN

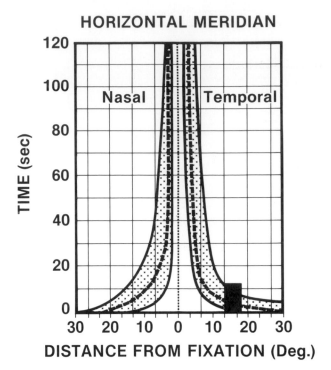

Fig. 1-13. Local adaptation timer as a function of retinal eccentricity. The ordinate represents the time in seconds for the test spot to disappear with most nearly perfect free fixation as possible. The dotted lines represent mean value, while the shaded area represents deviations. (*Redrawn from Cibis P: Zur Pathologie der Lokaladaptation. I. Mitteilung. Physiologische und klinische Untersuchungen zur quantitativen Analyse der örtlichen Umstimmungserscheinungen des Licht-und Farbensinnes unter besonderer Berücksichtigung hirnpathologischer Fälle. Albrecht von Graefes Arch Ophthalmol 148:1–92, 1947–1948. With permission.*)

There are two basic forms of eye movements. One is voluntary eye movements, the direction and magnitude of which can be willfully controlled. The second is physiological fixation nystagmus that occurs universally, free of volition. Voluntary movements range from small saccadic movements of a few degrees up to a full saccade of 80 or more arc degrees. The velocity that the eye will achieve during a saccadic eye movement varies and is proportional to the length of the saccade with a maximum velocity of 700 arc degrees per second being possible in a full side-to side saccade. The profile of the velocity consists of four basic phases: a latent period of about 150 msec to 250 msec, a period of acceleration, a short peak velocity, and a period of deceleration, the whole profile resembling half of a sine-wave.[51] Lynn and Tate have proposed a method of compensating for this type of movement based on monitoring the movement of an eye with a measuring device, such as an oculometer, and moving the test spot to instantly compensate for this movement so that the image of the spot remains in a constant position on the subject's retina.[13] Such techniques fall upon hard times if large eye movements are allowed. In addition to extreme saccadic velocities, increasing amounts of tor-

sional eye movements may be seen with increasingly eccentric oblique gaze, especially if the oculomotor system is impaired.[52] New devices, such as the scanning laser ophthalmoscope,[53,54] may shortly permit a new form of perimetry with stabilized images.

Physiological fixation nystagmus is another story. This subject has been nicely dicussed by Greve,[55] Alpern[52] and a number of other authors.[56,57] Basically, three types of fixation nystagmus have been demonstrated. The first is a tremor with a regular high frequency ranging between 70 and 150 Hz and only a small amplitude up to about 30 seconds of arc. Torsional tremors may also be observed up to 45 seconds of arc. The second type is a slow drift with a frequency of approximately 2 Hz and an average amplitude around 0.8 seconds of arc to 6.0 min of arc. These drifts have a rather slow velocity, something on the order of 6 min of arc per second. The third type is rapid microsaccades that occur at regular intervals with an average amplitude of under a degree, typically being between 2 and 50 min of arc, but usually under 20 min of arc. They are of rather short duration, something on the order of 10 to 20 msec, and are thought to correct deviations from fixation that result from the slow drift. There are, of course, considerable interindividual differences in the various forms of the physiological fixation nystagmus. The first two forms of physiological fixation nystagmus, tremor and drift, are probably due to oculomotor instability. As long as the drift is not outside the foveal receptive field area (approximately 6 min of arc) these variations in fixation, are not accompanied by correcting saccades. However, with larger drifts, saccades occur and the frequency and amplitude are subject to a number of variables. For example, when one is concentrating on fixation, they occur more frequently. It is believed that the basic function of these physiological movements is to prevent the fading of foveally dilated targets such as has been seen in the periphery in the local adaptation phenomenon. Of course, torsional eye movements exist with physiological fixation nystagmus as well but these movements are extremely difficult to measure and little literature about them exists.

Greve, using clinical perimetry, however, studied fixation with the blind spot as a marker in such a way that both translational and torsional movements would be measured.[55] He presented a strong superliminal stimulus about the blind spot and noted, via a frequency of seeing curve, the amplitude of eye movements either in the horizontal or the vertical/torsional directions. He found that the amplitude of horizontal drift was quite small, being something on the order of plus or minus 30 minutes of arc in length. The combination of vertical and torsional movements was somewhat greater, however, being on the order of 4 degrees of arc. Of course, his technique is unable to differentiate vertical and torsional movements and the problem is compounded by the report that vertical movements are normally greater than horizontal movements.[58] Roes-

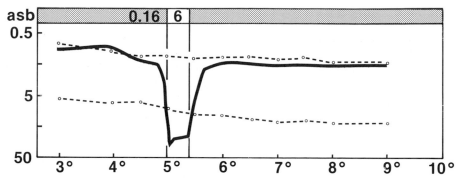

Fig. 1-14. Border contrast. The background contours areas of differing luminance, with the width of the brighter portion at 2°. Luminance of the darker background is 0.16 Asb, while that of the brighter portion is 6 Asb for a contrast ratio of 1:37. The dotted lines show the increment threshold across a uniform dark (upper line) or light (lower line) background. (*Redrawn from Aulhorn E, Harms H: Visual perimetry, in Jameson D, Hurvich LM (eds): Visual Psychophysics; Handbook of Sensory Physiology, vol. VII/4. Berlin, Springer-Verlag, 1972, pp 29–55. With permission.*)

sler[59] has found that torsional movements of 1–3 degrees are also present. In any event, as Greve himself points out, his figures must be considered the best fixation that a subject can maintain. Certainly fixational movements will become larger and larger as the visual acuity becomes poor, with less experienced subjects, with background luminances in the mesopic or scotopic region, and possibly also with the presence of increasing age or the physical fitness of the subject. It should also be noted that kinetic perimetry is more sensitive to unstable fixation than static perimetry since the spot is presented for longer periods.

BORDER CONTRAST

If the background screen of a perimeter is divided by a sharp edge into a light and a dark field, several phenomenon may occur at the border between the different brightnesses. The receptive field organization of the retina is such that those cells right along the border will have only half of their surround illuminated, while the other half will be in darkness. Also, the conditions of center illumination will differ from those across the border; the adaptation of those cells lying on one side of the border will thus change from those of their fellows on the other side of the border. Since the eye is never perfectly still, near the border an edge will move back and forth over the receptive fields of cells stimulating amacrine cells. Cortical cells respond exquisitely well to moving edges and some modification of the response at this level of anatomic organization is likely.

Such border phenomena have long been known to psychophysiological investigators in the form of Mach bands. These occur as subjective sensations upon viewing an edge, namely, just adjacent to the border there is a narrow whiter band present on the white side and a similar darker band present on the dark side. Harms and Aulhorn have studied the phenomenon from a perimetric point of view.[39,60] Their findings are given in Fig. 1-14 and may be summed up by saying that there is a depression of the sensitivity of the retina for the test objects at such borders. Since the subjective sensation is one of a darkening at the dark border, and a lightening on the light side of the border, one would expect this curve to be biphasic, yet no such increase in sensitivity is observed empirically. Aulhorn also noted (personal communication) that this depression occurs even when the border is presented essentially at the same time as the test, or when the border contrast is so low that it disappears as a result of local adaptation. From a practical standpoint, the perimetrist must maintain a uniform background, since changes in the retinal sensitivity above and beyond those produced by the adaptive states are caused by the presence of borders in the visual field.

THE EFFECT OF BLUR ON PERIMETRIC THRESHOLDS

If a spot of light is sharply focused on a surface and then progressively blurred by defocusing, two things happen simultaneously. The first is that the spot becomes dimmer; the second is that it becomes larger in diameter. How this affects its stimulus value will depend upon what part of the retina the stimulus falls. Area is a more efficient stimulus for vision in the peripheral retina than near the fovea. The original size of the focused spot is also of some interest since defocusing a large spot produces less diminution of brightness and relatively less enlargement for a given amount of blur than does a small spot. The effect of this phenomenon on perimetric threshold has been investigated by numerous workers.[61–63] Fankhauser and Enoch[61] demonstrated that the increment thresholds over the central 30 degrees are markedly affected by

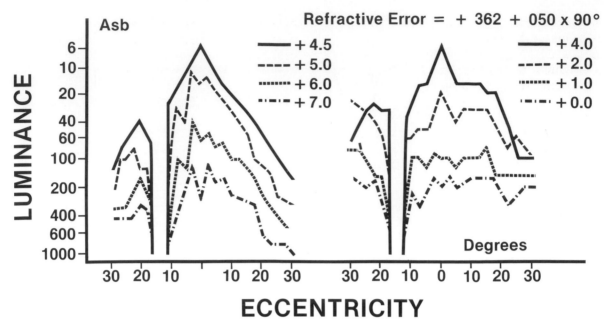

Fig. 1-15. The effect of differing refractions on increment threshold. The refraction of the patient at the surface of the bowl was +3.62 +0.50 × 90 (spherical equivalent of +3.87). Curves showing the effect of overplus are at left and overminus are at right. The overplus ranged from +0.62 diopters (+4.50 −3.87) to +4.12 (7.0 −3.87) while the overminus ranged from +.12 (4 −3.87) to −3.87 (0 −3.87). Ordinate is increment threshold in Apostilbs. (*Redrawn from Fankhauser F, Enoch JM: Archives of Ophthalmology. 68:240, 1962. Copyright 1962, America Medical Association. With permission.*)

blur (Fig. 1-15). Sloan has also investigated this phenomenon and notes that there is indeed a change in thresholds for test object size I and II on the Goldmann perimeter but that with the larger spot sizes (III, IV, and V) this effect is not seen (Fig. 1-16). According to present data, the effect of blur on perimetric thresholds is minimal beyond about 35 to 40 degrees with any size

object. This may be due to the fact that when the fundus periphery is compared with the center it is optically more hypermetropic and has more off-axis aberrations, but also due to the fact that the retina there has better spatial summation than the central area.

Certain fundus pathology that induces blur can have a profound effect on perimetric thresholds. Sev-

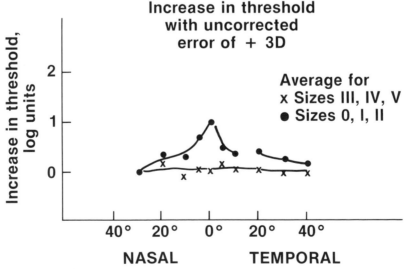

Fig. 1-16. Effect of stimulus size upon the effect of blur on increment threshold. The smaller Goldmann sizes (0, I, II) show an increased threshold (decreased sensitivity) with a +3.00 diopter error in refraction, while the larger sizes (III, IV, V) are unaffected by blur. (*Redrawn from Sloan LL: Area and luminance of test object as variables in examination of the visual field by projection perimetry. Vision Res 1:121–138, 1961–1962. With permission.*)

eral authors have called attention to the fact that refractive scotomas may appear,[1,64,65] but Schmidt[66] has published a field on a patient with a posterior staphyloma in which the scotomatous area became the only area seen with only a 4.0 diopter shift in refraction.

Refractive effects may be introduced unknowingly by physiological phenomenon as well, principally in the form of accommodative spasm or accommodation fatigue, the latter occurring primarily in undercorrected presbyopes. Either can give rise to a gradually decreasing light sensitivity in the central field and result in increased scatter. Accommodative spasm is perhaps more likely in the young uncorrected hyperope, but it can even be seen in myopes who have been chronically overcorrected or in the tense individual. This is generally best handled by refracting the patient at the bowl and stopping the test and, if central scatter is seen, by repeating the refraction. Some authorities who are plagued with this problem in their patients recommend the use of cycloplegics. Iatrogenically induced ammetropias may also occur, the most common of which results from the use of miotics for the treatment of glaucoma, particularly in the young. This induced myopia is variable, depending upon the age of the subject, the strength of the preparation and the time following its instillation. It can be as great as up to 7 diopters but averages around 2–3 diopters. It is at its peak 30 min after the instillation of the miotic and gradually disappears after about 1.5 to 2 h. The answer is to avoid the use of miotics within 2 h of performing a visual field test. Again, some have recommended the use of cycloplegics to help counteract the effect although this practice certainly introduces opportunities for additional variation in the field. Refracting patients during the test provides another possible, but if not convenient, form of control of this phenomenon.

Another thing to consider in the use of corrective lenses is that the lens itself may introduce artifacts in the field. It is obvious that the lens should be of quality colorless optical glass with a thin rim. The lens should be removed when the examination of the central field is finished lest lens edge artifact be introduced. According to Millodot, positive lenses have a slightly brighter image than negative lenses since they converge the light rays onto the pupil.[67] The effect is certainly minimal with normal amounts of refractive error. A much more significant source of error in the use of trial lenses lies in the fact that about 15 percent of the light is lost by reflection from each air-glass interface, a problem magnified by the use of multiple lenses to produce the required spherocylindrical correction.

With forward lenses of great power, some magnification and minification may be introduced and peripherally located stimuli will have some prismatic displacement as well. To counteract this effect, Beasly has proposed the use of contact lenses with aphakes.[68] The alert perimetrist thus should always consider the possibility of refractive effects and attempt to see how altering the patient's refraction changes the threshold of the area in question.

EFFECTS OF CHANGES IN PUPILLARY SIZE

Variations in the size of the pupil have a number of implications for the perimetrist. The pupil serves as an aperture stop for the optical system and as such can influence its performance in a number of ways. It may either enhance or degrade the image quality. The pupil also controls the amount of light entering the eye. It can also warn that pharmacological agents such as miotics, which can also affect the refractive state of the eye, are in use.

The effectiveness of the pupil in allowing light to pass to the periphery of the retina is somewhat diminished at more oblique angles. Because of the optical properties of the cornea, the available area of the pupil decreases more slowly than the cosine of the angle of eccentricity.[69,70] The decrease in pupillary area is offset because summation is to some extent better in peripheral than in central retina. Perimetrically, this effect is constant and therefore could be neglected in comparing one field with another. In any event, the effect is small, resulting only in a correction of about 0.07 db at 40 degrees eccentricity, about 2.8 db at 70 degrees, and 7.6 db at 96 degrees eccentricity.[55] A quantitative consideration of the issue has shown that light originating behind the iris plane may enter the pupil and defined the theoretical limit of the temporal visual field at 110 degrees, a level actually achieved clinically in a few individuals.[2]

With decreasing pupil size, the illumination of the retina also fails. The illumination of the retina is roughly proportional to the square of the diameter of the pupil or its area, and a change from a pupil that has a diameter of 4.75 mm to one that has a diameter of 1.5 mm decreases the illumination of the retina by approximately 1 Lu, which may be enough to shift from photopic to mesopic or from mesopic to scotopic light adaptation.

The effect of the pupil on the resolving power of the eye is more important than the way it theoretically limits the extent of the visual field. In any optical system, image quality ultimately reflects the sum of the effects of refraction and diffraction. The first effect is the relative ability of the lens to focus light, where the second is represented by "scattering" of light by edges within the optical system. Refractive effects may either improve or degrade image quality, while diffractive effects always degrade the image. The degrading refractive influences such as lens aberrations and shallow depth of field, are worse with large pupillary apertures, while the reverse is true of the diffractive effects. In the normal eye, as pupil diameter decreases from maxi-

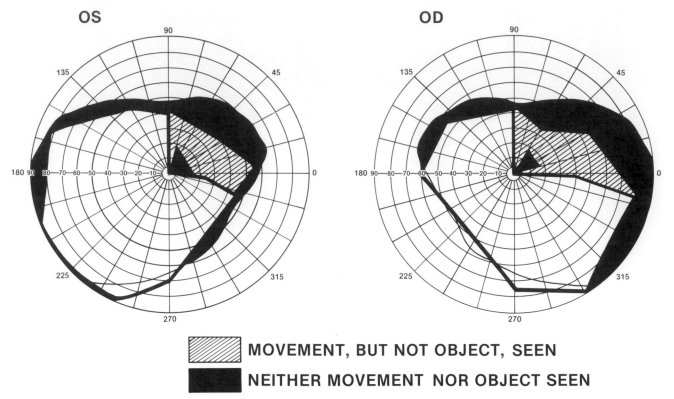

MOVEMENT, BUT NOT OBJECT, SEEN

NEITHER MOVEMENT NOR OBJECT SEEN

Fig. 1-17. Fields demonstrating the Riddoch phenomena. The black area shows an area of field in which neither movement nor a stationary object can be seen. The diagonally shaded area corresponds to area in which movement but no stationary objects, however large, can be seen. (*Redrawn from Riddoch G: Dissociation of visual perceptions due to occipital injuries, with especial reference to appreciation of movement. Brain 40:15–57, 1917. With permission.*)

mum to 2.5 mm, the image on the retina improves, because the small pupil size decreases the effect of the lens aberrations or small defects in focus similar to "stopping down" a camera. However, light is diffracted by the edge of the pupil, and as the pupil drops below about 2.4 mm in diameter, the diffraction effect becomes significant. In fact, with very small pupils, diffraction is the limiting factor for resolution.[71] The eye's optimal optical performance thus occurs at a pupil size of 2.4 mm. If pupil size falls much below 2.4 mm the combination of decreased resolving power along with changes in the adaptive state of the retina and a potentially greater significance of media opacities can significantly alter the shape of the visual field.

MEDIA OPACITIES AND PERIMETRY

The effect of cataract on perimetric threshold deserves some comment, since it is one of the most common problems facing the ophthalmologist. Cataracts and media opacities work their mischief by two basic mechanisms; defocusing the image of the test spot, and increased entopic light scattering. The scattering of light by the ocular media, even in the absence of degradation of focusing ability of the eye, may cause the depth of scotomata to be underestimated.[45] The problem of scattering is worsened in patients with

cataract or vitreous opacities and occurs with lower test luminances than in the normal individual. Miller and Benedick[72] report that 50 percent of the entopic stray light comes from the lens, while 25 percent each comes from the cornea and retina. The presence of a cataract will increase the amount from the lens, while a chorioretinal scar will increase the reflectivity of the retina. Obviously, the same can be said for corneal scarring and vitreous opacities.

It is important to note that such opacities not only increase the amount of scattered light, but they change its quality as well. Scattering of light can be described by a complex mathematical formula known as a Mie series. With small particles, such as molecules, the Mie series expansion describes Rayleigh scattering where the intensity of the scattered light is proportional to the reciprocal of the fourth power wavelength. If the particle size increases so that it is roughly on the order of the one wavelength of light, the scattering is proportional to the reciprocal of the square of the wavelength. With larger particles, which would be opacities, the scattering is less and less dependent on wavelength as the particle size progressively increases. That portion of entopic stray light from the normal lens and cornea thus could, theoretically, be diminished by filtering out the blue end of the spectrum, but such a simple defense is not available against light scattered from the retina nor from pathological opacities within the eye. Al-

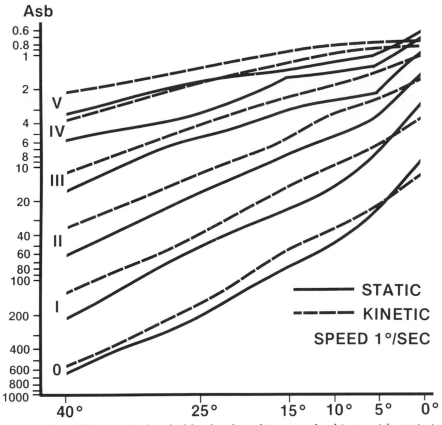

Fig. 1-18. The difference in threshold value found in normal subjects with static (solid line) and kinetic (dotted line) perimetry. The ordinate is the test luminance in asb. The abscissa is the eccentricity in degrees. The roman numeral (0 through V) to the left of each pair of lines gives the corresponding size of the test object on the Goldmann Perimeter. Note that kinetic thresholds are lower (thus, a higher line) in the periphery than static thresholds, where the reverse is true centrally. (*Redrawn from Fankhauser F, Schmidt T: Die optimalen Bedingungen für die Untersuchung der räumlichen Summation mit stehender Reizmarke nach der Methode der quantitativen Lichtsinnperimetrie. Ophthalmologica 139:409–423, 1960. With permission.*)

though most authorities agree that cataract can influence the visual field, a recent paper by Radius[73] points out that while the 1-2-e isopter (Goldmann perimeter) could be affected with only trivial opacities, the other isopters were relatively well preserved with visual acuities of 20/80. The III-4-e isopter remained intact at the 20/400 level.

On the other hand, all rules are made to be broken, and this author had the privilege of examining a patient of Dr. John Lynn's in whom a large cataractous cortical spoke caused a quadrantic field that resolved when the cataract was removed.

MOTION AS A STIMULUS

Anatomically, the stage is set for moving test objects to behave differently than static ones. Indeed, experiences from daily life where objects are frequently first noted because of their motion should convince us that motion can play an important role in perception,

even if logic based on anatomy and physiology does not.

Perhaps the first studies to differentiate the perception of movement from the perception of form were those by George Riddoch, a British physician, who published in 1917 a series of cases of patients who had suffered occipital injuries.[74] His patients had large areas of visual field in which stationary stimuli could not be seen, but movement was readily recognized. Figure 1-17 shows an example of the visual fields of one of Dr. Riddoch's patients. Later, Zappia et al.[75] published a series of cases that show the Riddoch phenomenon is associated with lesions other than those in the occipital lobe, notably with lesions in the optic tract. Safran and Glaser[76] studied statokinetic dissociation in normals and patients with tumors of the anterior optic pathway with chromatic and achromatic stimuli and found it enhanced in areas of field defect.

McColgin carried out perimetry on normal subjects in which the perception of motion was the end point.[77] He found that an individual's movement sensitivity

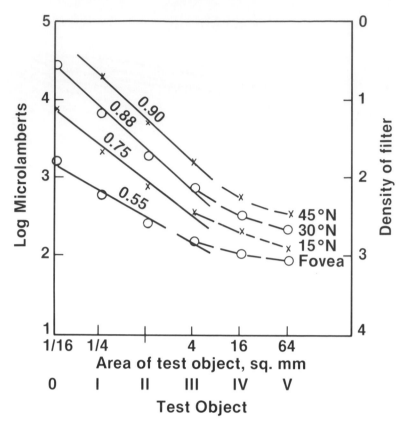

Fig. 1-19. The relationship of retinal location to summation coefficient K. The ordinate is the target luminance in log microlamberts. The abscissa is the target area in square millimeters. The parameters above each curve are the summation coefficients, while the parameters to the right of each curve give retinal position in degrees from fixation (here, all nasal). Although the principle of a K that varies with retinal location is undoubtedly true, other investigators have found different values for K, and that K also depends on target size (as did Sloan, et al,[63] for areas over 4 mm²) and differing adaptation conditions. (*Drawn after Sloan LL: Area and luminance of test object as variables in examination of the visual field by projection perimetry. Vision Res 1:121–138, 1961–1962. With permission.*)

decreases linearly from the fovea to the retinal periphery. The isograms obtained for either rotary or linear motion are elliptical in shape with the horizontal axis approximately twice as long as the vertical axis. He also noted that the sensitivity to rotary movement is less for a uniocular field than for binocular fields. Finally, Fankhauser and Schmidt showed in a beautiful set of curves (Fig. 1-18) that static thresholds are generally slightly higher than kinetic thresholds at the periphery of the visual field, whereas the reverse is true centrally.[78] This result correlates with the smaller receptive fields that are generally found near the fovea. These smaller receptive fields theoretically decrease the opportunity for lateral interaction.

These data put to rest the idea that kinetic and static fields are exactly identical, although the differences are subtle ones and for practical clinical purposes they may be considered as equivalent. Nevertheless, the fact that movement itself is a stimulus to the retina

means that the kinetic perimetrist must be careful to standardize the test velocity.

TEMPORAL AND SPATIAL SUMMATION

Large, long-lasting spots are empirically more effective as visual stimuli than spots of a small size and short duration. Spatial and temporal summation (or integration) operate quantitatively within limits and interact with one another to some extent. Temporal integration means that there are transmission delays along the visual pathway and that additional photons, in striking a given receptor, cause an increase in that receptor's potential if they arrive before the effects of the preceding photons have worn off completely. Spatial summation means that impulses from many adjacent receptor cells converge on a single ganglion cell;

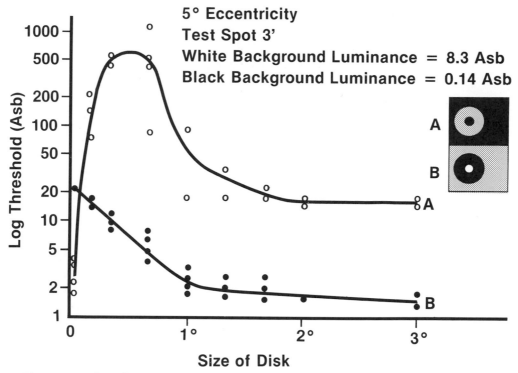

Fig. 1-20. The effect of varying illuminated surrounds on the increment threshold. Curve A shows the classical Westheimer effect with a light surround on a dark background. Curve B is a similar curve with a dark surround on a light background. Ordinate is increment threshold is Log Asb. The abscissa is the radius of the surround in degrees.

hence, the more receptor cells are stimulated by increasing the area of the stimulus, the more the combined outputs these receptor cells are likely to reach the threshold of their ganglion cell. Both of these summation mechanisms are progressively active in eccentric retinal positions.

Spatial summation is perhaps the more obviously important of the two for perimetry and certainly has spawned the most controversy. Although an extensive psychophysical literature exists on the subject which dates back to the studies of Ricco in 1877,[78,79] it was catapulted into clinical importance in 1945 by Goldmann[65,80] who based the design of a perimeter that has become a de facto clinical standard on the phenomenon.

The concept of spatial summation is that the brightness and size of a test object are interchangeable. This is mathematically stated either as $AB^K = C$ or $\log A + K.\log B = C'$ where A is the area of the test object, B the brightness, C and C' are constants, and K is the coefficient of summation, which is in theory a constant but in reality is a variable. The tacit assumption by investigators that K was constant led to the formation of a variety of laws. Thus, when $K = 1$, we say Ricco's law[79] holds, Piper's law[81] corresponds to $K = 0.5$, while Pieron's law[82] refers to $K = 0.33$. Goldmann was well aware that K varied as a function of retinal position, but concluded $K = 0.8$ was a useful approximation.[1,65]

Sloan has examined this question in great detail and finds that the summation coefficient in reality varies from 0.55 at the fovea to 0.9 at 45 degrees nasally (Fig. 1-19).[62,63] These values were all obtained under photopic conditions, and Fankhauser and Schmidt point out that the summation ability of the retina increases as the retina becomes more dark adapted.[78,83] They agree that the summation coefficient is not constant across the entire retina. Gougnard[84] found extreme variation of K not only with retinal position, but also between different sized stimuli. He also found a large interindividual difference.

The confusion concerning K may be summarized by stating that K is a function of the spectral composition of the light, the status of dark adaptation, the eccentricity of the retinal position under test, the presentation time of the stimulus and the subject under test. It may also vary with the age and presence of pathology in the patient. As a general rule, it increases with increasing dark adaptation, greater eccentricity of the test and shorter stimulus times.

The physiological basis for all this variability in the values of K harkens back to the variable anatomy and physiology of the retina. The inhibitory surround of the receptive field seems to be the cause of summation coefficients less than 1.0. Gougnard found that for small test objects, K closely approximated 1.0 past about 10 degrees eccentricity, but that K was less with

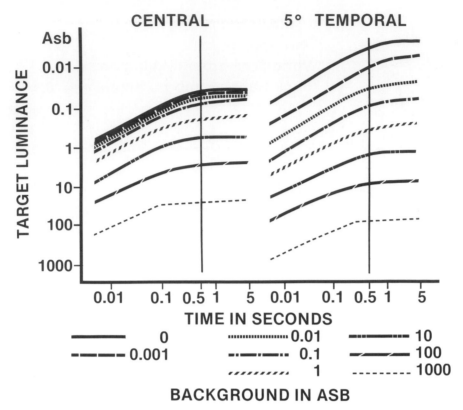

Fig. 1-21. Temporal summation: the effect of different exposure times on light difference thresholds in normal subjects under differing degrees of adaptation. The ordinate is the increment threshold in Asb. The abscissa is the exposure time in seconds. The parameter on each curve is the background luminance. (*Redrawn from Aulhorn E, Harms H: Visual perimetry, in Jameson D, Hurvich LM (eds): Visual Psychophysics; Handbook of Sensory Physiology, vol II/4. Berlin, Springer-Verlag, 1972, pp 29–55. With permission.*)

larger test objects[82] that would be expected to encroach upon the inhibitory surround.

The facility and inhibitory phases of spatial summation were originally explicitly tested by a technique devised by Westheimer[18–20] and more recently exploited clinically by Enoch and coworkers.[26,31] Tate, working in Aulhorn's laboratory, verified the existence of a facilitory and inhibitory phase if a light surround was used, but only a facilitory phase if a dark surround was used (Fig. 1-20).

Temporal integration is described by Bloch's Law ($B \times T$ = constant). This applies only to very small targets for short exposures since the light difference sensitivity fails to increase once the exposure passes a certain length of time (Bloch's time Tc).

With presentation times shorter than Bloch's time, only the luminous flux is of importance in determining threshold, but as the neural mechanism is saturated, summation becomes partial and then ceases. Most investigators find that Bloch's time is short, on the order of 0.06 seconds, but the entire process is affected by a host of factors, including stimulus size, eccentricity, background luminosity, stimulus color, and even the type of cognitive tasks to be performed, which implicates cortical factors.[85,86] The influence of higher

centers in this process is underlined by the fact that stimuli to the fellow eye[87,88] and even auditory stimuli[89,90] may have some affect on performance.

Dannheim and Drance[91] found that perimetrically some summation appeared to occur centrally after 0.1 seconds. Aulhorn and Harms have also investigated this phenomenon[40] and find that with exposure times longer than 0.5 seconds, no further decrease in the light difference threshold is noted (Fig. 1-21). This has been substantiated by Alexandres[92] who notes that the time to saturation for the temporal summation effect also varies somewhat as a function of retinal location as well as the light-dark adaptation status of the eye. Therefore, if exposure times during static perimetry are kept as long as one half second, the effect of temporal integration is neutralized. This solution is less than ideal, for with long stimulus times, fixation may wander. Greve observes that the interindividual variance in temporal summation is small[55] and feels that electric shutters with short stimulus presentations provide a more suitable solution to the problems of temporal summation in clinical patients who fixate irregularly. With kinetic perimetry, the temporal summation effect cannot be neutralized, and the degree to which it

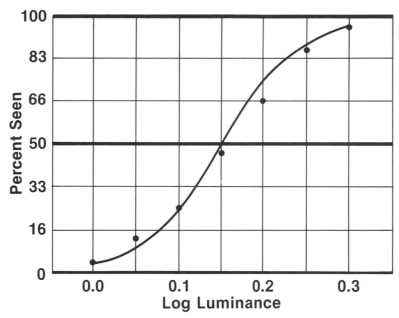

Fig. 1-22. A frequency of seeing curve.

influences the threshold is uncertain, largely because reaction time variance often exceeds the summation effect. The combined effects of temporal and spatial summation may make the shape of the test object just as important to the kinetic perimetrist as the area. A small rectangle with its short axis parallel to the direction of movement is a less efficient stimulus under some conditions than with its long axis parallel to the direction of movement, since the opportunity for temporal summation is decreased in the former case.

SUCCESSIVE LATERAL SPATIAL SUMMATION

In 1971, Greve and Verriest described a phenomenon called "successive lateral spatial summation" based on the fact that a kinetic stimulus may excite receptors while it is just infraliminal and that spatial summation can therefore occur, especially in the peripheral retina.[55] In fact, this phenomenon is likely to be a combination of temporal and spatial summation, based on Bloch's time (Tc) of the retina and the receptive field size. For example, consider an average $Tc = 0.06$ seconds and a receptive field (central portion only) of about 6 degrees of arc at the fovea, 15 degrees of arc at about 3 degrees eccentricity with larger receptive fields more peripherally, and a test velocity of 5 degrees per second. This corresponds to a receptive field transit time of 0.02 seconds at the fovea, 0.05 seconds at 3 degrees eccentricity, which is just about equal to Tc, and progressively larger values for more peripheral locations. If static perimetry were to be compared to this, using 0.5 seconds test exposure, it should be seen better than kinetic perimetry at the fovea and equal to kinetic at 3 degrees eccentricity, just from temporal

summation data alone. The receptor potentials likely decay along the same time course over which they build, so some effect of the stimulus likely lingers for a period equal to Rc after the stimulus has passed. Increasing spatial summation up to a track length of about 30 degrees with the test velocity may thus occur with the kinetic stimulus, pushing its effectiveness higher in the periphery. If this is true, it would be expected that the kinetic threshold curve would rise above the static threshold curve, then roughly parallel it once receptive fields larger than 30 degrees were reached. Moreover, with larger stimuli, the timing would be such that the crossing point between the static and kinetic curves would be pushed more centrally. Indeed, one need only to examine the curves of Fankhauser et al.[78] (Fig. 1-18) to see that this is exactly what happens.

In truth, it would be surprising if the mechanism were not a good bit more complicated than portrayed above since some interaction must occur with the inhibitory surrounding and motion-sensitive cells. Yet, from this simple analysis it seems reasonable to assume that both temporal and spatial summation are at work. Perhaps the phenomenon should be called, simply and noncommittally, successive lateral summation.

SLOPE OF THE VISUAL FIELD

The phenomenon of successive lateral summation was described above as though the test stimulus was equally effective everywhere along its course, that is, as though the slope of the visual field were flat. Such is not the case, however, in real life. The visual field has a slope to it and thus a kinetic test spot that is destined to reach threshold will start out quite infraliminal,

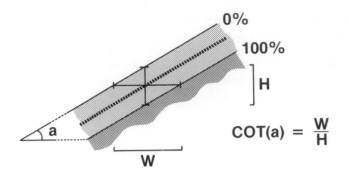

$$COT(a) = \frac{W}{H}$$

Fig. 1-23. Diagrammatic representation of how spatial summation and the "frequency of seeing curve" affect scatter. The distance H is a function of the underlying receptor and is thus more or less independent of slope. W is the length of the path that a kinetic stimulus must traverse through the "partial response zone" to get to the 100% response surface; thus, the length of W is proportional to the chance for scatter. Since the slope can be measured from the field, whereas the length of W cannot, the cotangent of the slope a provides us with a convenient measure of scatter. Since W is dependent on slope and H is not, one would also expect that a flat slope would be far more damaging to a kinetic field than a steep slope would be to a static field.

become progressively less infraliminal, reach threshold, then become progressively more and more supraliminal as it traverses its course from the periphery to fixation. In those areas where the test spot is too far below threshold, the various summation mechanisms will be ineffective in bringing the test spot above threshold, but as the moving test spot nears the threshold location, successive lateral summation can cause threshold to be reached more quickly. When the gradient of the visual field is flat, summation may reach threshold over a wider band than when the slope is steep. Thus, there is more potential for scatter with kinetic tests when the slope is flat than with steeper gradients.

To understand why this is so, one must realize that threshold does not always occur at a sharply defined stimulus, but rather over a band of values, each of which has its unique probability (or frequency) of being seen.

A "frequency of seeing" curve for a given area in the visual field may be plotted by repeatedly presenting a test spot of a given size at each of a graded series of luminances and by recording the subjective response to each presentation. The results of such an effort reveal a range of luminances over which the spot is never seen (probability of seeing = 0), a range over which the spot is always seen (probability of seeing = 100 percent), and a range of luminances over which the spot is seen some of the time (Fig. 1-22). This "uncertain range" spans approximately 3 db in trained observers. The variation in threshold due to this effect is called short-term fluctuation.

Since in any current form of clinical perimetry the stimulus is gradually brought closer and closer to threshold until it is first seen, a certain percentage of the responses will be seen "early" (toward the low end of the frequency of seeing zone) where others are seen "late," allowing a kinetic test to penetrate more deeply before being seen. The width of this zone of uncertainty varies with the sensitivity gradient, or slope of that portion of the field under investigation (Fig. 2-23).

An alternative way of explaining this same phenomenon is to consider that each point in the visual field has its own frequency of seeing curve associated with it which defines a set of stimulus values that correspond to probabilities of 0 percent to 100 percent being seen. In aggregate, these define a band overlying the surface of the visual field that can be traversed in either the horizontal or vertical direction (Fig. 1-23). Since the vertical dimension (H) is the width of the frequency of seeing curve of the underlying receptor, this value is fixed and independent of slope. The horizontal dimension (W) is directly determined by the slope and is in fact proportional to the cotangent of the angle of the slope. The scatter associated with moving tests is thus inextricably linked to the slope of the field, while the scatter of static tests is virtually immune to variations in the field gradient. The sole exception of this rule is near steep slopes where small eye movements may cause significant changes in threshold that some authorities call pseudoscatter.

Finally, it should be noted that the steepest any slope can be is when it is approached perpendicular to the isopter. The more obliquely the slope is approached, the flatter it appears, and if the isopter is paralleled, the slope is perfectly flat. Although this phenomenon does not get out of hand so long as the line of approach is within 30 degrees of perpendicular to the isopter, every effort should be made to keep the line of approach as close to perpendicular as possible if scatter is to be held to an absolute minimum in kinetic testing.

PATHOLOGY AND SCATTER

There are many possible causes of scatter even in the normal visual field. Indeed, Lynn has offered the mnemonic "the five P's of scatter"[13,93] to jog our memories concerning the various physical, pharmacologic, physiologic, psychologic, and pathologic factors capable of producing scatter in any visual field. The majority of these factors that contribute to the short-term fluctuation of perimetric thresholds has been discussed, but the last of these, pathologic, is of special interest to the clinical perimetrist.

Focal pathological areas of the visual field increase the scatter of threshold determination to both static and kinetic perimetry. It has been pointed out by Werner and Drance[94] that scatter in static tests increases in such areas even before definite defects can be found. This scatter may revert to normal amounts if the cause abates, such as a prolonged lowering of intraocular pressure in glaucoma. The effect in such areas is as though the frequency of seeing curve simply widened. Kinetically such areas show up as a widened geographical area where the test stimulus is seen, but in addition isopters just central to the defective area may show some concavity or the phenomenon called "penetraters" by Tate and Lynn[13] may be seen. These are spots that travel through the area of increased scatter without being detected, then traverse a defective area where the probability of being seen is zero or nearly so, and are possibly seen at the location of the next central isopter. They may also be seen before the development of a definite scotoma and disappear if the condition improves.

Pathologic areas of the visual field are unique in other ways. Although several authors[95–97] have noted some decrement in performance of some form or another of visual threshold testing with fatigue, Heijl[96] noted that in normal areas, the fatigue effect was minimal, on the order of 1.5 db, while decrements of 6 to 10 db were seen in areas destined to become defective in glaucoma patients. This has been confirmed by Heijl and Drance.[98] The presence of this increased fatiguability in glaucoma would certainly seem to place the defect in the retina, most likely the ganglion cell layer, but studies by Enoch and his coworkers[26–29,99] dispute this. These workers found a "fatiguelike effect" in lesions of the central visual pathway, but not in glaucoma. Indeed, if a bit of speculation based on extrapolating common experience from other diseases of the central nervous system is permitted, it is easy to conclude that increased fatiguability is a common trait of diseased neurons, although different means of eliciting this fatiguability may be required depending upon which neuron is affected. This important topic merits further investigation, both because it may provide a provocative test for visual field defects and because it is another element that must be controlled if serial visual fields are to be obtained that truly reflect the state of patients with chronic diseases.

LONG-TERM FLUCTUATION

In addition to the above variations in retinal sensitivity, fluctuations may occur in the visual field over a period of hours to years. If the prominent causes of such changes, aging and training are eliminated, and the causes of short-term fluctuation neutralized, some variation in threshold still exists. This component of the fluctuation had been named long-term fluctuation by Bebie and coworkers.[100]

The long-term fluctuation has been described as having two components, one that affects all points in the visual field equally and a second component that affects points in different areas by differing amounts. Bebie, Fankhauser, and Spahr[100] christened these components the synchronous and the uncorrelated components respectively, but Flammer, Drance, and Schulzer[101] have suggested the alternate terms homogenous and heterogenous, which seem a bit more descriptive.

Both groups agree on the magnitude of the homogenous component, the Swiss group finding a value of about 1.0 db, while the Vancouver group found a range from 1.1 to 1.2 db. The two groups parted company sharply on the estimated magnitude of the heterogenous component. Bebie et al.[100] pegged the heterogenous component at 1.3 db but Flammer et al.[101] determined it to be 0.8 db and concluded that the heterogenous component was likely a consequence of the factors determining the short-term fluctuation. The groups of patients analyzed in the two centers were not exactly comparable and, as Flammer, Drance, and Schulzer point out, it is possible that the heterogenous component is influenced by various diseases of the visual system. The final word in the chapter on long-term fluctuation thus has yet to be written.

PSYCHOLOGICAL AND MISCELLANEOUS PHENOMENA

The previous sections have dealt mainly with the physiology of the isolated retina or the psychophysics of the visual system as a whole in research subjects. The clinical perimetrist must deal with real world patients who may have certain psychologic features that may modify the results obtained perimetrically. Obviously the patient intent on malingering, or one who is hysterical, can profoundly influence the results that the perimetrist obtains, even if the visual apparatus is completely sound. A perfectly cooperative patient with full intention to provide the perimetrist with the best, most reliable results possible may still have his performance altered, however, by psychological influences. Psychological phenomena may make reliable testing of some patients with definite pathology impossible with certain varieties of tests.

One pitfall of a specific type of visual field study technique is the so-called completion phenomenon. It has been pointed out by several authors[1,102] that patients with damage to their posterior visual pathway may not be adequately tested for progression of their lesion by devices such as the Amsler grid. These patients tend to complete repeating patterns or objects of a familiar shape in the blind field.

The tendency of the human eye to complete figures has been examined by Fankhauser and Geiger, who find that most normal individuals tend to organize random arrays of points into figures.[102] Other workers have found that the presence of multiple spots can influence the apparent brightness of each individual spot and even change the flicker frequency. Binocular

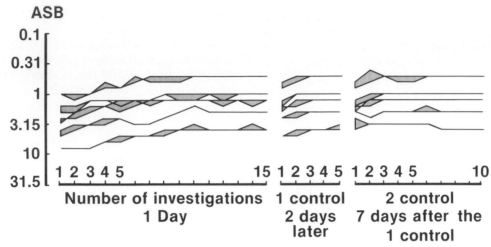

Fig. 1-24. The effect of training on static thresholds initially, then 2 and 9 days later. All five lines are from the same observer, taken at 0°, 2.5°, 5°, 10°, and 18° eccentricity from top to bottom. Two thresholds were consecutively determined for each location. Once each eccentricity had been tested, the cycle was repeated for 15 cycles (total of 30 tests at each eccentricity) on the first day, 5 cycles 2 days later, and 10 cycles 1 wk after the second session. The difference between the two consecutive thresholds for a given time is represented by the shaded area. A single line indicates that the two determinations were identical. Note that threshold improves a few tenths of a log unit with practice and the scatter likewise decreases. Moreover, the effect of practice seems to persist. (*Redrawn from Aulhorn E, Harms H: Early visual field defects in glaucoma, in Glaucoma Symposium, Tutzing Castle, 1966. Basel, Karger, 1967, pp 151–185.*)

presentation of stimuli may vary their threshold as well as their critical flicker frequency.[103,104,105] Nevertheless, multiple-stimulus devices may be clinically useful as rapid screeners.[55,102,106,107]

Patients with parieto-occipital lesions may show the so-called extinction phenomenon when examined by a simultaneous double stimulation technique. Bender[108] has investigated the extinction phenomenon in many sensory systems, including the tactile, auditory, and visual. He found that extinction is normally a part of tactile sensation but is made more prominent by cortical disease. He has reported several patients whose visual fields were "normal" when tested by routine perimetric techniques but showed a hemianopic defect when investigated with double simultaneous stimulation. He did not thoroughly investigate the extinction phenomenon perimetrically but instead concentrated on the other sensory systems.

Lynn and Aulhorn (personal communication) investigated the visual fields of normal individuals and glaucoma patients by double simultaneous stimulation and were unable to detect extinction in this group of subjects. Greve likewise carried out multiple-stimulus perimetry in a similar group of subjects[55] and found no threshold shift with up to eight simultaneous stimuli. It would thus appear that extinction with regard to the monocular visual field is likely to occur only in persons with disease of the higher centers.

Training is another factor that influences the perimetric threshold of a subject. Aulhorn and Harms[40] have studied the influence of training on perimetric threshold and find that there may be nearly an entire log unit shift in threshold with practice. This effect is greatest in the early trial sessions, and tends to be maintained in subsequent test sessions (Fig. 1-24). The amount of feedback given a patient can speed his learning and improve his performance significantly.[109] It has been shown that when the patient is forced to make a choice as to the direction in which he sees the test object, and is then told immediately whether his choice was right or wrong, he will attain lower thresholds (i.e., greater sensitivity) with less scatter sooner than by other methods.[110] These results underscore the importance of immediately telling the patient when performance is not adequate during the test and how it can be corrected to obtain optimal reproducible results.

The foregoing variables all relate to and influence a phenomenon known as the criterion effect. This is a temporal variation in response to a stimulus as the subject's criterion for making a response changes. A common example with an untrained subject is waiting until the spot is clearly visible before making a response. As the subject learns to "see the spot" further eccentrically, the isopter enlarges. Nothing has changed physiologically: the subject's criterion for reporting a seen stimulus has changed. Simply stated, the stimulus strength that a subject is willing to report as "seen" is influenced by psychological factors that affect his perception of how important it is to be absolutely sure he sees the test spot, even though he has some "misses," versus the importance of not missing a spot, even though this leads to some "false alarms." This process of changing one's criteria for responding to a stimulus lends itself to a mathematical description through the language of signal detection theory.[111–114] A simplified summary of these concepts has been given by Bernstein.[115] Baumgartner[41] provides a criticism of the signal detection approach to perimetry. Nevertheless, it is the opinion of many workers in this area that a subject's responses are colored by his psychological state, a fact certainly borne out by clinical experience.

Age is certainly another factor that has a profound effect on visual field thresholds. Drance has shown a progressive decrease in the size of isopters of a visual field with age.[116] Wolfe concurs, and points out that changes in physiological variables such as oxygen tension also affect threshold values.[117]

Obviously, these factors only scratch the surface of psychological variables. Fatigue[95,97] anxiety, preoccupation, various forms of stress,[118] drugs, intelligence, and many other factors can influence the patient's performance during a visual field test. Some of these may be recognized and neutralized and some cannot. When the perimetrist notes a degradation in performance from previous studies, the possibility of a spurious change due to psychological variables should thus be considered along with the common assumption that the disease has progressed.

REFERENCES

1. Goldmann H: Lichtsinn mit besonderer Berücksichtigung der Perimetrie. Ophthalmologica 158:362–386, 1969

2. LeGrand Y: Light, Colour and Vision. London, Chapman and Hall, 1957

3. Bartoli F, Liuzzi L: Laser perimetry: diagnostic application in six cases of pituitary chromophobe adenoma. Acta Ophthalmol 51:841–852, 1973

4. Greve EL, Verduin WM, Ledeboer M: Two-colour threshold in static perimetry. Mod Probl Ophthalmol 13:113–118, 1974

5. Nolte W: Bestimmung achromatischer Schwellen für verschiedene Spektrallichter. Inaugural-Dissertation. Universität Tübingen, 1962

6. Dowling JE: Organization of vertebrate retinas. Invest Ophthalmol 9:655–680, 1970

7. Dowling JE, Boycott BB: Organization of the primate retina: electron microscopy. Proc R Soc [Biol] 166: 80–111, 1966

8. Dowling JE, Ehinger B: Synaptic organization of the amine-containing interplexiform cells of the goldfish and Cebus monkey retinas. Science 188:270–273, 1975

9. Werblin FS: Control of retinal sensitivity. II. Lateral interactions at the outer plexiform layer. J Gen Physiol 63:62–87, 1974

10. Werblin FS: Response of retinal cells to moving spots: intracellular recording in Necturus maculosus. J Neurophysiol 33:342–350, 1970

11. Werblin FS, Copenhagen DR: Control of retinal sensitivity. III. Lateral interactions at the inner plexiform layer. J Gen Physiol 63:88–110, 1974

12. Hogan MJ, Alvarado JA, Weddell JE: Histology of the Human Eye; An Atlas and Textbook. Philadelphia, WB Saunders, 1971, p 687

13. Tate GW Jr, Lynn JR: Principles of Quantitative Perimetry: Testing and Interpreting the Visual Field. New York, Grune & Stratton, 1977

14. Normann RA, Werblin FS: Control of retinal sensitivity. I. Light and dark adaptation of vertebrate rods and cones. J Gen Physiol 63:37–61, 1974

15. Kuffler SW: Discharge patterns and functional organization of mammalian retina. J Neurophysiol 16:37–68, 1953

16. Wiesel TN: Receptive fields of ganglion cells in the cat's retina. J Physiol 153:583–594, 1960

17. Burkhardt DA: Sensitization and centre-surround antagonism in Necturus retina. J Physiol 236:593–610, 1974

18. Westheimer G: Spatial interaction in the human retina during scotopic vision. J Physiol 181:881–894, 1965

19. Westheimer G: Spatial interaction in human cone vision. J Physiol 190:139–154, 1967

20. Westheimer G: Bleached rhodopsin and retinal interaction. J Physiol 195:97–105, 1968

21. Teller DY: Sensitization by annular surrounds: temporal (masking) properties. Vision Res 11:1325–1335, 1971

22. Teller DY: Visual sensitization by annular surrounds. J Opt Soc Am 59:509, 1969

23. Teller DY, Gestrin PJ: Sensitization by annular surrounds: sensitization and dark adaptation. Vision Res 9:1481–1489, 1969

24. Teller DY, Lindsey B: Sensitization by annular surrounds: individual differences. Vision Res 10: 1045–1055, 1970

25. Teller DY, Matter CF, Phillips WD: Sensitization by annular surrounds: spatial summation properties. Vision Res 10:549–561, 1970

26. Enoch JM: Quantitative layer-by-layer perimetry: an update. Am J Optom Physiol Opt 59:952–953, 1982

27. Enoch JM, Berger R, Birns R: A static perimetric technique believed to test receptive field properties: extension and verification of the analysis. Doc Ophthalmol 29:127–153, 1970

28. Enoch JM, Fitzgerald CR, Campos EC: Quantitative Layer-By-Layer Perimetry: An Extended Analysis. New York, Grune & Stratton, 1981

29. Enoch JM, Lawrence B: A perimetric technique believed to test receptive field properties: sequential evaluation in glaucoma and other conditions. Am J Ophthalmol 80:734–758, 1975

30. Enoch JM, Sunga RN, Bachmann E: Static perimetric technique believed to test receptive field properties. I. Extension of Westheimer's experiments on spatial interaction. Am J Ophthalmol 70:113–126, 1970

31. Enoch JM, Sunga RN, Bachmann E: Static perimetric technique believed to test receptive field properties. II. Adaption of the method to the quantitative perimeter. Am J Ophthalmol 70:126–137, 1970

32. Hartline HK: Inhibitory interaction in the retina, in Straatsma BR, Hall MO, Allen RA, Crescitelli F. (eds):

The Retina; Morphology, Function and Clinical Characteristics. Berkeley, University of California Press, 1969, pp 297–317

33. Norton AL, Spekreijse H, Wagner HG, Wolbarsht ML: Responses to directional stimuli in retinal preganglionic units. J Physiol 206:93–107, 1970

34. Rushton WAH: Visual adaptation. Proc R Soc Lond (Biol) 162:20–46, 1965

35. Barlow HB, Hill RM, Levick WR: Retinal ganglion cells responding selectively to direction and speed of image motion in the rabbit. J Physiol 173:377–407, 1964

36. Barlow HB, Levick WR: The mechanism of directionally selective units in rabbit's retina. J Physiol 178:477–504, 1965

37. Østerberg G: Topography of the layer of rods and cones in the human retina. Acta Ophthalmol Suppl 6, 1935

38. Polyak SL: The Retina. Chicago, University of Chicago Press, 1941

39. Aulhorn E: Psychophysische Gesetzmässigkeiten des normalen Sehens. Ber Dtsch Ophthalmol Ges 66: 144–161, 1964

40. Aulhorn E, Harms H: Visual perimetry, in Jameson D, Hurvich LM (eds): Visual Psychophysics; Handbook of Sensory Physiology, vol. VII/4. Berlin, Springer-Verlag, pp 102–145

41. Baumgardt E: Threshold quantal problems, in Jameson D, Hurvich LM (eds): Visual Psychophysics; Handbook of Sensory Physiology, vol. VII/4. Berlin, Springer-Verlag, 1972, pp 29–55

42. Barlow HB: Dark and light adaptation: psychophysics, in Jameson D, Hurvich LM (eds): Visual Psychophysics; Handbook of Sensory Physiology, vol. VII/4. Berlin, Springer-Verlag, 1972, pp 1–28

43. Fankhauser F: Problems related to the design of automatic perimeters. Doc Ophthalmol 47:89–139, 1979

44. Dannheim F: Ueber die Untersuchung der Dunkelanpassung mit hellen und dunklen Pruefpunkten. Inaugural Dissertation, Universität Tubingen

45. Fankhauser F, Haeberlin H: Dynamic range and stray light. An estimate of the falsifying effects of stray light in perimetry. Doc Ophthalmol 50:143–167, 1980

46. Rose A: Vision: Human and Electronic. New York, Plenum Press, 1973

47. Troxler D: Über das Verschwinden gegenuber Gegenstände innerhalb unseres Gesichtskreisses. Ophthalmol Bibliothek 2:51, 1804

48. Cibis P: Zur Pathologie der Lokaladaptation. I. Mitteilung. Physiologische und klinische Untersuchungen zur quantitativen Analyse der örtlichen Umstimmungserscheinungen des Licht- und Farbensinnes unter besonderer Berücksichtigung hirnpathologischer Fälle. Albrecht von Graefes Arch Ophthalmol 148:1–92, 1947–1948

49. Cibis P: Zur Pathologie der Lokaladaptation. II. Mitteilung. Konstruktive Darstellung des Ablaufs der Erregungsvorgänge im normalen und erkrankten Sehorgan bei konstanter und phasischer Reizung umschriebener Sehfeldstellen. Albrecht von Graefes Arch Ophthalmol 148:216–257, 1947–1948

50. Yarbus AL: Eye Movements and Vision. New York, Plenum Press, 1967

51. Fuchs AF: The saccadic system, in Bach-Y-Rita P, Collins CC (eds): The Control of Eye Movements. New York, Academic Press, 1971, pp 343–362

52. Alpern M: Eye movements, in Jameson D, Hurvich LM (eds): Visual Psychophysics; Handbook of Sensory Physiology, vol. VII/4. Berlin, Springer-Verlag, 1972, pp 303–330

53. Mainster MA, Timberlake GT, Webb RH, Hughes GW: Scanning laser ophthalmoscopy: clinical applications. Ophthalmology 89:852–857, 1982

54. Timberlake GT, Mainster MA, Webb RH, Hughes GW, Trempe CL: Retinal localization of scotomata by scanning laser ophthalmoscopy. Invest Ophthalmol Vis Sci 22:91–97, 1982

55. Greve EL: Single and multiple stimulus static perimetry in glaucoma; the two phases of perimetry. Doc Ophthalmol 36:1–355, 1973

56. Aulhorn E, Harms H, Karmeyer H: The influence of spontaneous eye-rotation on the perimetric determination of small scotomas. Doc Ophthalmol Proc Ser 19:363–367, 1979

57. Burde RM: Control of eye movements, in Moses RA (ed): Adler's Physiology of the Eye; Clinical Application (ed 7). St Louis, CV Mosby, 1981, pp 122-165

58. Ditchburn RW, Foley-Fisher JA: Assembled data in eye movements. Opt Acta 14:113–118, 1967

59. Rossler F: Die Hohenstellung des blinden Fleckes in normalen Augen. Arch Augenheilkd 86:55–88, 1920

60. Harms H, Aulhorn E: Studien uber den Grenzkontrast. I. Mitteilung. Ein neues Grenzphanomen. Albrecht von Graefes Arch Ophthalmol 157:3–23, 1955–1956

61. Fankhauser F, Enoch JM: The effects of blur upon perimetric thresholds; a method for determining a quantitative estimate of retinal contour. Arch Ophthalmol 68:240–251, 1962

62. Sloan LL: Area and luminance of test object as variables in examination of the visual field by projection perimetry. Vision Res 1:121–138, 1961–1962

63. Sloan LL, Brown DJ: Area and luminance of test object as variables in projection perimetry; clinical studies of photometric dysharmony. Vision Res 2:527–541, 1962

64. Fankhauser F: Kinetische Perimetrie. Ophthalmologica 158:406–418, 1969

65. Goldmann H: Grundlagen exakter Perimetrie. Ophthalmologica 109:57–70, 1945

66. Schmidt T: Perimetrie relativer Skotome. Ophthalmologica 129:303–315, 1955

67. Millodot M: The effect of lenses on light transmission to the eye. Am J Optom 47:211–216, 1970

68. Beasley H: The visual fields in aphakia. Trans Am Ophthalmol Soc 63:363–416, 1965

69. Jay BS: The effective pupillary area at varying perimetric angles. Vision Res 1:418–424, 1961–1962

70. Spring KH, Stiles WS: Apparent shape and size of the pupil viewed obliquely. Br J Ophthalmol 32:347–354, 1948

71. Campbell FW, Gubisch RW: Optical quality of the human eye. J Physiol 186:558–578, 1966

72. Miller D, Benedek G: Intraocular Light Scattering; Theory and Clinical Application. Springfield IL, Charles C Thomas, 1973

73. Radius RL: Perimetry in cataract patients. Arch Ophthalmol 96:1574–1579, 1978

74. Riddoch G: Dissociation of visual perceptions due to occipital injuries, with especial reference to appreciation of movement. Brain 40:15–57, 1917

75. Zappia RJ, Enoch JM, Stamper R, Winkelman JZ, Gay AJ: The Riddoch phenomenon revealed in non-occipital lobe lesions. Br J Ophthalmol 55:416–420, 1971

76. Safran AB, Glaser JS: Statokinetic dissociation in lesions of the anterior visual pathways. A reappraisal of the Riddoch phenomenon. Arch Ophthalmol 98:291–295, 1980

77. McColgin FH: Movement thresholds in peripheral vision. J Opt Soc Am 50:774–779, 1960

78. Fankhauser F, Schmidt T: Die optimalen Bedingungen für die Untersuchung der räumlichen Summation mit stehender Reizmarke nach der Methode der quantitativen Lichtsinnperimetrie. Ophthalmologica 139:409–423, 1960

79. Ricco A: Relazione fra il minimo angola visuale e l'intensità luminosa. Ann Ottalmol 6:373–479, 1877

80. Goldmann H: Ein selbstregistrierendes Projektionskugelperimeter. Ophthalmologica 109:71–79, 1945

81. Piper H: Ueber die Abhängigkeit des Reizwertes leuchtender Objekte von ihrer Flächen, beziehungsweise Winkelgrösse. Z Psychol Physiol Sinnesorg 32:98–112, 1903

82. Pieron H: De la valeur de l'energie liminaire en fonction de la surface rétinienne excitée pour la vision fovéale, et de l'influence réciproque de la durée et de la surface d'excitation sur la sommation spatiale ou temporelle pour la vision fovéale et peripherique. (Cones et batonnets). CR Soc Biol 83:1072–1076, 1920

83. Fankhauser F, Schmidt T: Die Untersuchung der räumlichen Summation mit stehender und bewegter Reizmarke nach der Methode der quantitativen Lichtsinnperimetrie. Ophthalmologica 135:660–666, 1958

84. Gougnard L: Etude des sommations spatiales chez le sujet normal par la périmétrie statique. Ophthalmologica 142:469–486, 1961

85. Adler FH: Adler's Physiology of the Eye; Clinical Application (ed 5), revised by Moses RA. St Louis, CV Mosby, 1970

86. Blackwell HR: Neural theories of simple visual discriminations. J Opt Soc Am 53:129–160, 1963

87. Battersby WS, Defabaugh GL: Neural limitations of visual excitability: after-effects of subliminal stimulation. Vision Res 9:757–768, 1969

88. Matin L: Binocular summation at the absolute threshold of peripheral vision. J Opt Soc Am 52:1276–1286, 1962

89. Bernstein IH, Chu PK, Briggs P, Schurman DL: Stimulus intensity and foreperiod effects in intersensory facilitation. Q J Exp Psychol 25:171–181, 1973

90. Treisman M: The effect of one stimulus on the threshold for another: an application of signal detectability theory. Br J Stat Psychol 17:15–35, 1964

91. Dannheim F, Drance SM: Studies of temporal summation of central retinal areas in normal people of all ages. Ophthalmic Res 2:295–303, 1971

92. Alexandridis E: Raumliche und zeitliche Summation pupillomotorisch wirksamer Lichtreize beim Menschen. Albrecht von Graefes Arch Klin Exp Ophthalmol 180:12–19, 1970

93. Lynn JR: Examination of the visual field in glaucoma. Invest Ophthalmol 8:76–84, 1969

94. Werner EB, Drance SM: Early visual field disturbances in glaucoma. Arch Ophthalmol 95:1173–1175, 1977

95. Haider M, Dixon NF: Influences of training and fatigue on the continuous recording of a visual differential threshold. Br J Psychol 52:227–237, 1961

96. Heijl A: Time changes of contrast thresholds during automatic perimetry. Acta Ophthalmol 55:696–708, 1977

97. Ronchi L, Salvi G: Performance decrement, under prolonged testing, across the visual field. Ophthalmic Res 5:113–120, 1973

98. Heijl A, Drance SM: Changes in differential threshold in patients with glaucoma during prolonged perimetry. Br J Ophthalmol 67:512–516, 1983

99. Sunga RN, Enoch JM: Further perimetric analysis of patients with lesions of the visual pathways. Am J Ophthalmol 70:403–422, 1970

100. Bebie H, Fankhauser F, Spahr J: Static perimetry: accuracy and fluctuations. Acta Ophthalmol 54:339–348, 1976

101. Flammer J, Drance SM, Schulzer M: The estimation and testing of the components of long-term fluctuation of the differential light threshold. Doc Ophthalmol Proc Ser 35:383–389, 1983

102. Fankhauser F, Giger H: Die perzeptorische Organisation von Punktfeldern. Vision Res 8:1349–1366, 1968

103. Granit R, Harper P: Comparative studies on the peripheral and central retina. II. Synaptic reactions in the eye. Am J Physiol 95:211–228, 1930

104. Thomas JP: Brightness-contrast effects among several points of light. J Opt Soc Am 55:323–327, 1965

105. Sperling G: Linear theory and the psychophysics of flicker. Doc Ophthalmol 18:3–15, 1964

106. Harrington DO, Flocks M: The multiple pattern method of visual field examination. Trans Am Acad Ophthalmol Otolaryngol 59:126–142, 1955

107. Friedmann AI: Serial analysis of changes in visual field defects, employing a new instrument, to determine the activity of diseases involving the visual pathways. Ophthalmologica 152:1–12, 1966

108. Bender MB: Disorders in Perception; With Particular Reference to the Phenomena of Extinction and Displacement. Springfield, IL, Charles C Thomas, 1952

109. Abernethy CN III, Leibowitz HW: The effect of feedback on luminance thresholds for peripherally presented stimuli. Percept Psychophys 10:172–174, 1971

110. Blackwell HR: Studies of psychophysical methods for measuring visual thresholds. J Opt Soc Am 42:606–616, 1952

111. Green DM: Signal Detection Theory and Psychophysics. New York, John Wiley and Sons, 1966

112. Nachmias J: Signal detection theory and its application to problems in vision, in Jameson D, Hurvich LM (eds): Visual Psychophysics; Handbook of Sensory Physiology, vol. VII/7. Berlin, Springer-Verlag, 1972, pp 56–77

113. Swets JA, Tanner WP Jr, Birdsall TG: Decision processes in perception. Psychol Rev 68:301–340, 1961

114. Egan JP: Signal Detection Theory and ROC-Analysis. New York, Academic Press, 1975

115. Bernstein IH: The criterion effect and signal detection theory, in Tate GW Jr, Lynn JR (eds): Principles of

Quantitative Perimetry: Testing and Interpreting the Visual Field. New York, Grune & Stratton, 1977, pp 295–305

116. Aulhorn E, Harms H: Early visual field defects in glaucoma, in Glaucoma Symposium, Tutzing Castle, 1966. Basel, Karger, 1967, pp 151–185

117. Wolf E, Nadroski AS: Extent of the visual field; changes with age and oxygen tension. Arch Ophthalmol 86:637–642, 1971

118. Bursill AE: The restriction of peripheral vision during exposure to hot and humid conditions. Q J Exp Psychol 10:113–129, 1958

2

Principles of Static Perimetry

Douglas R. Anderson

Within the field of vision, every point is characterized by a certain level of visual sensation. One measure of this is the differential luminosity threshold, which is tested in most forms of perimetry. The threshold at a location is roughly considered to be the weakest stimulus that is just barely visible at that spot (see Chapter 1 for more exact definition). The line that joins all adjacent points with identical thresholds is the isopter for that stimulus.

A stimulus is just barely visible at its isopter, and is more easily seen at all points within the isopter, because in a normal field visual sensation is progressively better as fixation is approached (Fig. 2-1). Contrariwise, the stimulus is not seen in regions more peripheral than its isopter. The isopter is thus the boundary that separates the region within which the stimulus is visible from the region in which the stimulus is not visible. This feature is the basis of classic kinetic perimetry, in which a stimulus is moved from the periphery (where it is not seen) toward the center. The place at which it is first seen is a point on the isopter for that stimulus. This procedure is repeated with the same stimulus along many meridians until the ovoid contour of the isopter can be plotted by joining the points. Concentric isopters are plotted at various distances from the center to the periphery with each of several additional appropriate stimuli. Although kinetic technique is used to good advantage in manual perimetry, none of the currently available perimeters utilize kinetic stimuli automatically.

An equivalent representation of the hill of vision can be obtained by performing static threshold determinations at representative locations throughout the field. By trial and error, with stimuli of various strengths it can be determined at each location what is the weakest stimulus visible. A line joining the points

at which, for example, stimulus strength 27 is visible, would be the isopter for the stimulus strength 27 (Fig. 2-2). The isopter separates the region in which weaker stimuli (with larger numbers) are seen from the more peripheral region in which the thresholds are stronger stimuli (with smaller numbers). At points inside the isopter where weaker stimuli are visible, the stimulus strength 27 is suprathreshold.

STATIC SPOT-CHECKING WITH A SUPRATHRESHOLD STIMULUS

If a stimulus of appropriate intensity is presented at many locations in a normal visual field, the stimulus will be seen over a central region but will not be seen at more peripheral points. By this procedure the isopter for that stimulus has been determined to be in the zone that separates the points where the stimulus is visible from the points where it is not (Fig. 2-3). When spot-checking is done in this manner, a judgment can be made whether or not the isopter is depressed inward at some or all meridians compared to its expected normal position. In addition, if the stimulus is not seen at one or several points within the region bounded by the isopter, a scotoma has been discovered. (Fig. 2-4). The ability to detect a field defect by presenting a certain stimulus at a certain pattern of points is described in terms of sensitivity and specificity (see Chapter 5). It should be noted that with suprathreshold spot-checking the defects are detected, but the depth of the depressed sensitivity is not determined, nor is the extent for the abnormal region fully mapped. This would require repeating the procedure with several stimuli.

AUTOMATIC PERIMETRY IN GLAUCOMA
ISBN 0–8089–1705–6

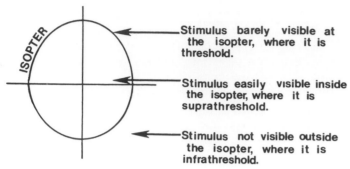

Fig. 2-1. Isopter separating the inner region in which the stimulus is seen from the outer region where it is not seen.

In a typical automated application of the spot-checking technique, a certain portion of the field (for example, the central 25 degrees) is tested with a single stimulus intensity that in a normal field would be suprathreshold (visible) over the area tested; that is, a stimulus is used whose isopter is normally outside 25 degrees. This suprathreshold spot-checking (also called supraliminal screening, see Chapter 5) is the essential feature of the "selective perimetry" devised by Armaly and modified by Drance to search selected regions of the field for glaucomatous abnormalities. Ideally, the stimulus used should be the one that is normally not visible much beyond the region tested. If a stimulus strong enough to be seen out to 60 degrees is used to test the central 25 degrees, it may be so strong that it is

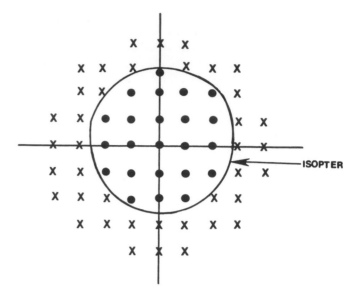

Fig. 2-3. Pattern of suprathreshold static spot-checking, showing an "isopter" separating locations where the stimulus is seen (●) from those where the stimulus is not seen (X). Compare to Figure 1-1.

also seen within a shallow scotoma, and the presence of the scotoma would be missed. On the other hand, if a weak stimulus is used that may normally have its isopter as far inward as 15 degrees, the region from 15 to 25 degrees is effectively not tested, because this zone would be judged normal whether or not the stimulus is seen.

For this "one-level screening" there are two fundamental approaches to the selection of the stimulus to be used. The first approach is to choose a standard stimulus that is normally threshold at 30 degrees. The

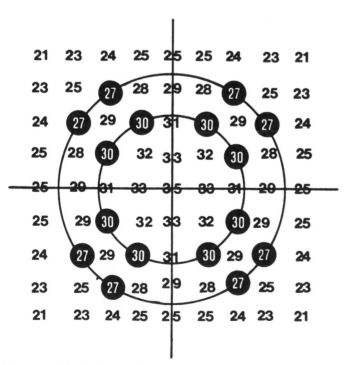

Fig. 2-2. Grid of static thresholds at 81 points. The isopters for stimuli 27 and 30 are drawn. The isopter for stimulus 27 encloses all points at which weaker stimuli (with larger numbers) are visible. Outside the isopter lie points at which only stronger stimuli (with smaller numbers) are visible.

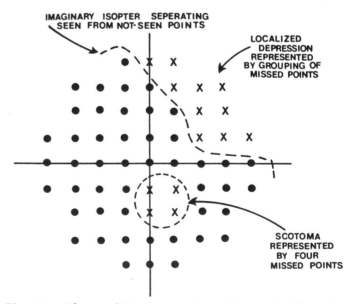

Fig. 2-4. Abnormalities in a pattern of spot-checking. An "X" represents where the stimulus was not seen. An upper nasal step and a paracentral scotoma are illustrated.

selection is best adjusted for age. With such one-level screening with a standard-for-age stimulus, generalized depression (reduced static threshold at all points, concentric inward movement of all isopters) is represented as a constricted area over which the stimulus is seen. In the case of a depressed field, scotomas can be detected only within the contracted area within which the stimulus is seen.

The second approach for stimulus selection is to use a threshold-related stimulus in order to adjust for any generalized depression that may be present. This is done by determining what stimulus is threshold 30 degrees from fixation in each individual eye, and using that stimulus to test the central field. An appropriate location at which to determine threshold is 30 degrees temporally somewhat above and below the horizontal meridian, selecting the weaker stimulus if the two thresholds are different. These locations will be affected by generalized depression, but it is unlikely that both locations will be affected by scotomas or localized depressions (nasal steps and temporal wedges). The individual selection of the stimulus enhances the detection of scotomas and nasal steps, which can be detected anywhere in the central field even in the presence of a generalized depression. This is important because such localized defects are more specific for glaucoma than is generalized depression. The ability to judge the presence of generalized depression is not lost. Depression is recognized to be present if the threshold stimulus at 30 degrees is stronger than usual for the person's age. Individual selection of threshold also prevents the inadvertent use of a stimulus excessively strong for that individual, which would reduce the ability to detect shallow scotomas near the center. In most settings, the benefit of using an individually selected stimulus is worth the slight expenditure of time needed to determine threshold at two or more points.

With either a standard-for-age stimulus or an individually selected stimulus, an optimum strategy may also adjust the strength of the stimulus for eccentricity from fixation (eccentricity-compensated screening). The purpose is to use of a progressively weaker supraliminal stimulus the closer one is to fixation. This would allow detection of a more shallow scotoma inside 15 degrees (for example one in which the 30-degree threshold stimulus is visible) than is possible by one-level screening with a 30-degree threshold stimulus. This eccentricity-compensated screening can be done with a standard-for-age stimulus, but more often is combined with a threshold-related strategy. The individual's threshold may be determined at several representative eccentricities, or an appropriate stimulus can be selected for the different eccentricities by using only the individually measured 30-degree threshold and assuming the usual slope of the normal hill of vision.

To summarize about the stimulus used for suprathreshold (supraliminal) spot-checking: Screening can be done as a one-level screening with a single standard stimulus for a person of that age, or eccentricity-compensated screening can be done with stimuli of different strength depending on the distance from the point of fixation. With either, the test can be made better by using a threshold-related stimulus selection, i.e., by adjusting the strength of stimuli according to the individual's threshold at a reasonably normal position in the field. Further details and considerations with regard to the ideal use of stimuli that are both threshold related and eccentricity compensated are found in Chapter 5.

For optimum detection (and for characterization of the topography of the defect), an adequate number of points must be tested in locations appropriate for the disease under consideration. For glaucoma, usually 75 to 150 points are tested within the central 25 to 30 degrees to detect scotomas in the arcuate regions. Additional points outside 30 degrees are often also tested to detect nasal steps and temporal wedges. If eccentricity-compensated stimuli are not being used, it is at least important to use two different stimuli for the peripheral and central fields. The same stimulus cannot be used for both, because a stimulus strong enough to be seen at the periphery will be excessively suprathreshold in the central field. The rate of detection improves as the number of points tested is increased, but so does the time for the test. The usual pattern of 75 to 150 points used in most instruments represents a concensus of what constitutes a reasonably compulsive screening examination that does not demand an unreasonable length of time.

It is very important that all isolated points at which the patient fails to respond be retested. It is quite common for individuals with normal fields to fail to see some stimulus presentations because of a blink, momentary inattention, or hesitation of response beyond the time allowed. To conclude that a missed response represents a field defect there must be confirmation by repeated presentation, unless the missed response is considered confirmed by being part of a cluster of missed points. In some testing strategies, locations at which the suprathreshold stimulus is not seen are then tested with stronger stimuli. The location may first be tested with a somewhat stronger stimulus and then with a maximal stimulus, so that each missed point is classified as a shallow, deep, or absolute defect. Other programs may quantitate the depth of the defect by a more carefully measured static threshold.

For manual suprathreshold testing, a stimulus duration of 0.33 to 0.5 seconds is recommended so that full temporal summation occurs. Shorter stimulus durations are permissible with automated stimulus presentations, provided the duration is reliably reproducible so that the stimulus presentations are all equivalent. An advantage of a stimulus 0.1 seconds or shorter is that the duration is too brief for the patient to perform a saccade toward the stimulus (although it may not matter too much, because the patient can make a saccade toward a stimulus presented in a random location only if he did in fact see the stimulus).

The stimulus presentation is followed by an interval of time during which the patient may respond. The interval during which a response is accepted may or may not occupy the entire interval until the next stimulus presentation. The length of the test is related to the number of stimulus presentations and the interval of time between them. The interval must not be made so short that the patient is unable to respond within the interval or that he finds the pace too hectic, nor so long that the test seems to take forever. An automated adjustment according to the quickness of the individual's response time, and a somewhat irregular rhythm of presentation (to avoid a tendency for rhythmic responses) are ideal.

STATIC THRESHOLD QUANTITATION

To determine the stimulus intensity that separates visibility and nonvisibility at a certain point (that is, the threshold stimulus that is just barely visible), there must be an absolute minimum of two stimulus presentations, one seen and one not seen. Because all individuals will give some inconsistent responses, particularly to marginally visible stimuli, the seen and unseen responses bounding threshold need to be confirmed. Therefore, four stimulus presentations at each point are in fact the minimal for an accurate examination, but more will inevitably be needed at most points because the threshold value is not known in advance and several stimulus presentations will be needed to approach and define the threshold. If six stimulus presentations are needed on the average at each point tested, the examination will take six times longer than suprathreshold testing for a given number of points.

Threshold can be measured in two ways: the ascending method of limits, and the up-and-down bracketing "staircase" method. In the method of limits, traditionally used for manual perimetry, successive stimulus presentations approach threshold from the infrathreshold (invisible) side. Each stimulus presentation is somewhat more intense than the last. If the first stimulus is seen (or for that matter the second stimulus, as the first response could have been a false one), the procedure is started again beginning with a weaker stimulus, as one seemingly did not start sufficiently infrathreshold. After at least two negative responses to seeming infrathreshold stimuli, the first stimulus seen is the apparent threshold, but should be presented a second time to be sure that the "seen" response was not a false one. (In some manual strategies the presentation is not repeated if the apparent threshold is in keeping with adjacent previously tested points.) If the stimulus is not seen on the second presentation, then the procedure continues with increasing strength of stimuli. To save time in case the first seen response was a false one, Greve introduced the clever method of making the presentation after a seen response one step more intense, just as if it had not been seen, accepting the first response as threshold if it is confirmed by a seen response on the second slightly more intense presentation.

The staircase, up-and-down, or bracketing method, is typically used in automated perimeters. If the first stimulus is seen (suprathreshold), the next stimulus at that location is made weaker. Contrariwise, the stimulus is strengthened if the previous presentation at that location was not seen (i.e., it was infrathreshold). By these means, when successive stimulus presentations seem to have crossed threshold (that is, when two successive presentations are seen and not seen, respectively, or vice-versa), the direction of the intensity change for the subsequent stimulus is reversed. The process continues until a computer algorithm accepts as threshold a point that in essence is straddled by at least two seen and two unseen stimulus presentations. To save time, large steps of intensity may be taken until threshold is first crossed, but after the direction of the intensity change reverses, smaller steps are used to determine the threshold more accurately. With computer help, it is not necessary to test completely the threshold at one point before moving on to another. Instead, successive stimulus presentations can be made at different points in the field (thereby reducing the tendency for the patient to lose fixation), but with the strength of the next stimulus presented at any given point being determined by the last response given at that particular location.

The time of the test is reduced if the first stimulus presentation at each location is close to the actual threshold. To accomplish this, the first presentation at each point may be chosen according to known normal values for age at each point. The first stimulus to present may instead be chosen according to the threshold of that point recorded in a previous examination, if that data is available to the memory of the computer. Alternatively, especially if the field is abnormal, it is of advantage to determine actual threshold at a limited number of points (say one in each quadrant), and then to threshold neighboring points starting with stimuli selected according to the known threshold at nearby points. This procedure mimics some of the time-saving advantage of kinetic perimetry. For example, if a point has an absolute defect, then adjacent points are tested with stimuli of maximal luminosity, to confirm quickly the extent of the absolute defect.

The accuracy of the threshold determination is limited by the luminosity interval between the final stimulus presentations that straddle threshold. In manual perimetry 1 db steps was most often used, but larger steps were chosen for most automated strategies in order to save time. The accuracy is not really reduced, because accuracy is also limited by unavoidably inconsistent responses that occur in a range of luminous intensities around threshold (strictly defined as the intensity at which the person responds to the stimulus half the time). The accuracy is also affected by the patient's alertness and his consistency of response. The variability of the measured threshold on several repeated measurements at the same sitting is called short-term fluctuation. It can be estimated by root mean square of duplicate measures at selected points within the field, so that the significance of a seemingly deviant value can be judged. This value indicates the unavoidable short-term fluctuation (which may be increased in abnormal regions of the field), and also the perhaps avoidable variability due to unreliable patient responses. The component due to unreliability of the patient's responses can be judged by noting such things as the frequency with which he responds when no stimulus is presented, the frequency with which he fails to respond when a bright stimulus is presented, and the frequency with which a response is given prematurely (before stimulus is presented).

An accurate threshold could be taken as the average of several successive measurements with smaller intervals of luminosity, but for routine purposes the small clinical utility of such high accuracy does not justify the additional time utilized. For example, there is no need to have better accuracy than the magnitude of the normal change in the physiologic state of the visual system from one time to another (the long-term fluctuation defined in Chapter 10).

The duration of the stimuli and the interval between them are governed by the same considerations as for suprathreshold spot-checking. An optimum compromise between allowing sufficient time for the patient to respond and shortening the time of the test can be achieved if the computer varies the interval between stimuli according to the response time shown by the individual being tested. The time of the perimetric test must be kept under control, not only to keep the test practical and cost effective, but also because the test quality may deteriorate with fatigue.

The number of points tested and their location vary according to the clinical circumstance for which a visual field test is being performed. The user typically has a choice of such things as a meridional static cut; a pattern of points of certain spatial density covering the central field, or the peripheral field, or both; or a concentrated grid of points that can be placed in an area of particular interest, such as covering the macula or the region of a suspected scotoma. At present the user might select a general purpose program covering the central field, and based on the results then decide to perform a static cut or a closer grid of points in a certain suspicious area. Future software development may provide for automatic retesting of points with threshold values out of line with the value predicted by the threshold of neighboring points, or automatic exploration of the area with a finer grid of points or a static cut.

SELECTION OF TESTING STRATEGY

Screening

Suprathreshold testing is a rapid way to screen relevant areas of the visual field. It requires only one presentation (question) per location tested (two presentations at missed points). Suprathreshold spot-checking is particularly used when a rapid screen of a large group of individuals is undertaken, especially if most of the group will be normal. It is important to keep the test short so that the time spent per case detected is at a reasonable level (i.e., to keep the screening project cost effective). Specificity of the test must be kept high (see Chapter 5) as time spent in more detailed examination of false positive results must be counted in the cost of the screening effort.

In a group with a very high prevalence of glaucoma (for example, office patients that have an elevated intraocular pressure), the higher sensitivity for shallow defects may make a quantitated static threshold test worthwhile even for simple detection. In fact, it may actually take less time to do a quantitative field on every one than to do a sensitive spot-checking field on everyone plus a quantitative field on a large proportion of the group with a positive result (including false positives) from suprathreshold testing. Threshold testing is wise anyway in a group at risk of developing a field defect, even if they don't have it now (for example those with elevated intraocular pressure or strong family history of glaucoma), because in such suspects one wants a baseline threshold determination so that the future development of a defect can be judged against the individual's previous status, rather than judged less accurately against the norm for age (see Chapter 8).

Diagnosis

A suprathreshold spot-checking strategy is often adequate not only for detecting a defect, but for establishing the nature of the defect. It may be obvious, for example, that the patient has a central scotoma, an arcuate defect, or a hemianopia. Occasionally, however, it may be necessary to repeat the suprathreshold testing with another stimulus or to perform a fully quantitative field to establish the topographical nature of a vague wedge-shaped depression or other indistinct abnormality.

Progression

Suprathreshold testing with a single stimulus on successive occasions gives a very crude and usually inadequate estimation of progression, which is equivalent to the mapping of a single isopter in kinetic perimetry. Careful quantitation of both the normal and abnormal areas of the visual field by static threshold determination is required to detect the occurrence of new defects, to detect the deepening of existing defects, to detect the spread of existing defects into new regions, and to help distinguish glaucomatous progression from other alterations in the visual system (small pupil and cataract, for example).

After three or four stable threshold examinations, subsequent examinations can theoretically be conducted to good advantage by a modified suprathreshold technique that is fundamentally different from the ones used for screening. For example, the field may be tested with a stimulus at each point that is a set amount slightly stronger than the average past threshold at that point. This fast strategy for ruling out progression is available on the Humphrey perimeter. Another possible strategy would be to use a stimulus only very slightly stronger than the worst previously recorded threshold of that point. With either plan, if the patient sees the single stimulus presentation at each point, it would seem that the field has not worsened.

3

The Glaucoma Visual Field Defect and Its Progression

Stephen M. Drance

The classical visual field defects of chronic open angle glaucoma are well known and our understanding of them has evolved since campimetry was first used by Von Graefe over a hundred years ago. Central and/or peripheral field changes have been highlighted in the last century, depending on the introduction of new instruments and the refinement of visual field techniques. The successful plotting of certain glaucomatous defects in the visual field depends on the method chosen or available to the perimetrist who is investigating the disease. One only finds the things that one is looking for. This explains some of the apparent contradictions found in the literature and some of the differences of emphasis of the importance of certain aspects of the glaucomatous field defect.

The first techniques used during the last century in evaluating the glaucomatous visual field used the campimeter and were then followed by the introduction of the perimeter, which remained in vogue for a number of years. The reintroduction of the campimeter or the tangent screen by Bjerrum was followed by the excellent studies of Ronne,[1] Traquair,[2] Harrington[3] and others, which re-emphasized and refined the understanding of the central visual field defects of the disease. Using both the perimeter and campimeter with kinetic stimuli produced a fairly comprehensive representation of glaucomatous field defects.

The introduction of the static perimetry by Sloane in 1966 led to a reevaluation of the earliest glaucomatous defects by Harms and Aulhorn[4] and confirmed by others,[5] which showed that isolated paracentral scotomata were common early defects of the visual field and that central and peripheral nasal steps could occur

on their own, without paracentral scotoma, but were more often associated with the paracentral defects. The defects were either relative or absolute and finally resulted in the classical arcuate scotoma with peripheral nasal loss. It was then realized that peripheral field loss, particularly on the nasal side could occur on its own and that even unusual temporal and other sectors could become affected in isolation and were therefore sometimes the earliest localized visual field defects. The frequency of various types of scotoma in glaucoma have been studied in a cross sectional manner by Aulhorn,[6] Armaly,[7] and Phelps.[8] The defects occur more frequently in the upper part of the visual field and they are closer to fixation in the upper field. The refinement in techniques has led to earlier detection of field damage and the mapping of subtler visual field defects. Generalized contraction of the isopters and an enlargement of the blind spot, including baring of the blind spot, has been known and emphasized for a long time but such changes occur also as a result of altered transparency of the optical media, miosis, uncorrected refractive error and aging, which made these changes difficult to interpret and too nonspecific.

In 1978 Werner and Drance[9] showed that localized scatter in both kinetic and static responses was a precursor to subsequent visual field defects in glaucomatous patients. Shortly afterward, the introduction of the threshold measuring computerized perimeters as well as the realization that the nerve fibers in the retina can be lost without any localized nerve fiber bundle defects being seen in the visual field[10] has made it clear that generalized changes in differential threshold and increased localized scatter occur prior to the nerve fiber bundle defects in the central visual field.

AUTOMATIC PERIMETRY IN GLAUCOMA
ISBN 0–8089–1705–6

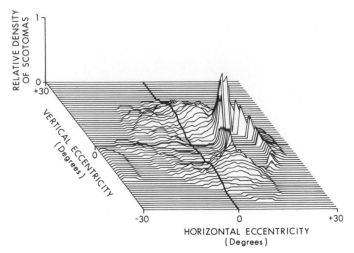

Fig. 3-1. Topographical distribution of relative density of earliest detectable glaucomatous scotomas of 98 eyes. Densities of scotomas were summed at each position and data were normalized by dividing all values by maximum. Heavy lines mark vertical and horizontal meridians. The physiologic blind spot was eliminated from consideration and appears flat. (Reprinted with permission from: Hart and Becker, *Ophthalmology* 89:268–279, 1983.)

It is proposed now to describe: generalized disturbances in visual function, localized nerve fiber bundle defects, and the modes of progression of visual field defects.

GENERALIZED CHANGES IN THE DIFFERENTIAL LIGHT SENSE

In 1966 Aulhorn and Harms[4] reported on 2684 eyes of glaucoma patients and glaucoma suspects who had been examined with static perimetry. Thirty-one percent had normal visual fields and of the remainder, 38% had a generalized contraction of the isopters. Armaly[7] found that 6 of 100 patients, with elevated intraocular pressure and examined by his method of selective perimetry, had a contraction of isopters that was pressure dependent. In 1981 I[11] showed that in asymmetric patients in whom one eye already had a nerve fiber bundle field defect, the central isopters of that eye were contracted compared with the fellow eye without a defect in only about 30 percent of the cases. Werner, Saheb, and Patel[12] independently recorded similar findings. If a generalized isopter contraction always preceded a localized nerve fiber bundle defect, then one would expect the damaged eyes to have contracted isopters, compared with the undamaged fellow eye 100 percent of the time, which was not the case. Hart and Becker[13] found that 35.6 percent of eyes that developed localized field defects showed blind spot enlargement and 31 percent showed central isopter constriction. In all of these studies, in approximately two thirds of fields there was no contraction of

the isopters associated with the development of a classical nerve fiber bundle defect. Hart and Becker found that isopter constriction occurred significantly more frequently during the year prior to the onset of the definitive field defects when compared with a control group who did not subsequently develop field defects. It can be concluded that while contraction of the central isopters occurs quite commonly in eyes that subsequently develop localized visual field defects, the majority of localized visual field defects is not preceded or accompanied by such an isopter contraction.

The interest in generalized isopter contraction was rekindled by the studies of the optic nerve counts made by Quigley[10] who showed that 40 to 50 percent of nerve fibers could be lost without a field defect and by the findings of Airaksinen[14] who showed that localized nerve fiber bundle loss and diffuse loss of nerve fibers in the retina preceded visual field defects. The abnormalities of other psychophysical functions such as foveal function,[15] color sense,[11] temporal,[17] spatial[16] contrast sensitivity, and receptive fieldlike functions[18] occurred before the development of visual field defects that further suggested some generalized disturbances prior to field defects.

LOCALIZED NERVE FIBER BUNDLE DEFECTS

The now classical features of paracentral scotomata along the course of the arcuate nerve fibers, the associated or independent central and peripheral nasal steps, the classical arcuate nerve fiber bundle defects, the temporal and other sector-shaped defects are well known. To identify the earliest visual field defects, I presented a study in 1978[9] of 35 eyes of patients who developed reproducible nerve fiber bundle field defects with previously normal visual fields. These patients had field-plotted every 4 mo. The appearance of the first reproducible defect therefore denoted an early field defect but that does not imply early disease. In 51 percent of the patients the first visual field disturbance was a paracentral scotoma with a nasal step, an additional 26 percent had a paracentral scotoma alone, 20 percent showed only nasal steps, two thirds of which were in the central isopters and one third only in the peripheral isopters. The remaining 3 percent developed sector-shaped defects in other quadrants as the first defect. The study also revealed that the upper and lower hemifields could become involved at almost the same time, that a scotoma was often relative initially but could be very dense from the beginning. In 1983, Hart and Becker[13] studied the initial glaucomatous defects of 98 eyes of 72 patients and reported that 54 percent had nasal steps, 41 percent had paracentral or Bjerrum scotomata, 30 percent had arcuate blind spot enlargement, 90 percent had isolated arcuate scotomata separated from the blind spot, and 3 percent had temporal defects as their initial defects. These authors also found that the upper visual field was more commonly involved than the lower in a 3:2 ratio. In some of their patients the nasal steps involved both the central and peripheral isopters, but there were some eyes with only a peripheral nasal step and others with only a central nasal step. These authors also showed that the most common area of paracentral disturbance was adjacent to the superior nasal pole of the blind spot (Fig. 3-1). Phelps[5] illustrated the location of paracentral defects of varying severity (Fig. 3-2.). Werner and Drance[9] found a localized scatter of both static and kinetic responses that preceded the subsequent development of visual field defects. Flammer, Drance, and Zulauf[19] used quantitative threshold perimetry to show an increase in short-term fluctuation in areas without an increased threshold to be present in early glaucoma that was confirmed by the studies of Sturmer, Gloor, and Tobler.[20] They traced the sequence of early glaucomatous disturbances to be a localized one of increased short-term fluctuation with a normal threshold. Increased fluctuation, with a reduction in sensitivity (increased threshold) was the next stage of the visual field disturbance, followed by a relative scotoma found to be in an area in which the threshold was difficult to determine because of the increased fluctuation, and which they felt was therefore not a clearly demarcated disturbance as had been previously suggested by kinetic perimetrists.

It would now appear, judging from longitudinal studies, that the earliest localized defects have been described as to nature, location, density, and frequency. These disturbances are preceded by increase in the short term fluctuation in the area in which a defect subsequently develops.

PROGRESSION OF GLAUCOMATOUS DAMAGE

Very little has been written about the way in which the glaucomatous visual field progresses apart from the well known sequence of an arcuate scotoma, breaking through to the periphery in the upper and lower field and gradually leading to a central island of vision and/or a peripheral temporal field remnant. The manner in which the progression occurs has not been fully explored. There are at least five ways in which progression can occur: (1) Scotomas can continuously increase in size and depth (Fig. 3-3); (2) Scotomas can become larger and/or deeper in an episodic manner (Fig. 3-4); (3) Fresh scotomas or sector shaped defects may develop (Fig. 3-5); (4) There may be a generalized loss of retinal sensitivity as manifested by a gradual constriction of all isopters and not accounted for by opacities of the media (Fig. 3-6); and (5) There may be improvement in the field.

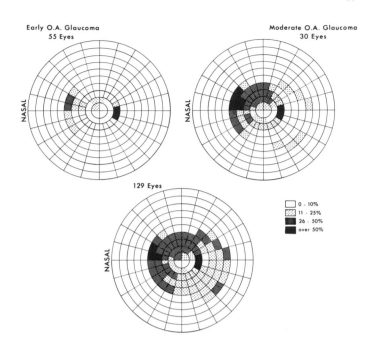

Fig. 3-2. Frequency distribution of mild, moderate, and all visual field defects in eyes with chronic open angle glaucoma whose maximum intraocular pressures were 22–34 mm Hg. (Modified with permission from: Phelps, Hayreh and Montague, Doc Ophthalmol Proc Ser 35:113–123, 1983.)

Hart and Becker[13] described the chronology of 98 developing field defects in which the initial defects were relative. Of the 98 eyes examined, 22 showed a disappearance of the scotoma on medical therapy. The disappearance of the early scotoma was not related to pressure reduction and in all 22 the defects recurred and were more dense within 5 yr in the territory of the nerve fiber bundle originally disturbed. Of the 98 eyes examined, 67 showed a similar gradual onset but had no temporary improvement and in the remaining 9 of the 98 eyes there was a relatively abrupt onset followed by rapid progression in the size and density of the defect. Although the onset of the defects appeared to be gradual in their patients, the progression of established defects seemed to occur in episodic fashion so that the defect would increase in size and density, after which there would be many eyes without further progression. Sixty-three of the eyes were observed for at least a decade and 13 involved both hemifields from the outset, whereas in the remaining 50, the defects were confined to either the superior or inferior hemifield. Of those 50 eyes, 22 percent showed defects in the other hemifield at the end of the decade but in the other 78 percent the defect remained confined to the same hemifield. All showed marked progression over the 10-yr period, so that in 72 percent of them the loss was marked and dense, and in 6 percent the loss was absolute, while only 4 percent were left with a shallow relative defect. In those eyes in whom both hemifields were initially involved the progression was even more marked, so that 54 percent developed absolute field

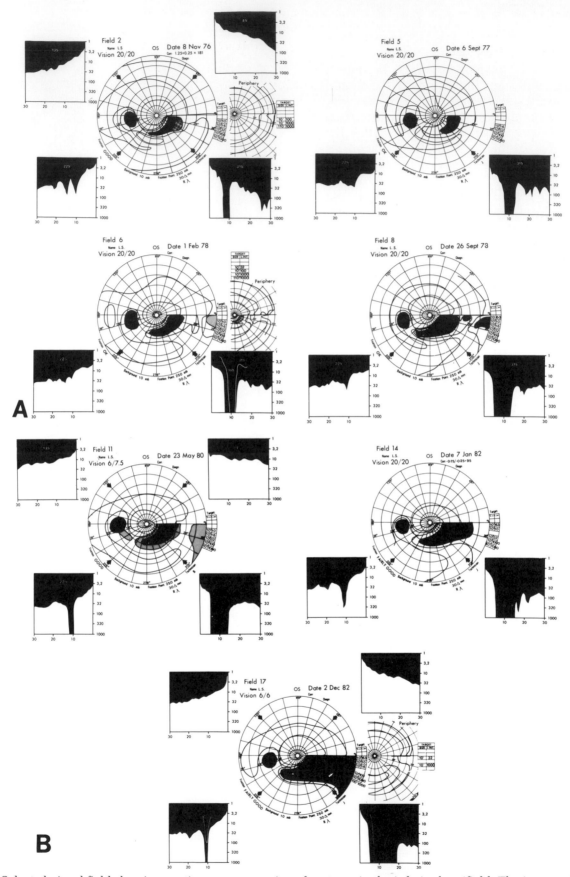

Fig. 3-3. Selected visual field showing continuous progression of scotoma in the inferior hemifield. The intervening fields, not illustrated, confirm the continuous progression.

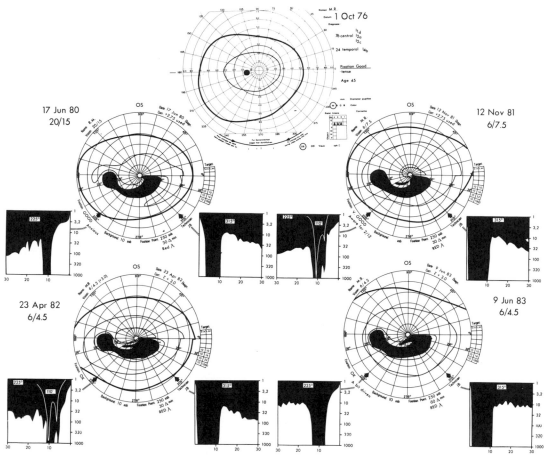

Fig. 3-4. Visual fields indicating sudden onset of scotoma noticed by patient (June 17, 1980). The occurrence of a fresh episode is shown statically and kinetically (November 12, 1981) with subsequent lack of further damage.

loss in the decade. There was no significant difference in the mean intraocular pressure or age that could be related to the degree of progression. Most of the eyes had well-controlled low pressures but the mean pressures were slightly lower, but not statistically significantly lower in the group of eyes suffering the greatest extent of field loss.

Some questions should be addressed to progression of the defect. Do scotomata increase in size and density at the same time? How often do fresh scotomata occur? Is there a diffuse change in the sensitivity of the visual field? Is it greater or smaller than the changes in the scotoma? Is there always change in the central field when the peripheral field changes? Is the rate of loss related to intraocular pressure? Can rate of progression be affected by therapy?

To try and answer some of these questions the following study was recently carried out.[21] Of 48 patients (28 males and 20 females), 48 eyes were selected on the basis of having chronic open-angle glaucoma, an accurate perimetric follow-up for a number of years was made. At least two follow-ups must have been with a scotoma. The initial visual acuity had to be 6/9 or better and the final acuity had to be 6/12 or better. All the fields had planimetry carried out of all scotomata as well as planimetry of the static profiles of the island of

vision through the scotoma. The central sensitivity of each field was known. The mean duration of follow-up was 8 yr ± 3.5 yr with a median of 7.5 yr, and range from 2 to 15 yr. Forty-two (87.5 percent) of the eyes showed progression, five (10.4 percent) remained stable and one (2.1 percent) improved. An increase in density of a scotoma was the most common mode of progression and occurred in 78 percent of progressing defects while an increase in the size of the scotoma occurred in 52 percent and a new scotoma appeared in 49 percent of the eyes showing progression. Of 45 eyes that had only one hemifield involved by the scotoma at the onset, 22 (63 percent) remained in that hemifield, whereas 13 (37 percent) showed involvement of the other hemifield over the period of observation. Many of the eyes showed combinations of all three modes of progression. The duration of follow-up was related to the chance of developing a new scotoma and the involvement of the second hemifield. The age at diagnosis and the intraocular pressure did not appear to be statistically significantly related to qualitative progression. The study of the relationship of rates of progression to intraocular pressure may be rewarding in the future.

It appears that most scotomas progress by increasing in depth and a smaller number increase in size and

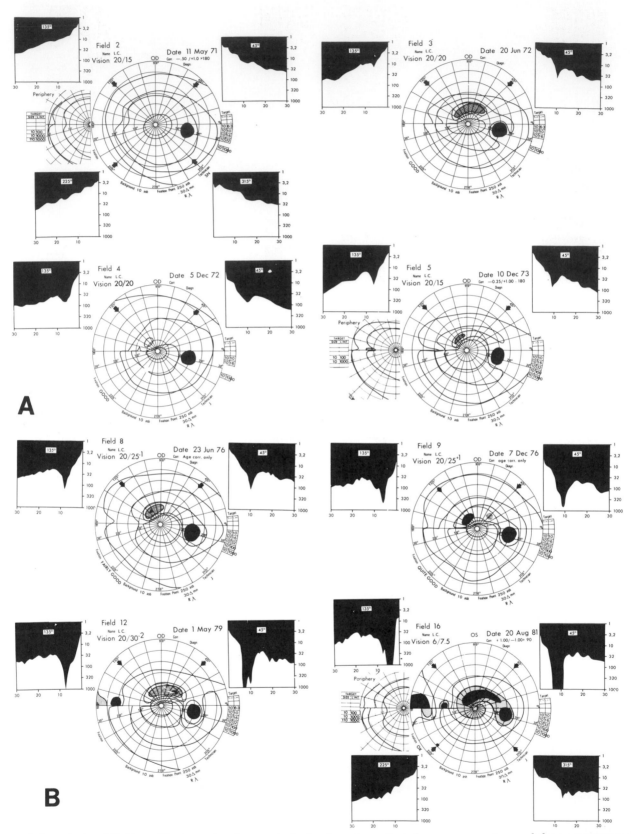

Fig. 3-5. Selected visual fields to illustrate development of a fresh scotoma that shows progression and the appearance of a new scotoma in the inferior hemifield (field 16).

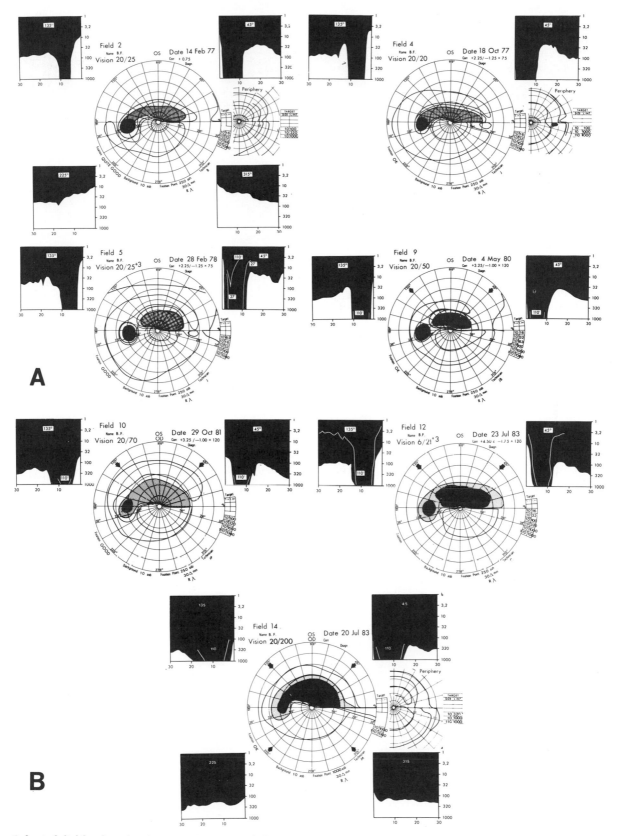

Fig. 3-6. Selected fields showing increase in size and density of scotoma in upper hemifield but with decreased vision due to lens opacity and overall loss of sensitivity.

about half of the eyes developed a new scotoma. One third of those with a single hemifield involvement developed involvement of the other half. Progression appears to be related to the length of follow-up and not to the age at the time of diagnosis nor to the level of intraocular pressure. Most of the studies reported in literature show that the majority of patients with field loss progress over time; our own studies confirm that.

The implications for perimetry of field defects in glaucoma are that threshold information of disturbed points in a scotoma or its quantification with kinetic perimetry are necessary in the most common mode of progression, which indicates deterioration of the disease is to be detected. Careful delineation of the area of scotomas and examination of the unaffected field are necessary since these types of change can also occur as isolated signs of progression.

It is essential that further work be done to elucidate whether pressure reduction plays an important role in determining the course and rate of the progression of glaucomatous visual field defects.

REFERENCES

1. Rönne H: Ueber das Gesichtsfeld beim Glaukom. Klin Monatsbl Augenheilkd 47 Part I:12–33, 1909
2. Traquair HM: The nerve-fibre bundle defect. Trans Ophthalmol Soc UK 64:3–23, 1944
3. Harrington DO: The art of perimetry. Am J Ophthalmol 80:414–416, 1975
4. Aulhorn E, Harms H: Early visual field defects in glaucoma, in Leydhecker W (Ed): Glaucoma; Tutzing Symposium 1966. Basel, Karger, 1967, pp 151–185
5. Drance SM: The early field defects in glaucoma. Invest Ophthalmol 8:84–91, 1969
6. Aulhorn E, Karmeyer H: Frequency distribution in early glaucomatous visual field defects. Doc Ophthalmol Proc Ser 14:75–83, 1977
7. Armaly MF: Selective perimetry for glaucomatous defects in ocular hypertension. Arch Ophthalmol 87:518–524, 1972
8. Phelps CD, Hayreh SS, Montague PR: Visual fields in low-tension glaucoma, primary open angle glaucoma, and anterior ischemic optic neuropathy. Doc Ophthalmol Proc Ser 35:113–124, 1983
9. Werner EB, Drance SM: Early visual field disturbances in glaucoma. Arch Ophthalmol 95:1173–1175, 1977
10. Quigley HA, Addicks EM, Green WR: Optic nerve damage in human glaucoma. III. Quantitative correlation of nerve fiber loss and visual field defect in glaucoma, ischemic neuropathy, papilledema and toxic neuropathy. Arch Ophthalmol 100:135–146, 1982
11. Drance SM, Lakowski R: Early psychophysical disturbances in chronic open angle glaucoma, in Symposium on Glaucoma; Transactions of the New Orleans Academy of Ophthalmology. St. Louis, CV Mosby, 1981, pp 107– 113
12. Werner EB, Saheb N, Patel S: Lack of generalized constriction of affected visual field in glaucoma patients with visual field defects in one eye. Can J Ophthalmol 17:53– 55, 1982
13. Hart WM Jr, Becker B: The onset and evolution of glaucomatous visual field defects. Ophthalmology 89:268–279, 1982
14. Airaksinen PJ, Tuulonen A: Early glaucoma changes in patients with and without an optic disc haemorrhage. Acta Ophthalmol 62:197–202, 1984
15. Anctil JL, Anderson DR: Early foveal involvement and generalized depression of the visual field in glaucoma. Arch Ophthalmol 102:363–370, 1984
16. Atkin A, Bodis-Wollner I, Wolkstein M, Moss A, Podos SM: Abnormalities of central contrast sensitivity in glaucoma. Am J Ophthalmol 88:205–211, 1979
17. Tyler CW: Specific deficits of flicker sensitivity in glaucoma and ocular hypertension. Invest Ophthalmol Vis Sci 20:204–212, 1981
18. Enoch JM, Campos EC: Analysis of patients with open-angle glaucoma using perimetric techniques reflecting receptive field-like properties. Doc Ophthalmol Proc Ser 19:137–149, 1978
19. Flammer J, Drance SM, Zulauf M: Differential light threshold; the short- and long-term fluctuation in patients with glaucoma, normal controls, and patients with suspected glaucoma. Arch Ophthalmol 102:704–706, 1984
20. Gloor B, Stürmer J, Vökt B: Was hat die automatisierte Perimetrie mit dem Octopus für nee Kenntnisse uber glaukomatose gesichtfeldveranderungen gebracht. Klin Monatsbl Augenheilkd 184:249–253, 1984
21. Mikelberg FS, Drance SM: The mode of progression of visual field defects in glaucoma. Am J Ophthalmol 98: 443–445, 1984

4

Strategies for Detection of Glaucoma Defects

Anders Heijl

The detection of glaucomatous field loss at an early stage is much more crucial today, when we tend to distinguish between ocular hypertension and manifest glaucoma with field loss, than before when all patients with elevated intraocular pressure were considered to suffer from glaucoma and were subjected to pressure-reducing therapy. Research performed during the last two decades has demonstrated that the risk of patients with mild ocular hypertension developing clear-cut glaucomatous damage within a 10-year period is actually quite low though higher than in normals. This justifies the modern no-therapy approach in most patients with increased ocular pressure and normal discs and fields.

The importance of using criteria other than the intraocular pressure to make a diagnosis of glaucoma is even more obvious when we consider the fact that population studies have shown that cases with low-tension glaucoma constitute a large part of all patients with glaucoma. There are indications that in the future tests other than visual field examination, for instance, examination of color perception, contrast sensitivity and retinal nerve fiber photography, may play a more important diagnostic role, but at this time the demonstration of glaucomatous visual field loss is still the most reliable sign when establishing a diagnosis of glaucoma.

Since the number of patients with suspect glaucoma is large, a heavy burden is placed on ophthalmologists as an acceptable standard of visual field examination must be maintained in a great number of tests. The problem of the large number of tests of acceptable quality has actually spurred the development of semi-automated and automated perimeters and is the main reason why computerized perimetry has been so widely accepted in the few years after its inception.

In this chapter the term screening for glaucoma defects is used in its meaning of winnowing out fields with glaucomatous visual field damage from a larger population of normal and pathological fields. Screening is thus used not as a synonym for supraliminal screening but as a synonym for detection of scotomas.

AIM

The aim of screening for glaucoma defects is to identify as many of the existing glaucomatous field defects as possible (to use a test with a high sensitivity) without creating too many false positive field defects (to use a test with a high specificity). These are partially conflicting requirements and generally a sensitive test will create more false positives than an insensitive one and vice versa.

THE IMPORTANT AREAS OF THE VISUAL FIELD

The current thoughts on the nature of glaucomatous visual field defects originate from the work of Aulhorn and Harms during the 1960s. The common early defects are paracentral scotomata in the Bjerrum area inside 25-30° and nasal steps.[1] Several frequency distributions showing the locations of glaucomatous field defects have been published.[2–6] Manual[2] as well as semi-automatic[3,4] and computerized[5,6] perimetry have been used in these studies. These studies all agree

AUTOMATIC PERIMETRY IN GLAUCOMA
ISBN 0–8089–1705–6

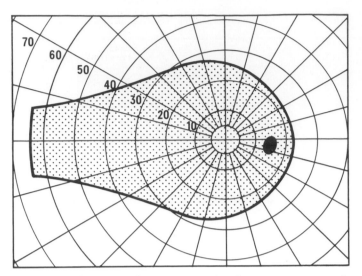

Fig. 4-1. The area where most early glaucomatous visual field defects occur.

that glaucomatous field loss is more common in the nasal field than temporally. Defects close to the fixation point occur more commonly above than below. All studies except that of Aulhorn and Karmeyer[2] have found a higher incidence of field defects in the superior than in the inferior half of the visual field.[3–6] A longitudinal study[6] where only the first defects occurring in a large population of ocular hypertensives were studied gave results similar to those of the transsectional studies.

While glaucomatous field loss is most common centrally and nasally it may occur anywhere in the visual field. Drance and collaborators have shown that even isolated temporal sector defects may occur in glaucoma although with a very low frequency.[7] A question that remains unsolved is the frequency of glaucomatous fields in which defects occur only peripherally (outside 30°). The figures in the literature vary widely from less than 1 percent[1] to over 10 percent.[8,9] It is clear that the frequency of peripheral field defects will vary with the technique used for the examining of the central visual field. If very sensitive techniques are used for the central visual field examination, fewer isolated peripheral defects will be found.[9] An educated guess might be that the frequency of isolated peripheral glaucomatous field loss is 3 to 6 percent. This is in accordance with figures published by Werner and Drance[10] in a paper on the earliest field change in glaucoma. If the frequency was much higher it would be difficult to explain why such high sensitivities have been reported when using tests where the peripheral field is not examined at all.[11–13]

The important area where most glaucomatous field loss occurs is shown in Fig. 4-1. The earlier idea of enlargement of the blind spot being a sign of glaucoma has been abandoned. Most glaucomatous early field defects are not connected to the blind spot and it is usually not until a later stage, when a more or less complete Bjerrum scotoma has formed, that the defect joins the blind spot. Baring of the blind spot lacks diagnostic value and can be elicited in almost all normal eyes.[14] Although most authors now stress the preponderance of early field defects in the nasal part of the field, other results have been presented, where the superior temporal quadrant has been considered very important.[15] Perimeteric results from the pericecal area are, however, unreliable even in normal subjects.[16] Angioscotomata that seldom disturb manual kinetic testing frequently give rise to reduced sensivities below and particularly above the blind spot when static, computerized techniques are used.[17]

STRATEGIES

In computerized perimetry static perimetric techniques are almost exclusively used. This is particularly appropriate for glaucoma screening since circumscribed, early glaucomatous field defects are easily missed when kinetic testing is used. In any static visual field screening there are two components: the pattern of tested points and the actual test strategy used at each point. To detect field loss two quite different strategies can be used: these are supraliminal screening and actual threshold determinations. Almost all computerized perimeters expose stimuli in a randomized, nonpredictable sequence. This improves the patient's fixation thus facilitating the detection of defects.[18]

Supraliminal Screening

The concept behind supraliminal screening is to save time by exposing a stimulus slightly above the expected normal threshold at each tested point, not trying to determine the actual threshold, but accepting the point as normal if the supraliminal stimulus is seen. According to the choice of the stimulus intensities computerized screening may be performed in three principally different ways: (1) one-level screening; (2) eccentricity-compensated screening; (3) threshold-related screening (used either as a one-level screening or preferably with eccentricity compensated stimuli).

One-level Screening

In the simplest form of supraliminal screening, targets of the same intensity are used at all points regardless of their position in the visual field. This has been the most common screening method in some of the simpler first generation automatic screeners. The sensitivity of the normal eye is highest at the fovea and decreases with increasing distance from the point of fixation. The sensitivity of a one-level test therefore will be higher further away from the point of fixation than more centrally, where relative defects might escape detection (Fig. 4-2). The sensitivity is increased if a lower stimulus intensity is used, but the number of false positives will then increase particularly further away from fixations.

Eccentricity-compensated Screening

A more rational and effective screening can be obtained by compensating for the normal gradient of sensitivity with increasing eccentricity (Fig. 4-2). The stimulus will then be similarly supraliminal at all points and field defects will be detected with a similar probability regardless of their location in the field.

Threshold-related Stimulus Selection

To adapt the stimulus intensity levels to the normal shape of the island of vision is a good first step but it does not solve the whole problem. The reason for this is the large interindividual variation of sensitivity between persons with normal fields that may exceed 1 log unit. Part of this variation is due to a general reduction of sensitivity with age that starts at about 40 yr of age. The age-dependent component of the variation can be taken care of by using threshold data obtained from groups of normals in different age brackets when deciding target intensities for supraliminal screening in various parts of the visual field. In doing so we approach a true threshold-related screening procedure. However, there is still a fairly large variation of threshold values even in patients of the same age with normal fields. This can be due to opacities of the media, variation in pupillary size, or different levels of alertness. In a test where target intensities are based on age-corrected normal values, patients with media opacities and miosis will seem to have field defects even if their visual fields are normal (apart from a general, nonspecific depression of sensitivity).

The only way to obtain a true threshold-related, supraliminal screening is to measure the actual threshold of the eye in one or more test points, correct for the location of the tested points in the visual field and add a suitable amount of stimulus intensity (usually 0.5 to 0.8 log units) at each point in order to make the test supraliminal (Fig. 4-2). Such threshold related supraliminal tests will have better sensitivity and specificity than a simple one-level test (compare Fig. 4-3). The initial threshold determinations may be performed automatically by the computerized instrument, or manually and followed by the automated supraliminal part of the test. Many modern instruments use this approach. Not even this approach is free from risk, however. If the initial threshold determination(s) are either faulty or performed in areas with pathologically increased increment threshold the choice of supraliminal screening intensities may be erroneous and the whole test jeopardized. If for example only a foveal threshold determination is performed, in a patient with macular disease, all intensities of the supraliminal

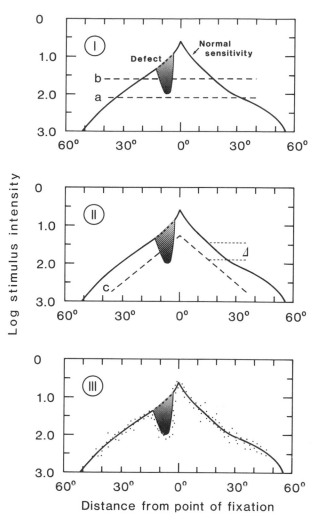

Fig. 4-2   In the normal visual field the sensitivity is highest at the fovea and decreases with the distance from the point of fixation. One-level supraliminal screening will either miss relative defects in the paracentral visual field (level a in graph I), or create many false positive defects (level b in graph I). Much more efficient screening is obtained if stimulus intensities are adjusted for the normal decrease of sensitivity with eccentricity, particularly if some initial threshold determinations are performed to adjust the screening levels for the general sensitivity level of the tested field (II). Threshold determinations (III) at each tested point will give the most accurate results, but at the cost of an increased test time.

screening might be too high and relative field defects missed. Most computerized instruments try to eliminate or diminish this risk by performing threshold determinations at 2–4 points and use the most sensitive point or an average of the most sensitive points as the reference level supposed to represent the normal area of the field being tested. Computerized comparisons of the obtained threshold values might be used in an effort to determine whether any of the initial points are likely to be situated in a defective area, where the measured threshold should not be allowed to influence the selection of the intensities used for the subsequent screening.[12] The accuracy of the initial threshold determina-

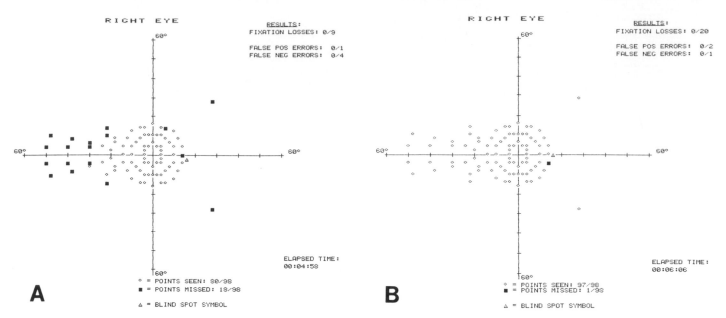

Fig. 4-3. Results obtained with a one-level (a) and a threshold-related, eccentricity-compensated (b) test in the same normal eye (Armaly tests performed with the Humphrey field analyzer). The one-level test has many false positive points, more so peripherally than centrally. The threshold-related test has just one missed point, in the blind spot of the tested eye.

tions might be increased by using a test logic with more than one reversal at each point[19] or by repeating the threshold determinations.[20] If all the initial test points are situated in defective parts of the field the result of the screening might still be completely misleading.

Retesting, Two-level Tests, and Quantification of Defects

Some early automatic field screeners exposed the stimulus once at every test point, registered whether it was perceived or not but did not carry the test any further. This lead to an unacceptably high frequency of

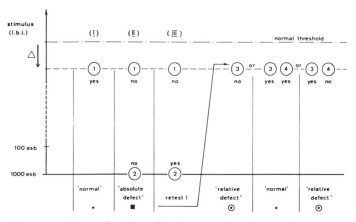

Fig. 4-4. Example of two-level screening strategy (programs 03 and 07 of the Octopus perimeter), permitting classification of tested points into three categories: normal, relative defect and absolute defect. (Reproduced with permission from Bebie H, Fankhauser F, Jenni A, et al: First Int Meeting on Automated Perimetry System Octopus, Interzeag AG, Schlieren, pp. 155–78)

isolated false positive points.[12,21] Retesting reduces the number of false positives dramatically[12,22] and therefore an automatic retest of initially missed points should be mandatory.

It is possible to carry the test further by exposing a maximum intensity stimulus at all missed points. This procedure allows a classification of tested points into three categories: normal points, points in relative defects and points in absolute (maximum luminosity) defects (Fig. 4-4). This type of testing is available in several instruments.

A further refinement is to measure the depth of all defects identified by the supraliminal test. This feature, which has been standard in the Competer supraliminal screening program for many years, is available also in some other instruments (compare Fig. 10-3, Chapter 10, and Fig. 12-4, Chapter 12).

It is obvious that a printout, which allows the user to separate between relative and absolute defects or shows the depth of all identified defects, makes interpretation much easier than a chart, where only missed and seen points are indicated (Fig. 4-5).

The available supraliminal screening strategies of each point can then be summarized in order of increasing sophistication: Stimulus shown only once—no retesting; Missed points retested; Missed points classified into relative and absolute defects; Depth of defect ascertained by measuring threshold at all missed points.

All extra testing, beyond the first of the above alternatives, requires increased test time. In normal fields, the use of more complex test protocols requires very little extra time. The extra time input however is a small price to pay for a more accurate separation

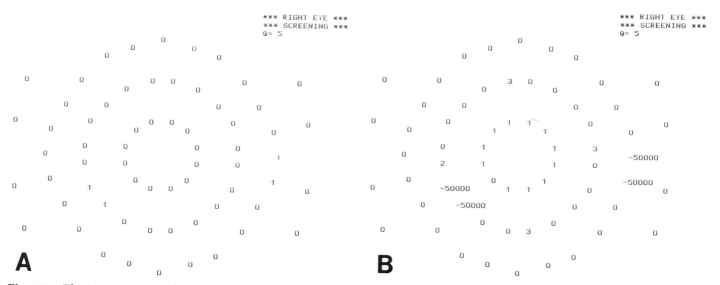

Fig. 4-5. The interpretation of screening results is much facilitated if the depth of the identified defects is shown. A and B show the same glaucomatous visual field displayed in two different ways. In A (a simulated printout) all seen points are indicated by 0 and all missed points by 1. The standard Competer print-out (B) shows that all four missed points, two in the blind spot and two in an inferior, nasal paracentral scotoma, are absolute defects.

between normal and pathological fields, particularly since a screening test with some quantification of defects also gives a much better assessment of the nature of the field defects than a screening test without any quantification.

Spatially Adaptive Screening

It is possible to design test algorithms where the computer will automatically increase spatial resolution in areas where defects are found, just as a human perimetrist would do. More data would then be collected from suspicious areas facilitating separation between normal and abnormal fields and resulting in a partial assessment of detected field loss (see Fig. 12-9, Chapter 12). Spatially adaptive programs for detailed investigation of small preselected areas of the visual field were described several years ago.[23] Adaptive screening tests covering larger areas of the field,[20] on the other hand, are new and one might foresee that increasing research efforts will be invested in this area. In this context it might be appropriate to point out that the human eye is an excellent image analyzer and presently it could be equally effective to have the user interpret the result of a basic screening test and decide whether to conduct high-resolution custom tests in areas where the results of the initial screening are uncertain.

Threshold Determinations

The search for glaucomatous field loss may be conducted not only with supraliminal screening techniques, but also with tests where the computerized instrument performs true increment threshold measurements at each tested point.

Threshold determinations will map the actual sensitivity contour of the tested eye within the limitations of its accuracy (Fig. 4-2, lower profile) and will detect subtle defects more easily than with a supraliminal test. The threshold-measuring tests will also give meaningful results in cases where there is not only a general depression of sensitivity, but also a change of the shape of the sensitivity profile for example in patients with dense cataracts. Such patients exhibit not only a general depression of sensitivity but a flattening of the central sensitivity profile as well. Supraliminal screening may encounter problems when the initial points are situated in a field defect, but a test program in which threshold determinations are performed at all tested points will have no problems in the same situation. The price of these advantages is an increased test time. Threshold determination usually requires three to six questions per tested point. Hence, a threshold test tends to take approximately three times as long as a supraliminal test with the same number of points. Unfortunately, this sets a disturbingly low upper limit to the number of points that can be examined with threshold perimetry during one test session due to the acceptance of the test by patients.

Although a description of details of various test logics for threshold will not be undertaken in this chapter, it should be pointed out that most algorithms used for threshold determination in computerized perimetry have a certain tolerance for patient errors, more so in complex programs where the threshold is crossed several times before it is determined.[19,24] While test points in supraliminal screening tests might be subject to retesting or quantification if the result is out of line with adjacent points, some perimetric test logics for threshold determination can be regarded as having a built-in retest. The measured threshold after the first reversal of the test process (from seen to not seen or vice versa) can be compared to the expected threshold value for that test location. If this level is out of line with the expected, the test process continues until two more reversals have occurred, thus diminishing the risk of a resulting inaccurate threshold value.[19,25] Certain so-called fast-threshold programs, like programs 33 and 34 in the Octopus perimeter,[26] can be used in screening for glaucomatous defects. The initial screening stimuli of these Octopus programs are exposed at an intensity level equal to the expected local age-corrected normal threshold + 0.4 log units. Points not seen at this level are subjected to threshold determination, whereas points where the initial screening stimulus is seen are accepted as normal. It should be pointed out that such selectively quantitative threshold programs are very similar to supraliminal screening with quantification of all detected defective points.

THE INFLUENCE OF THE STRATEGY ON THE DETECTION OF SMALL SCOTOMATA

One-level Screening

The threshold difference between the fovea and more peripheral points in the central visual field (25° to 30° from fixation) is approximately 1 log unit using a 23-minute target and a 31.4-asb background (the size III target in the Goldmann perimeter). Similar combinations of stimulus size and background are frequently used in computerized perimeters. If a supraliminal central field test is therefore conducted with a stimulus intensity that is adjusted until it is readily seen 25–30° from fixation (e.g., 0.4 log units above the 50 percent threshold in that area) scotomata with a depth of 1 log unit situated close to fixation will be missed. If the peripheral field, e.g., out to 60°, is also tested the results will be even less satisfactory. The difference between the normal threshold at the fovea and at 60° (with same stimulus and background perameters as above) is of the magnitude 1.5 log units or more. Quite substantial defects can thus escape detection if such an approach is used (compare Fig. 4-2, top diagram). With smaller targets or higher background luminosities the normal sensitivity gradient steepens and the difficulties in conducting an effective one-level screening will be even greater. Conversely, larger stimuli or lower background luminosities flatten the normal contour and diminish the disadvantages of tests where one intensity level is used in all points tested.

Eccentricity-compensated Threshold-related Screening

In this type of screening the target intensity is usually adjusted to 0.5–0.8 log units above the expected threshold and scotomatata with a depth exceeding this

should theoretically be detected. Strategies where the screening is conducted with substantially less supraliminal stimuli are not effective since the normal threshold variation is quite large and too many false positive defects would be created. Should the slope of the tested field differ from that programmed into the computer such as is seen in eyes with cataracts the sensitivity might increase or decrease in different areas. A "trigger-happy" patient might drive the sensitivity of the initial points up to such a high level that the subsequent test will be conducted with stimulus intensities that are very close to threshold. While this makes the test more sensitive it will also lead to an increased frequency of false positive defects. As mentioned, a supraliminal threshold-related test may sometimes fail because the initial test points are located in defective areas of the field.

Screening with Threshold-measuring Programs

It is difficult to state the minimum depth of a field defect detectable with this type of test. The minimum step size between the various intensity levels of the automatic instrument plays only a minor role. The main limiting factor is the patient's threshold fluctuation. Repeated computerized threshold determinations often have a standard deviation of 0.15 to 0.30 log units.[19, 27] Therefore isolated depressions involving only one test point should be interpreted very conservatively even when they equal 1 log unit. If the affected area is larger, covering many test points, and the irregularities in the rest of the field are small, much shallower defects can be identified. It is often stated that in manual perimetry depressions of less than 0.5 log units should be disregarded and not considered pathologic.[28] Nevertheless, nasal steps of 5° or more are often considered significant in manual kinetic perimetry.[10, 29] Assuming that the field is plotted with a Goldmann perimeter using stimulus size I, a threshold difference above and below the horizontal meridian of only 0.2 log units can result in a 5° nasal step in the region 30° nasal to the point of fixation. It is fortunate that this type of field defect, without any localized deeper scotomata in the same area, is uncommon since such minor depressions would be difficult to find with computerized static perimetry even when using threshold measuring techniques.

TEST POINT PATTERNS FOR DETECTION OF GLAUCOMATOUS FIELD LOSS

Although the actual strategy at each point might be the most important factor in deciding the efficacy of a computerized screening for glaucomatous field loss it is also very important that most of the testing is per-

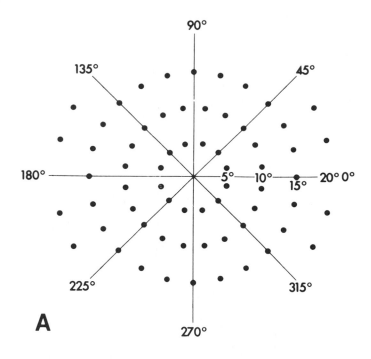

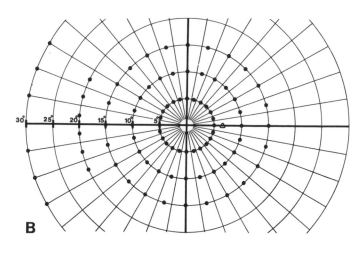

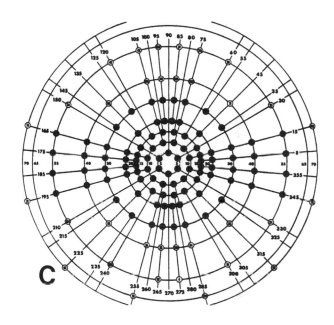

Fig. 4-6. Specific glaucoma screening patterns from some computerized perimeters. *A* Original Competer central pattern (primarily developed for glaucoma testing). *B* Humphrey Field Analyzer central Armaly pattern. *C* Fieldmaster 200 glaucoma screening pattern.

formed in areas where most early glaucomatous field defects occur (Fig. 4-1). Most test programs covering the central 30° of the visual field should screen efficiently, however some instruments have specific test point patterns for detection of glaucoma (Fig 4-6). Several of these are similar to the Armaly screening protocol. It is obvious that small scotomata may escape detection because they happen to fall between the points tested. Arcuate glaucomatous defects may in fact be very narrow even if they are deep and sometimes such defects will be missed even when a rather high density test point pattern is used (Fig. 4-7).

CLINICAL RESULTS

Many clinical studies dealing with detection of glaucomatous field loss have been published where the ability of various computerized perimeters are compared with that of different manual methods or with results obtained with other automatic instruments. Sensitivity and specificity figures from studies of various instruments and test logics should be compared with great caution. A high sensitivity alone is not a guarantee of clinical usefulness. Unless one has an appropriate standard against which the performance of the automatic instrument is measured, a high sensitivity figure might just reflect either a lack of sensitivity in the standard method, or the fact that the automatic instrument has a low specificity and tends to produce false "defects" in normal eyes.

It is not surprising that many studies have demonstrated that threshold-measuring computerized perimetry detects glaucomatous field loss better than manual kinetic perimetry.[30-32] It is also logical that different instruments using threshold-measuring techniques may give very similar sensitivity and specificity figures in detecting glaucomatous field defects when tested on the same patient material (13). Threshold-measuring

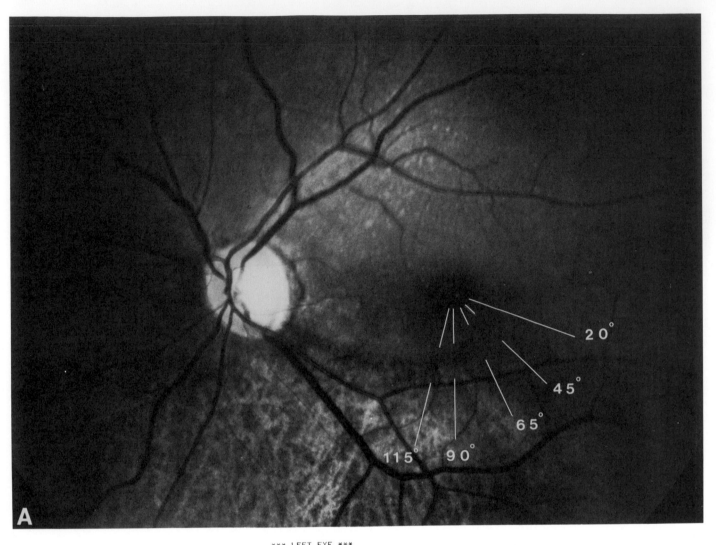

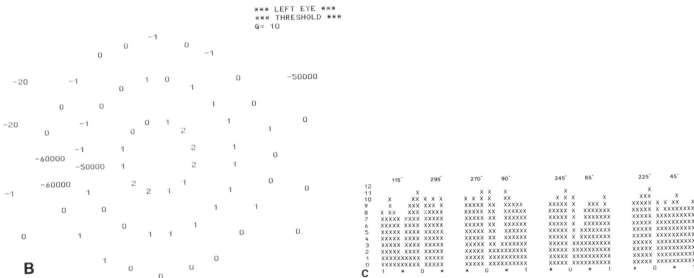

Fig. 4-7. Some small visual field defects will escape detection even when a rather tight test point pattern and threshold-measuring techniques are used. A glaucomatous retinal nerve fiber layer defect is seen in *A*. Despite this the central test point pattern, *B* is normal. High resolution profile perimetry *C* demonstrates a deep and narrow defect corresponding to the nerve fiber layer defect. (Reproduced with permission from Airaksinen PJ, Heijl A, *Acta Ophthalmol* 61:186–94, 1983)

Table 4-1.
Some Advantages (+) and Disadvantages (−) of
Supraliminal Screening Strategies as Compared with
Threshold-measuring Strategies in Screening for
Glaucomatous Field Loss

	Supraliminal Screening	Screening with Threshold Determination at Each Tested Point
Detection of shallow defects	−	+
Possible resolution	+	−
Time-consumption	+	−
Patient acceptance	+	−

techniques should detect glaucomatous field defects with the same precision as extremely detailed and time-consuming manual tests (11). This means that this advanced mode of computerized perimetry may be able to perform on a level that is difficult to attain and even harder to maintain in a clinical setting.

Threshold-related eccentricity-compensated screening procedures detect defects earlier than routine manual kinetic perimetry with or without sparse static testing[12,33] and the results surpass those of, for example, Armaly screening under ordinary clinical conditions.[12]

Despite the fact that one-level screening procedures have definite theoretical shortcomings compared with the more advanced detection strategies, high sensitivity figures have been quoted in studies using this type of test.[22,34] Doubts as to the specificity of such tests have been raised,[35,36] but there are indications that this type of test detects defects equally well or better than much of the manual screening performed today, even in larger centers.[37] If one-level screening is repeated with different stimulus intensities the detection rate can come quite close to that obtained even with thorough manual testing.[38]

Some of the advantages and disadvantages of threshold-measuring and supraliminal protocols are shown in Table 4-1.

AREAS FOR FUTURE STUDY

Although efficient and useful routines for computerized detection of glaucomatous field defects are a reality today several questions still remain unanswered and must be clarified before more efficient tests can be designed.

1. How important is the peripheral field? This question can only be answered through large clinical tests using high-resolution testing over the whole visual field.

2. What is a suitable trade-off between resolution (number of test points) and precision at each point? A more precise test logic requires more questions per point, thus limiting the number of points that can be tested at one single session. If glaucomatous field defects contain deep nuclei a high-resolution, low-precision test might be preferable to a test where fewer points are tested with a higher precision. If, on the other hand, glaucomatous field loss frequently starts with large but shallow field defects the opposite should be true. The probability of identifying small areas with only slightly diminished sensitivity will always be low, if the test time is kept reasonably short. A feasible method might be to combine a low-resolution, high-precision thresholding pattern with an intervening high-density pattern in which only supraliminal testing is done.

3. Is it an advantage to use kinetic or pseudo-kinetic instead of static techniques to explore the area round the nasal horizontal meridian in order to detect nasal steps?

4. What is a suitable duration of a computerized field screening? Patients certainly prefer short tests, but it has been shown that glaucomatous field defects tend to become deeper and larger during prolonged testing.[39] On the other hand, will longer tests lead to increased patient fatigue and variation, resulting in too many false positive results?

5. Is the size of the stimulus and the exposure time of only minor importance, or should short presentation times and small stimuli be preferred? Earlier results indicated that these factors may be important[40,41] but subsequent well-performed investigations have shown that spatial and temporal summation is normal or near normal in glaucoma,[42] and if this is true stimulus size and duration should be unimportant (except for other effects on such things as fixation and refraction scotoma.) Nevertheless, results obtained by computerized perimetry are available indicating that glaucomatous field defects become more obvious when short stimulus exposures[43] and small targets[44] are used.

6. Are white stimuli on a white background the best combination? It has been claimed that blue stimuli on a yellow background may be more sensitive in screening for glaucomatous field loss.[45]

7. Is the background luminance important? Some early results[46] indicate that mesopic perimetry is a more sensitive method for detecting glaucomatous field loss than standard perimetry

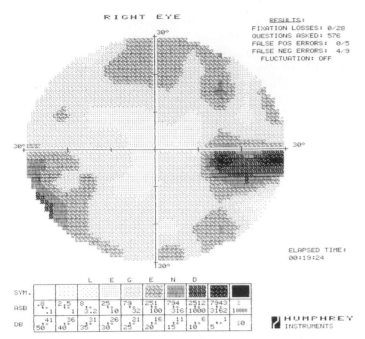

RIGHT EYE

RESULTS:
FIXATION LOSSES: 0/28
QUESTIONS ASKED: 576
FALSE POS ERRORS: 0/5
FALSE NEG ERRORS: 4/9
FLUCTUATION: OFF

ELAPSED TIME:
00:19:24

Fig. 4-8. False positive defects due to correction lens artifacts and ptosis are common 25° to 30° from the point of fixation, as in this field from a normal test subject.

in the superior or peripheral part of the central field are commonly false positive defects (Fig. 4-8).

ADVANTAGES AND DISADVANTAGES OF COMPUTERIZED SCREENING

The main advantages of computerized screening for glaucomatous visual field defects when compared with manual methods are:

1. High-quality perimetry possible without specially trained personnel.
2. The elimination of perimetrist error.
3. The reproducibility of test algorithms and time parameters.
4. The static testing, facilitating the detection of small, circumscribed field defects.
5. The randomized stimulus sequence, facilitating fixation.
6. The increased volume of visual field testing possible.
7. The reduced cost per test because of automation.
8. Numerical results suited for statistical analysis.

The main disadvantages are:

1. Some instruments still lack effective strategies.
2. The difficulties in interpretation of new types of charts and overinterpretation of printed information.
3. The increased risks for lens rim artifacts and false positive field defects due to drooping lids.
4. The frequently limited flexibility of programs.
5. The high initial investment cost of the instrument.

The general conclusion must be that computerized screening for glaucomatous field loss is of great benefit to the large number of patients with suspected glaucoma. Automatic perimeters are able to perform well conceived complicated tests over and over again without any fatigue, which is impossible to be matched even by a "perfect" human perimetrist. It is only by using these modern tests that the ophthalmic community may be able to perform the necessary large volume of field tests in these patients. This in turn makes it possible to differentiate between glaucoma with damage and ocular hypertension and to relieve many patients of the worries of pressure-reducing therapy and of a diagnosis of glaucoma.

performed at photopic levels but this has subsequently been questioned.

INTERPRETATION

The fact that automatic perimetry field charts are printed out by computers should not make us believe that they represent the ultimate truth. No doubt the perimetrist error is eliminated by the use of computerized techniques, but visual field examination remains a subjective test where we have to rely on the patient's responses. The intraindividual variation is large in field testing and small areas of decreased sensitivity should be interpreted with great care, especially if not shown to be reproducible. Angioscotomata may disturb the field around the blind spot. Lens rim artifacts are a larger problem in computerized than in manual perimetry, possibly because of the lack of feedback between patient and perimetrist, which in manual perimetry might ensure that the corrective lens is kept close to eye tested and well centered. Droopy lids seem to be a larger problem in automatic than in manual perimetry. The spatially randomized stimulus presentation pattern, which is so widely used in computerized perimetry because of its favorable effect on fixation, has the inherent disadvantage of not stimulating the patient to raise his upper lid as effectively as in a manual test where he can anticipate a stimulus to appear in the superior field. These problems can be reduced by paying attention to the alignment of corrective lenses and by instructing the patient properly and taping lids when necessary. Nevertheless, defects appearing only

REFERENCES

1. Aulhorn E, Harms H: Early visual field defects in glaucoma, in Leydhecker W (Ed): Glaucoma; Tutzing Symposium 1966. Basel, Karger, 1967, pp. 151–186

2. Aulhorn E, Karmeyer H: Frequency distribution in early glaucomatous visual field defects. Doc Ophthalmol Proc Ser 14:75–83, 1977

3. Coughlan M, Friedmann AI: The frequency distribution of early field defects in glaucoma. Doc Ophthalmol Proc Ser 26:345–349, 1981

4. Furuno F, Matsuo H: Early stage progression in glaucomatous visual field changes. Doc Ophthalmol Proc Ser 19:247–253, 1979

5. Gramer E, Gerlach R, Krieglstein GK, et al: Zur Topographie früher glaukomatöser Gesichtsfeldausfälle bei der Computerperimetrie. Klin Monatsbl Augenheilkd 180:515–523, 1982

6. Heijl A, Lundqvist L: The location of earliest glaucomatous visual field defects documented by automatic perimetry. Doc Ophthalmol Proc Ser 35:153–158, 1983

7. Brais P, Drance SM: The temporal field in chronic simple glaucoma. Arch Ophthalmol 88:518–522, 1972

8. LeBlanc RP, Becker B: Peripheral nasal field defects. Am J Ophthalmol 72:415–419, 1971

9. LeBlanc RP: Peripheral nasal field defects. Doc Ophthalmol Proc Ser 14:131–133, 1977

10. Werner EB, Drance SM: Early visual field disturbances in glaucoma. Arch Ophthalmol 95:1173–1175, 1977

11. Heiji A, Drance SM, Douglas GR: Automatic perimetry (COMPETER); ability to detect early glaucomatous field loss. Arch Ophthalmol 98:1560–1563, 1980

12. Heijl A: Automatic perimetry in glaucoma visual field screening; a clinical study. Albrecht von Graefes Arch Klin Exp Ophthalmol 200:21–37, 1976

13. Heijl A, Drance SM: A clinical comparison of three computerized automatic perimeters in the detection of glaucoma defects. Arch Ophthalmol 99:832–836, 1981

14. Drance SM: The glaucomatous visual field. Invest Ophthalmol 11:85–97, 1972

15. Hart WM Jr, Becker B: The onset and evolution of glaucomatous visual field defects. Ophthalmology 89:268–279, 1982

16. Zingirian M, Calabria G, Gandolfo E, et al: The normal pericoecal area. A static method for investigation. Doc Ophthalmol Proc Ser 26:393–403, 1981

17. Heijl A: Unpublished results.

18. Heijl A, Krakau CET: A note on fixation during perimetry. Acta Ophthalmol 55:854–861, 1977

19. Heijl A: Computer test logics for automatic perimetry. Acta Ophthalmol 55:837–853, 1977

20. Heijl A: The Humphrey field analyzer. [This volume, Chapter 12.]

21. Keltner JL, Johnson CA: Capabilities and limitations of automated suprathreshold static perimetry. Doc Ophthalmol Proc Ser 26:49–55, 1981

22. Johnson CA, Keltner JL: Comparative evaluation of the Autofield-I®, CFA-120®, and Fieldmaster Model 101-PR® automated perimeters. Ophthalmology 87:777–783, 1980

23. Fankhauser F, Haeberlin H, Jenni A: Octopus programs SAPRO and F. Two new principles for the analysis of the visual field. Albrecht von Graefes Arch Klin Exp Ophthalmol 216:155–165, 1981

24. Bebie H, Fankhauser F, Spahr J: Static perimetry: strategies. Acta Ophthalmol 54:325–338, 1976

25. Heijl A, Krakau CET: An automatic perimeter for glaucoma visual field screening and control; construction and clinical cases. Albrecht von Graefes Arch Klin Exp Ophthalmol 197:13–23, 1975

26. Jenni A, Fankhauser F, Bebie H: Neue Programme für das automatische Perimeter Octopus. Klin Monatsbl Augenheilkd 176:536–544, 1980

27. Bebie H, Fankhauser F, Spahr J: Static perimetry: accuracy and fluctuations. Acta Ophthalmol 54:339–348, 1976

28. Greve EL: Single and multiple stimulus static perimetry in glaucoma; the two phases of perimetry. Doc Ophthalmol 36:29, 1973

29. Phelps CD: The effect of myopia on prognosis in treated primary open-angle glaucoma. Am J Ophthalmol 93:622–628, 1982

30. Schmied U: Automatic (Octopus) and manual (Goldmann) perimetry in glaucoma. Albrecht von Graefes Arch Klin Exp Ophthalmol 213:239–244, 1980

31. Li SG, Spaeth GL, Scimeca HA, et al: Clinical experiences with the use of an automated perimeter (Octopus) in the diagnosis and management of patients with glaucoma and neurologic diseases. Ophthalmology 86:1302–1312, 1979

32. Krieglstein GK, Schrems W, Gramer E, et al: Detectability of early glaucomatous field defects. A controlled comparison of Goldmann versus Octopus perimetry. Doc Ophthalmol Proc Ser 26:19–24, 1981

33. Dyster-Aas K, Heijl A, Lundqvist L: Computerized visual field screening in the management of patients with ocular hypertension. Acta Ophthalmol 58:918–928, 1980

34. Bobrow JC, Drews RC: Clinical experiences with the Fieldmaster perimeter. Am J Ophthalmol 93:238–241, 1982

35. Hong C, Kitazawa Y, Shirato S: Use of Fieldmaster automated perimeter for the detection of early field changes in glaucoma. Int Ophthalmol 4:151–156, 1981/82

36. Gramer E, Krieglstein GK: Zur Spezifität der uberschwelligen Computerperimetrie. Klin Monatsbl Augenheilkd 181:373–375, 1982

37. Dannheim F: Clinical experiences with a semi-automated perimeter (Fieldmaster). Int Ophthalmol 2:11–18, 1980

38. Keltner JL, Johnson CA, Balestrery FG: Suprathreshold static perimetry; initial clinical trials with the Fieldmaster automated perimeter. Arch Ophthalmol 97:260–272, 1979

39. Heijl A, Drance SM: Changes in differential threshold in patients with glaucoma during prolonged perimetry. Br J Ophthalmol 67:512–516, 1983

40. Dubois-Poulsen A, Magis C, Ben-Mansour, et al: La dysharmonie photométrique dans le champ visuel des glaucomateux. Doc Ophthalmol 13:286–302, 1959

41. Wilson ME: Spatial and temporal summation in impaired regions of the visual field. J Physiol 189:189–208, 1967

42. Dannheim F, Drance SM: Psychovisual disturbances in glaucoma. A study of temporal and spatial summation. Arch Ophthalmol 91:463–468, 1974

43. Holmin C, Krakau CET: Variability of glaucomatous field defects in computerized perimetry. Albrecht von Graefes Arch Klin Exp Ophthalmol 210:235–250, 1979

44. Gramer E, Kontic D, Krieglstein GK: Die computerper-
    imetrische Darstellung glaukomatöser Gesichtsfeld-
    defekte in Abhängigkeit von der Stimulusgrösse.
    Ophthalmologica 183:162–167, 1981
45. Marré G, Marré M, Mierdel P, et al: Erfassung von
    Frühausfällen des Offenwinkelglaukoms durch kinetis-
    che Perimetrie des Blaufarbsehmechanismus, in: Zur
    Prognose und Therapie des Primären Glaukoms. Ros-
    tock, Wilhelm-Pieck-Universität, 1981
46. Jayle GE, Aubert L: Le champ visuel mésopique chez le
    sujet normal et en pathologie oculaire; son intérét clin-
    ique. Actualités Lat Ophtalmol 50–116, 1958

5

Epidemiological Considerations of Visual Field Screening for Glaucoma

Stephen M. Drance

The proper selection and interpretation of diagnostic procedures can be guided by the principles of diagnostic reasoning and by a knowledge of the test characteristics.[1-4] The detection and diagnosis of glaucoma may involve the use of several diagnostic tests (tonometry, ophthalmoscopy, perimetry), the net sensitivity and specificity of which is a complex function of the sensitivity and specificity of each test.

This chapter deals only with detecting scotomatous field loss, one of the chief cardinal physical signs on which the diagnosis of glaucoma depends.

GLOSSARY

Cut-off point: the arbitrary value used to separate positive from negative results for the screening procedure.

Negative predictive rate: probability that a scotoma is not present when the test is negative.

Positive predictive rate: probability that a scotoma is present when the test is positive.

Receiver operating characteristics: a graphic plot of sensitivity versus specificity at various definitions of the field abnormality (sensitivity/specificity trade-off curve).

Sensitivity: probability that the test will be positive when a scotoma is present.

Specificity: probability that the test result will be negative when no scotoma is present.

An ideal perimetric test to screen for scotomas is one that would be abnormal in almost all eyes that have a scotoma and would be normal in an eye free of scotomas. The arbitrarily selected criteria of the visual field test that constitute a positive or negative test are important, because the criteria can give the test either a high sensitivity or a high specificity. Altering the criteria to improve sensitivity usually reduced specificity, and vice versa. (Fig. 5-1) In practice, criteria are chosen that give an acceptably high sensitivity with a reasonably good specificity.

To achieve an optimum balance between sensitivity and specificity every perimetric screening test must have a set of characteristic features that reflect the information expected in patients with and without a scotoma. These test characteristics must be chosen to achieve optimum answers to two fundamental questions. If a scotoma is present, what is the likelihood that the test result will be positive? If a scotoma is not present, what is the likelihood that the test result will be normal? The answer to the first question determines the sensitivity of the test and the answer to the second question addresses itself to specificity.

These characteristics can be easily displayed by a simple binary table often referred to as a two-by-two table illustrated in Fig. 5-2. The sensitivity of the perimetric screening procedure is determined by identifying the proportion of patients (eyes) with a known scotoma in whom the test is positive $(A)/(A + C)$. The specificity of the screening procedure is determined by identifying the proportion of patients (eyes) without a scotoma in whom the test is negative $(D)/(B + D)$. The cell marked A of the two-by-two table reflects true positives, while the cell marked D reflects the true negatives.

AUTOMATIC PERIMETRY IN GLAUCOMA
ISBN 0-8089-1705-6

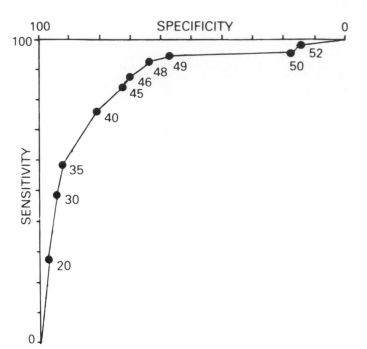

Fig. 5-1. A graphic plot of sensitivity against specificity of a scotoma screening method utilizing various criteria for the selection of positive and negative tests. As the sensitivity rises the specificity falls. Such a plot helps to select the optimal cut-off point for screening. (Reproduced with permission from: Daubs J, Crick RP: Epidemiological Analysis of K.C. Hospital Glaucoma data. Research and Clinical Forums 2:41–63, 1980.)

The sensitivity and specificity of a certain test with a certain criterion for interpretation can be determined empirically. For example, in a recently published paper[5] the results of using the threshold screening method on the Competer in patients with and without a known scotoma were studied. Criteria to identify the positive and therefore also negative tests were chosen and fully described in the paper. Of 74 patients, 74 eyes

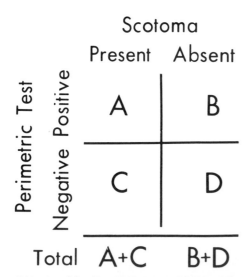

Fig. 5-2. Binary table illustrating sensitivity and specificity of screening for scotoma.

were tested, 42 had known abnormality in the visual field, and 39 of them were correctly identified by the Competer as positive. Using these data, a two-by-two table can be constructed as shown in Fig. 5-3. The sensitivity of the Competer program with the criteria arbitrarily chosen for the presence of the scotoma was 93 percent, whereas in those eyes without evidence of a field defect the screening test was normal in 81 percent. The test therefore failed to identify the presence of a known scotoma in 7 percent of eyes, and was positive in 19 percent of eyes without a scotoma. The fundamental test characteristics can thus be summarized: sensitivity is the positive tests divided by total number of eyes with scotomas $(A/(A+C) = 39/42 = 93\%)$. Specificity is equal to the negative results divided by the total number of eyes without a scotoma $(D/(B+D) = 26/32 = 81\%)$.

When screening a group for glaucoma, the sensitivity and specificity of the test is obviously important. When dealing with an individual patient, however the clinician is more interested in knowing the predictability of the test, namely the likelihood that a positive visual field screening test (which includes both true positives and false positives) indicates the presence of a scotoma and therefore of eye disease including glaucoma (positive predictive rate). He is also interested in the likelihood that a negative test indicates the true absence of a scotoma (negative predictive rate), which might be used to reassure the patient and to plan his future management. These predictive rates cannot be determined from the operating characteristics (sensitivity and specificity) of a screening test by themselves unless the test has the utopian characteristics of being always positive when a scotoma is present (sensitivity of 100 percent) and always negative when the scotoma is absent (specificity of 100 percent). None of the current field screening devices has those characteristics.

Scotoma

	Present	Absent
Competer Test Positive	39	6
Negative	3	26
Total	42	32

Fig. 5-3. Results of screening a glaucomatous and non-glaucomatous population with the computerized COMPETER

To calculate predictive rates, knowledge of the test's operating characteristics must be coupled with the clinician's knowledge of the proportion of eyes that have a scotoma in the population studied with the screening test.

The selection of the arbitrary criteria that will determine a positive or negative test result has to be done with an understanding of why the visual field screening test is being done. The general rule is that in a population consisting mainly of those suspected to have glaucoma, the criteria for the screening test must be so chosen that the sensitivity of the test is high; but in the screening of a population in whom a scotoma is unlikely to occur with any frequency, the specificity of the test must be high. This will become apparent from consideration of three hypothetical examples: screening a population with a 1 percent prevalence of glaucoma, screening office patients of whom 10 percent have a field defect, and screening an office group in which 30 percent have a scotoma.

If a test that is 90 percent sensitive and 90 percent specific is used to test a town of 1,000 people (of whom 10, or 1 percent, have glaucomatous field defects), 9 of the 10 with scotomas will be detected but 10 percent of the 990 normal individuals will also have a (falsely) positive test. There will therefore be 99 false positives and 9 true positives. When the prevalence of affected individuals is only 1 percent of the population, the positive predicted rate is thus less than 10 percent (that is, less than 10 percent of those with positive response will have a true defect). It may be deemed important to improve the specificity to 95 percent or 97 percent to reduce drastically the false positive responses, even if by altering the criterion for a positive test reduces the sensitivity to 80 percent and one additional case of glaucoma therefore is undetected.

If the same field test with 90 percent sensitivity and specificity is applied to an office practice in which half of 100 patients with elevated intraocular pressure have a scotoma, 45 of the 50 patients with glaucoma will be detected by 90 percent sensitivity. With a specificity of 90 percent, 45 of the 50 normal eyes will be normal, and there will be five false positives among the 50 without scotommas. Of the 50 with positive tests, 45 are true positives with a positive predictability rate of 90 percent (that is, 90 percent of those with a positive test will truly have a defect).

However, a 90 percent detection rate may not be satisfactory, because clinicians are anxious to detect the disease reliably at the earliest stage so that intervention that might be undertaken has the best chance of saving vision. In a disease such as glaucoma, one is required to develop tests that detect early damage at a time when it is still reliably reversible. It is necessary therefore, to select criteria that yield the highest sensitivity to make certain that not even the earliest small relative scotomas slip through the screening. If the criteria are chosen in such a way as to produce an

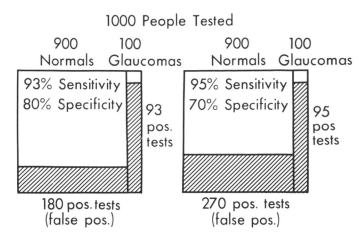

Fig. 5-4. The effects screening with tests of different sensitivities and specificities in 1,000 people of whom 90 percent are normal. The number of false positives and true positives is clearly shown and the importance of specificity is clear.

almost 100 percent sensitivity, then it is likely to be so sensitive that the normal fluctuation of all psychophysical tests and the methods used for threshold measurement would be bound to yield many false positive results.

Just how high one may go with the sensitivity (at the price of lowering specificity) depends on how high is the chance of a person having a defect. The best way to illustrate this is to consider the testing of 1,000 eyes in an office where 90 percent of patients had no field defect and 10 percent of patients had glaucoma. If a cut-off were chosen that gave a 93 percent sensitivity with an 80 percent specificity, then 93 of the 100 glaucoma patients in that population would be correctly identified and 7 would have been missed by the screening test (Fig. 5-4). If one chose different criteria to increase the sensitivity to 95 percent at the expense of decreasing the specificity, for example, to 70 percent then the detection rate of the glaucoma patients would have gone up from 93 to 95 but the number of false positives among the normal individuals would have gone up from 180 to 270. This is a considerable change in the false positives. With the 93 percent sensitivity and 80 percent specificity there would be 273 positives in the 1,000 eyes tested, but as only 93 of them actually have a glaucomatous scotoma, a positive screening test would therefore only have a 34 percent chance of discovering an eye with a scotoma. On the other hand, with the increased sensitivity to 95 percent and the resulting decrease in specificity to 70 percent, there would be 365 positives in the 1,000 eyes of whom 95 would be truly glaucomatous. The chances therefore of a positive response belonging to a glaucomatous patient would have dropped from 34 percent to 26 percent.

If 1000 eyes were tested in an entirely different office situation (Fig. 5-5.), however where 30 percent of the eyes were glaucomatous, a sensitivity of 93 percent

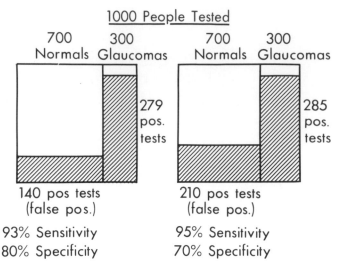

Fig. 5-5. Similar to Fig. 5-4 but in 1,000 people when only 70 percent are normal. The importance of sensitivity becomes clear from this example.

would correctly identify 279 of the 300 glaucomatous eyes and therefore the remaining 21 would be missed, but 140 of the 700 normal eyes would be screened as positive. An increase of the sensitivity to 95 percent, with the resultant loss of specificity for example to 70 percent, would correctly find 285 of the 300 glaucomatous eyes and therefore miss only 15, but 210 of the 700 normal eyes would now have a positive screening. This is a very large increase of false positives. With the first sensitivity and specificity a positive screening test would therefore have a 66 percent chance of indicating a glaucomatous eye and in the second instance a positive screening test would have a 58 percent chance of indicating a glaucomatous eye. This must be compared with the 34 percent and 26 percent chance of being glaucomatous when positive in the previous population where the prevalence of glaucoma was lower.

These examples illustrate the importance of sensitivity, specificity, and prevalence in screening procedures and should make it clear why different criteria for a positive test might be chosen for screening different populations.

One can actually assess the predictive value of a screening method by the use of Bayes' formula. It states that for a given triad of sensitivity, specificity, and prevalence, the proportion of truly positive cases among those diagnosed as "positive" (i.e., the positive predictive rate), is equal to the ratio, sensitivity × prevalence/(sensitivity × prevalence + [1 − specificity] × [1−prevalence]), and that the proportion of truly negative cases among those diagnosed as "negative" (i.e., the negative predictive rate), is equal to the ratio (specificity × [1−prevalence])/(specificity × [1−prevalence] + [1−sensitivity] × prevalence). In the example discussed above with 93 percent sensitivity, 80 percent specificity, and 10 percent prevalence, the

positive predictive rate would thus be (0.93 × 0.10)/(0.93 × 0.10 + [1−0.80][1−0.10]) = (0.93 × 0.10)/(0.93 × 0.10 + 0.20 × 0.90) = 0.34 or 34% as shown above, and the negative predictive rate would be (0.80 × [1−0.10])/(0.80 × [1−0.10] + [1−0.93] × 0.10) = (0.80 × 0.90)/(0.80 × 0.90 + 0.07 × 0.10) = 0.99 or 99%.

In the second example (95 percent sensitivity, 70 percent specificity, 10 percent prevalence), the positive predictive rate would be 0.95 × 0.10)/(0.95 × 0.10) + (0.30 × 0.90) = 0.26 or 26% as shown above, while the negative predictive rate would be (0.70 × 0.90)/(0.70 × 0.90) + (0.05 × 0.10) = 0.99 or 99% practically as before.

On the other hand, considering the triad of 93 percent sensitivity, 80 percent specificity, and 30 percent prevalence, the positive predictive rate would become (0.93 × 0.30)/(0.93 × 0.30 + 0.20 × 0.70) = 0.66 or 66%, while the negative predictive rate would be (0.80 × 0.70)/(0.80 × 0.70 + 0.70 × 0.30) = 0.96 or 96%. Finally, with 95 percent sensitivity, 70 percent specificity, and 30 percent prevalence the positive predictive rate would be (0.95 × 0.30)/(0.95 × 0.30 + 0.30 × 0.70) = 0.58 or 58%, as shown previously, whereas the negative predictive rate would now be (0.70 × 0.70)/(0.70 × 0.70 + 0.05 × 0.30) = 0.97 or 97%.

THE TESTING FOR SENSITIVITY AND SPECIFICITY

Unfortunately, even when the best technician performs a visual field test when a small relative scotoma is in fact present, the chances of finding that scotoma without access to previous information are less than 100 percent.

There are, however, very few tests in medicine that have a 100 percent sensitivity. It is erroneous, but perpetrated all too often, to take a group of glaucoma suspects and to subject them to manual and automatic perimetry in order to compare these two methods of screening. The finding of a higher number of positives by the automated perimetry is interpreted as meaning that automated screening has a higher sensitivity than manual screening. The fallacy unfortunately lies in the fact that some of the positives that were produced by the automatic screening may be false positives, depending on the criteria used to label an automatic screening as positive or negative (these are usually not given in the papers). Such a study design is useful only if a low false positive rate (high specificity) has been established in a separate group of normal eyes, or that the two tests under comparison have the same specificity. Only then can it be said that one test is more sensitive than the other.

A better design of a study to assess sensitivity and specificity of different methods of screening is to have a mix of proven patients with a visual field defect and preferably including some with early visual field defects, with a population of patients who have proven to have absolutely normal visual fields. This mixed population should then be exposed to the perimetric screening that is being evaluated whether it be a comparison of two automatic methods of screening or a comparison of an automatic with a manual method of screening. One can then look at the results, decide on one or several sets of criteria for what should be called positive, and evaluate the sensitivity and specificity that these screening methods would yield with the chosen criteria. If the sensitivity and specificity of several potentially useful criteria are calculated for each of the tests under comparison, a receiver operating curve could be generated for each and the relative usefulness of each test under different circumstances can be determined. The tests should be done "blindly" (which is always the case with automatic perimetry), and the number of those with defects and those without

defects who are selected for the tests should be approximately equal. Until all screening is properly subjected to this type of rigorous analysis we will not be in a position to know clearly the best methods of screening.

REFERENCES

1. Feinstein AR: Clinical Judgement. Baltimore, Williams and Wilkins, 1967
2. Luster LB: Introduction to Medical Decision Making. Springfield, Il, Charles C Thomas, 1968
3. Galen PS, Gambino SR: Beyond Normality; The Predictive Value and Efficiency of Medical Diagnosis. New York, John Wiley and Sons, 1975
4. McNeil BJ, Keller E, Adelstein SJ: Primer on certain elements of medical decision making. N Engl J Med 293:211–215, 1975
5. Heijl A, Drance SM: A clinical comparison of three computerized automatic perimeters in the detection of glaucoma defects. Arch Ophthalmol 99:832–836, 1981

6

The Graphical Display of a Computer Assisted Perimeter

Erik L. Greve

The graphic display or printout of a result produced by a computer assisted perimeter (CAP) is extremely important and deserves ample attention. A printout should give suitable information on the size and configuration, and on the intensity (depth) of a defect in relevant areas of the visual field. Relevant in this context means that if a defect is known to be limited to the central visual field, e.g., central serous retinopathy, a printout of the peripheral field is not necessary; in glaucoma we know that the central 25°-visual field and the nasal peripheral field are important and that this should be included in the printout. The printout possibilities depend on the areas of the visual field tested and the stimulus distribution within these areas. The printout furthermore depends on the examination strategy. In short, they logically depend on the programs. The possibilities for printout are shown in Table 6-1.

VISUAL FIELD AREA, STIMULUS DISTRIBUTION, AND CHART

Every printout should provide data on the central threshold and on the immediate paracentral sensitivity. In glaucoma important decisions have to be made on the basis of these values. It is well known that details of the central 25°-visual field are more important than those in the peripheral field. Therefore, 30°-charts usually have a greater resolution than total field charts. Only one CAP, the Peritest, provides a chart that has a gradual decrease of resolution from center toward periphery. This type of chart has advantages.[1,2]

In general the size of the chart should be adequate. In the past some CAPs have produced small charts that were difficult to read. The size of the Goldmann-perimeter chart seems to be appropriate. Charts can be blank or preprinted. The latter possibility has the advantage that after the examination the printer does not have to do all the time consuming work.

If stimuli are distributed as a regular grid interpolated greyscales are possible (Fig. 6-1). An irregular stimulus distribution does not allow such a type of presentation. The stimulus density (resolution) determines to a large extend the ease of interpretation of a printout unless interpolated values are used (Fig. 6-2). It is not advisable however to interpolate over large distances. A defect with the size of the blind spot can be missed with a 6°-interstimulus distance grid. Interpolation under such circumstances would provide an area that is falsely indicated in the printout as being normal. A single defect-position can be interpolated into a sizeable defect. It seems preferable to make it quite clear that areas between stimulus positions have not been measured.

The examination strategies that are most commonly used are listed in Table 6-2.[3,4] If a single-luminance strategy is used the only practical printout choice is the use of symbols. Suprathreshold, threshold-related techniques vary in their accuracy of defect intensity measurements. For a two-zone technique symbols can be used (Fig. 6-3). The more zones are used, the less attractive symbols are. Three-zones could still be expressed in symbols. For multizone strategies greyscales are better because they present a less confusing picture (Fig. 6-4). In all these techniques the use of numbers hardly makes sense.

Threshold techniques present sensitivity values that have been measured with small luminance steps

AUTOMATIC PERIMETRY IN GLAUCOMA
ISBN 0–8089–1705–6

Table 6-1	
Possibilities for Printout	
Graphical data	Symbols
	Grayscales noninterpolated
	Interpolated
	Numbers
	Profiles
	Isopters
	Three-dimensional displays
	Combination of the above
Additional data 1	Fluctuation
	Defect volume
	Statistical analysis
	Comparison
Additional data 2	Fixation
	False positives and false negatives
	Number of presentations
	Duration of examination
	Reaction time behavior
	Fatigue analysis

Table 6-2
Common Examination Strategies
Suprathreshold
Single luminance level
Threshold related, gradient adapted
2 Zones: normal-defect
3 Zones: normal-relative-maximum
Multizone: classes
Threshold

reduced. A four-zone printout will become a three-zone printout if the dynamic range is insufficient.

ABSOLUTE OR RELATIVE INTENSITY

Greyscales or numbers may express the absolute luminance values or an intensity value relative to normal values and comparable to visual acuity values (Fig. 6-5).

An absolute value simply presents the threshold luminance. Such presentations do not take in account the normal gradient of sensitivity nor the difference between general and local reduction of sensitivity (GRS and LRS). Absolute values leave a lot to the personal interpretations of the ophthalmologist. They may even lead to false interpretations.

It is logical to use defect-intensity values that are similar at every eccentricity. This means that one starts with the normal sensitivity at each position. The next step is the determination of general reduction of sensi-

(usually 0.2 log unit) and possibly also with a special threshold technique. The results of such threshold techniques can be expressed with virtually all printout possibilities. However, the method of choice is numbers.

For all these printout possibilities it should be remembered that the intensity printout is limited by the dynamic luminance range of the CAP. If, for instance, a patient has a cataract causing a general reduction of sensitivity of 1 log unit the possibility of measuring defect intensity in several classes or zones may be

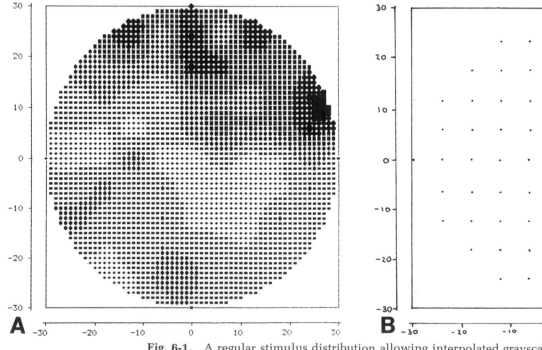

Fig. 6-1. A regular stimulus distribution allowing interpolated grayscales.

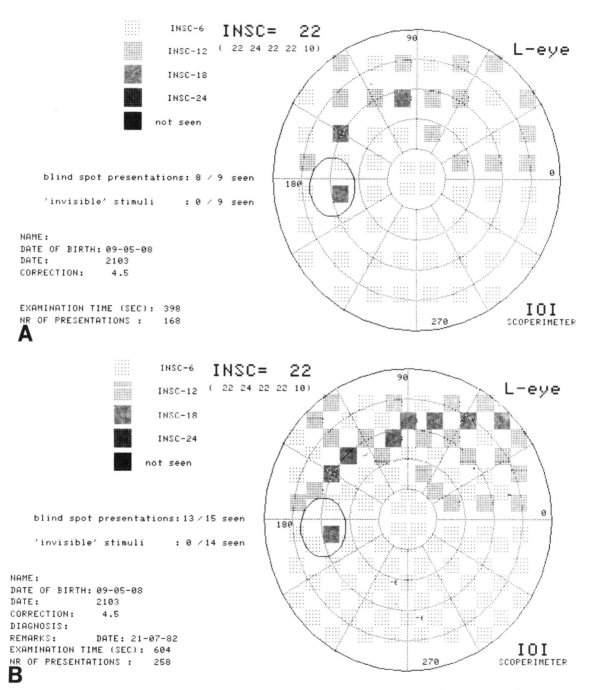

Fig. 6-2. A non-interpolated grayscale printout with two different stimulus densities (resolutions).

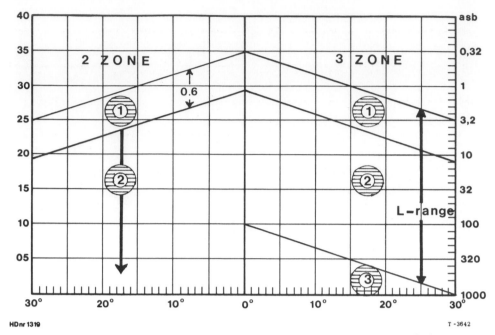

Fig. 6-3. Suprathreshold, threshold-related strategy with two-zone and three-zone assessment.

tivity. There are often a number of positions that have an equal sensitivity that is better than the sensitivity in other positions. Although their sensitivity may not be normal they still represent normal or near normal positions as far as glaucoma is concerned, the reduction being caused by a preretinal "filter", e.g., cataract. The remaining positions with a greater reduction of sensitivity are the "local" glaucomatous defects. The interpretation of the visual field printout is greatly facili-

tated if a relative intensity printout with separation of GRS and LRS is used. Such printout modes are available in the Octopus, Peritest, and Humphrey CAPs.[1,5,6]

At this point it may be useful to emphasize that a relative defect is a defect for a certain standard size stimulus with a threshold luminance between normal and maximal. If the maximal luminance is not seen the defect is logically called a defect for maximum luminance and not an absolute defect. The absolute defect

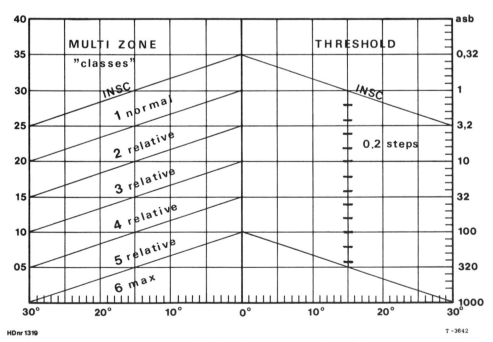

Fig. 6-4. Suprathreshold, threshold-related strategy with multizone assessment (L) threshold strategy (R).

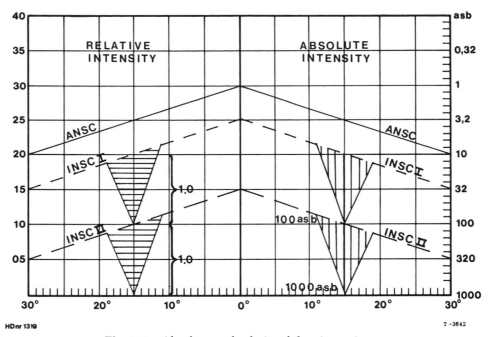

HDnr 1319   T -3642

Fig. 6-5. Absolute and relative defect intensity.

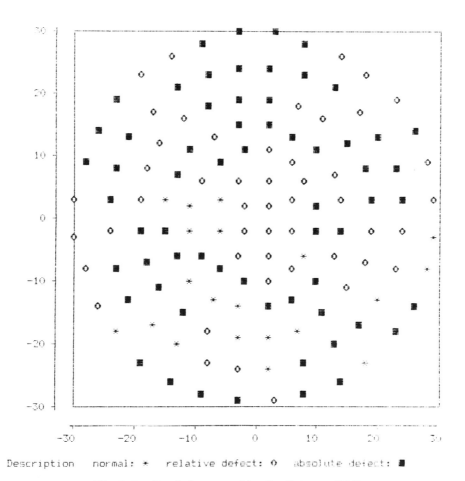

Description   normal: *   relative defect: O   absolute defect: ■

Fig. 6-6. Symbols as used by the Octopus CAP.

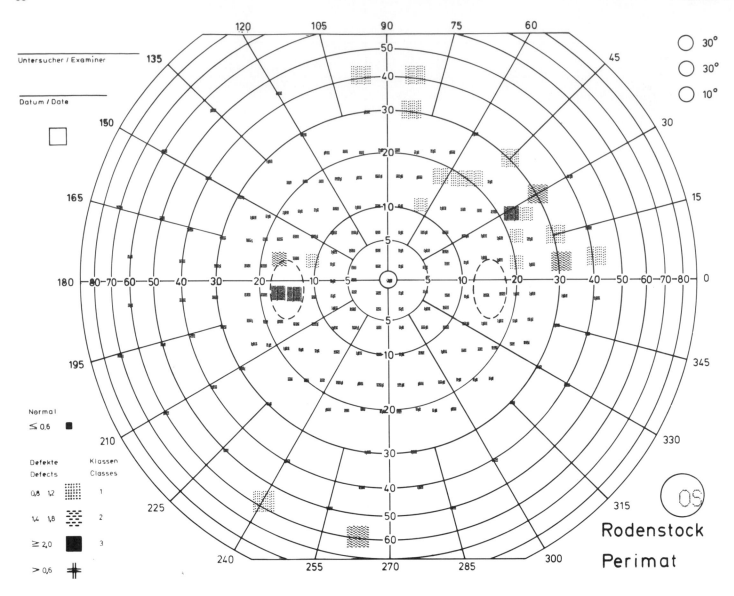

Fig. 6-7. Noninterpolated grayscales demonstrating a glaucomatous defect (Peritest).

on the Goldmann-perimeter is a defect measured with a size V stimulus and maximum luminance or a comparable defect.

The printout possibilities of table 6-1 will now be discussed. Symbols are mainly used for suprathreshold with a limited number of zones (Fig. 6-6). The choice of the actual symbols is critical. Grayscales give a very attractive and easily interpretable picture of the visual field provided the stimulus-density (resolution) is sufficient (Fig. 6-2). Noninterpolated grayscales provide adequate information on the configuration of a defect without loosing the possibility to read the individual values (Fig. 6-7). Only a limited number of grayscales should be used to avoid a confusing picture. Grayscales provide sufficient information on defect-intensities expressed in relatively large luminance steps.

Numbers may be difficult to read. They provide a highly unattractive picture of the size and configuration of defects. They make no sense in normal areas and

areas with defects for maximum luminance. They are necessary however to present small luminance step threshold values in relative defects. They are also indispensable for double-threshold measurements (Fig. 6-8). Profiles have always been an excellent means of presenting meridional (or other high resolution) static threshold measurements and should only be used in combination with such measurements (Fig. 6-9). Isopters are hardly used in CAP but could be valuable for the peripheral borders and the blind spot. Three-dimensional displays are impressive and have been advocated by some authors. Although we have made such three-dimensional printouts ourselves we have not seen a use for them clinically.

COMBINATIONS

Many of these printout possibilities can be combined, e.g., profiles and numbers. A very practical

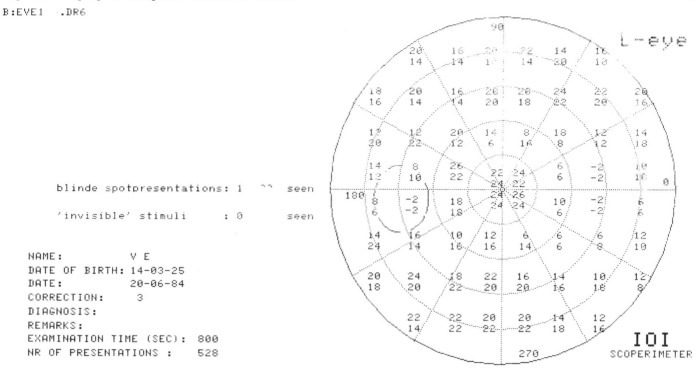

Fig. 6-8. Double-threshold measurements as performed by the Scoperimeter and expressed by numerical values.

combination is the use of grayscales or symbols for normal areas and defects, for maximal luminance and numbers for relative defects (Fig. 6-10).[1]

ADDITIONAL DATA

Data on fluctuation can be provided in a simple way by showing double-threshold measurements (see Fig. 6-8). This is really too simple however because fluctuation does not make much sense if not accompa-

nied by a statistical analysis. Such an analysis should provide separate data on fluctuation in normal areas and in defects. Defects for maximal luminance do not fluctuate.

Data on defect-volume are helpful, the more so when they are provided with a standard deviation of the defect-volume. The statistical handling of the threshold data is critical. It is all too easy to produce statistics that have no clinical relevance. At present I am not aware of a fool-proof statistical program for the analysis of fluctuation of defect-volume and conse-

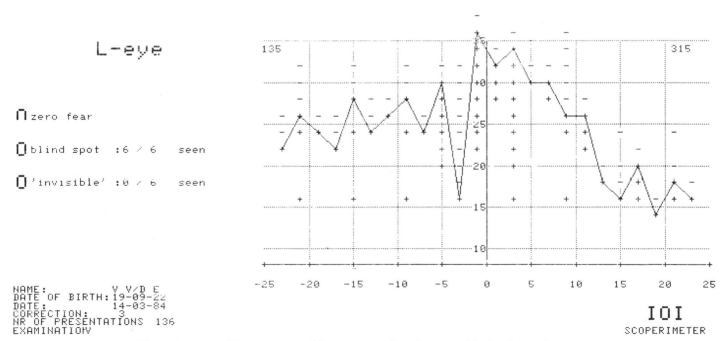

Fig. 6-9. A profile as measured by automated perimetry with the Scoperimeter.

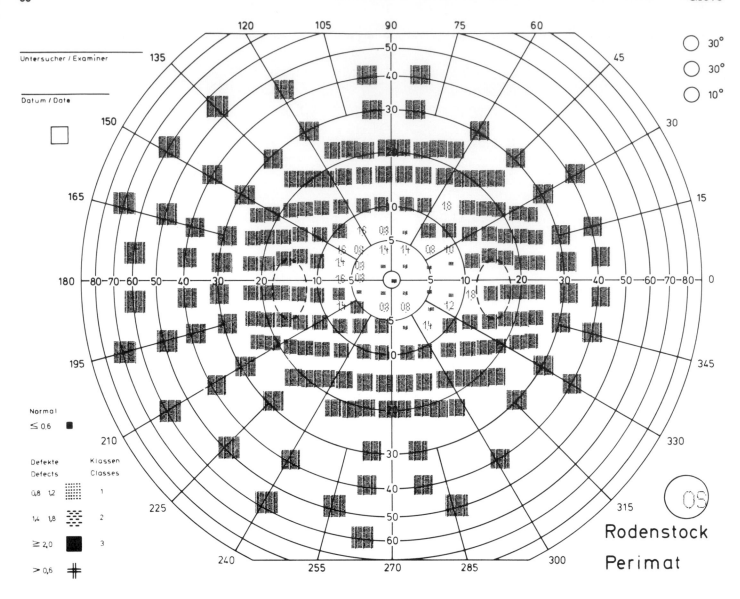

Fig. 6-10. A combination of symbols for maximal defects and normal areas and numerical values for relative defects.

quently for the analysis of change (comparison). There is no doubt however that such program will become available in the near future.

An indication of the reliability of fixation is recommended. Direct measurements are preferable to indirect measurements like the blind spot check. Similarly, data on false positive and false negative are important and should be provided by the printout. Number of target presentations and the duration of the examination are self explanatory. It would be interesting if a CAP printout could provide data on patient behavior indicating deterioration of responses. Such evaluations are not yet available. Finally, all these printout possibilities require a good printer.

REFERENCES

1. Greve EL: Peritest and Perimat 206. Chapter 11 of this book, 1985
2. Greve EL, Dannheim F, Bakker D: The Peritest, a new automatic and semi-automatic perimeter. *Int* Ophthalmol 5:201–214, 1982
3. Fankhauser F: Problems related to the design of automatic perimeters. Docum Ophthalmol 47:89–139, 1979
4. Greve EL: Performance of computer assisted perimeters. Docum Ophthalmol 53:343–380, 1982
5. Heijl A: The Humphrey Visual Field Analyzer. Chapter 12 of this book, 1984
6. LeBlanc R: The Octopus automatic perimeter. Chapter 7 of this book, 1984

7

The Octopus System

Ray P. LeBlanc

The Octopus Automated Perimetry system consists of a full line of automated projection perimetry systems with a wide variety of available programs for "threshold-related" screening and quantitative threshold measurement. Differences in both hardware and software in the three series in this system give to each a specific character that determines its appropriateness to a given research and/or clinical situation. The system was first introduced as the 201 instrument in 1976 based on the prototype developed by Fankhauser. Approximately five years later a more clinically oriented series (2000 model) was introduced and offered most of the features of the 201 series. Recently, an office version (500 series) has become available for individual physician use.

The wide spectrum of this system can be appreciated by a close look at the common features of each series as well as at the specific attributes of each model. (Table 7-1).

SOFTWARE

We owe the development of automated perimetry to the early work carried out by a handful of investigators and their commitment to programing. It is clear that the essence of excellent automated static examinations lies in the programing while differences in hardware are becoming less of a consideration. The Octopus system has approached this problem with methodic logic and has developed a number of standard programs for suprathreshold screening, quantitative threshold measurement, as well as research and user

programs. The availability of these programs varies in the three series as we will see further on.

Screening Programs

The Octopus system uses programs in which the test locations are closer together centrally than peripherally whether one is using a full field program (07) or a central field program (03). In each program the suprathreshold test target has a value that is spatially related, i.e., respects the increasing retinal sensitivity as one moves closer to fixation (Fig. 7-4).

The strategy used is meant to determine if a specific location has a sensitivity that is normal or abnormal. Further, if abnormal, whether the scotoma is relative or absolute (Fig. 7-5). No attempt is made to further quantitate the value in these screening programs. The starting point (test target intensity) is presented at 6 db above the normal threshold (dependent on patient's age and coordinates of test location).

Retests are an integral and automatic feature of the screening programs with all abnormal points (deviation > 6 dB) retested if less than 25 percent of points are abnormal (beyond that, a screening program is less appropriate and represents poor use of time). Also, isolated abnormal points in the field or isolated normal points in an area of an abnormal field are automatically retested.

Catch trials are randomly presented during both the 07 (full field) and 03 (central field) programs. These trials estimate patient reliability in the test situation by presenting an audible cue without test target (false positive if patient responds) and retesting at random

AUTOMATIC PERIMETRY IN GLAUCOMA
ISBN 0–8089–1705–6

Table 7-1
Description

	Series 201 (Fig. 7-1)	2000 R (Fig. 7-2)	500/500 E (Fig. 7-3)
General	Automated perimeter Storage of test results Storage of patient data Analysis programs Screening Quantitative threshold assessment Data transmission	Automated perimeter Storage of test results Storage of patient data Analysis programs Screening Quantitative threshold assessment Data transmission	Automated perimeter Screening Quantitative threshold assessment Data transmission
Stimulus	Goldmann 0 to V size .002–1000 Asb*	Goldmann III and V .002–1000 Asb*	Goldmann III .002–1000 Asb*
	Projection system with over 50,000 test locations for each series		
Cupola	100 cm diameter 4 Asb background*	85 cm diameter 4 Asb background*	85 cm diameter 4 Asb background*
Eye fixation	Infrared camera TV monitor	Electronic with monitor	500–Telescope 500E–Electronic
Operation	Keyboard–printer	Keyboard, CRT screen	Light pen, CRT

CRT, cathode ray tube.
* Computer calibrated.

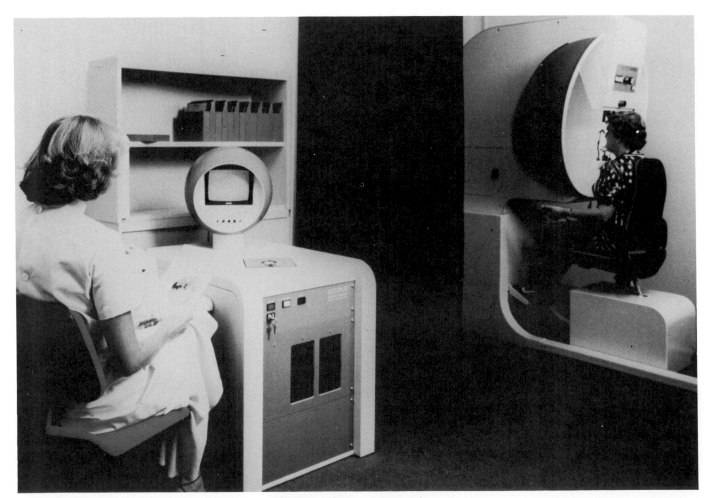

Fig. 7-1. Octopus 201 series.

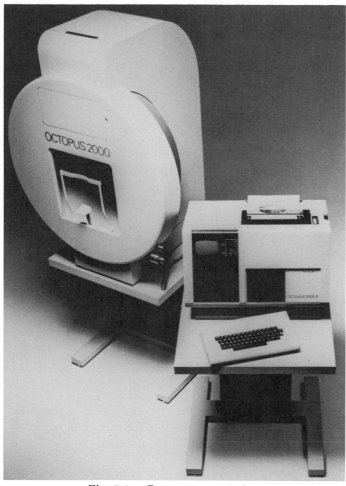

Fig. 7-2. Octopus 2000 series.

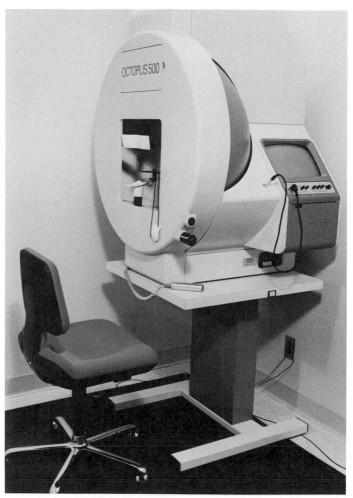

Fig. 7-3. Octopus 500 series

with maximal target intensity a point previously showing a response to a suprathreshold target (false negative if patient does not respond).

Quantitative Threshold Measurement

Quantitative threshold measurement can be carried out for an almost infinite (>50,000) number of locations in the visual field depending on the program used. The standard determination is carried out using stored patient data or master file visual field data (age corrected) as the starting point and the 4-2-1- test logic is used to determine accurate threshold values (Fig. 7-6). Double and even multiple determinations of some or all of the tested points are desirable at times and are an integral part of or can be built into the various programs.

Standard programs currently in use for the central 30 degrees of the field include programs 31, 32, which offer a 6-degree grid (separation along X, Y axis of each point). The difference between these two programs is that program 31 is centered on fixation, while 32 is offset 3 degrees (Fig. 7-7, 7-8). Combined use of these two programs allows a grid density of 4.2 degrees to effectively determine threshold measurements.

For midfield assessment, programs 41 and 42 allow a 12-degree grid assessment of the field between 30 and 60° using the same test logic. Once again combined use of the two programs allows a much tighter grid pattern (8.4°) (Fig. 7-9).

Program 61 and 11 are specific high density programs featuring three determinations per point with the grid having points with 3 degree separation along the X-Y axis. Program 11 is suitable for central testing offering a 3×3 point grid, while program 61 offers a 5×5 point grid that can be centered on any X-Y coordinate in the visual field.

Fast version programs of the standard 31, 32, 41, and 42 are available as an option or a standard feature (Table 7-2) and are meant to reduce the testing time while not altering any of the data of abnormal areas. In these programs (33, 34, 43, 44) grid patterns identical to those of programs 31, 32, 41, and 42 are used. The near threshold value is set at "expected threshold" minus 4 dB, and if the response to this target is positive on two repeated test presentations, it is assumed that this point has a normal value and the master field value is assigned rather than going through the 4-2-1 steps of actually determining the threshold. This approach re-

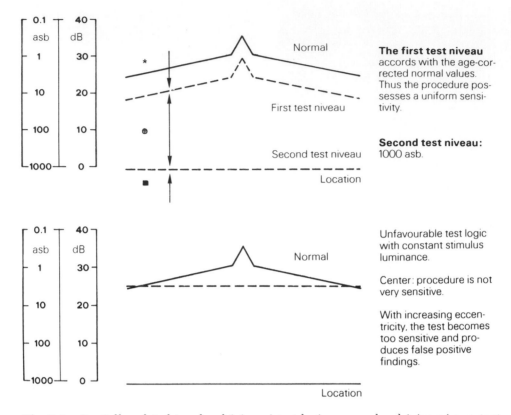

The first test niveau accords with the age-corrected normal values. Thus the procedure possesses a uniform sensitivity.

Second test niveau: 1000 asb.

Unfavourable test logic with constant stimulus luminance.

Center: procedure is not very sensitive.

With increasing eccentricity, the test becomes too sensitive and produces false positive findings.

Fig. 7-4. Spatially related two level (niveau) test logic vs. one level (niveau) constant stimulus logic.

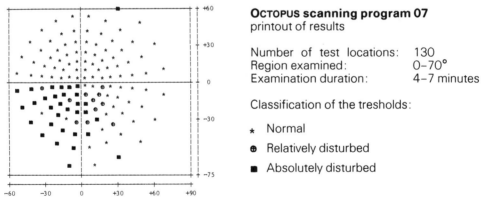

OCTOPUS scanning program 07 printout of results

Number of test locations: 130
Region examined: 0–70°
Examination duration: 4–7 minutes

Classification of the tresholds:

* Normal

⊕ Relatively disturbed

■ Absolutely disturbed

Fig. 7-5. Printout of two level screening program.

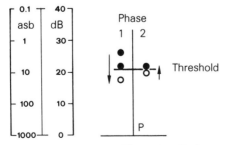

Double crossing of the threshold as base principle of the quantitative OCTOPUS perimetry. First in steps of 4 dB, then in steps of 2 dB to increase the precision and reliability.

Fig. 7-6. Staircase double threshold strategy.

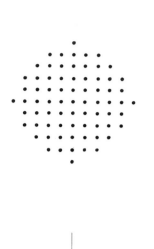

Fig. 7-7. Grid pattern program 31.

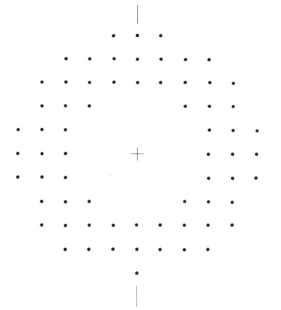

Fig. 7-9. Grid pattern program 41.

duces time of testing for all normal points but all abnormal points are actually fully tested as in the standard programs. In this way, no abnormal data are sacrificed but time is saved proportional to the extent to which the field is normal.

Reproducibility of test results and patient reliability are tested or monitored during the standard programs of the 30 and 40 series. In each of the programs 31, 32, 41, and 42, ten points are randomly retested to measure local scatter. The root mean square (RMS) of these ten points is then determined and is used as an index of reproducibility of test results during the same test session. At present in programs 31 and 32 five of the ten points are in locations near the periphery of the

central field and as such are vulnerable to fluctuations brought about by lens aberrations. Since normal points do not have actual threshold determinations in programs 33, 34, 43, and 44, the RMS is not determined in these programs.

In all 30 series and 40 series programs, catch trials are integrated to give the examiner an appreciation of patient reliability. Randomly throughout the program, the sound cue is not followed by a target; if the patient responds we consider this a false positive. Conversely, in random fashion in areas already tested and having shown a response, a maximal target (1,000 asb) is

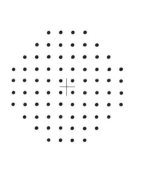

Fig. 7-8. Grid pattern program 32.

Table 7-2
Software/Storage/Printout

		Series 201	2000 R	500/500E
Screening Program (07, 03)				
2 level test	03	×	×	—
	07	×	×	×
Quantitative Threshold				
Assessment Program				
31, 32,		×	×	—
41, 42	×	×	×	—
Fast Version 33, 34, 43, 44		×	×	36, 44
Macula Program 11	×	×	—	—
High Density Program 61		×	—	—
62		—	×	—
Fast Version 64		—	×	×
Storage-internal		×	×	—
-remote		×	×	×
Delta Program		×	×	—
User Program		×	×	—
Printout-Gray Scale		×	×	×
-Value Table		×	×	×
-Comparison		×	×	×

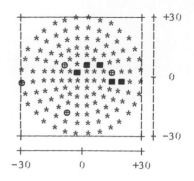

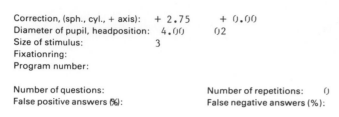

Correction, (sph., cyl., + axis):   + 2.75   + 0.00
Diameter of pupil, headposition: 4.00   02
Size of stimulus: 3
Fixationring:
Program number:

Number of questions: Number of repetitions: 0
False positive answers (%):   False negative answers (%):

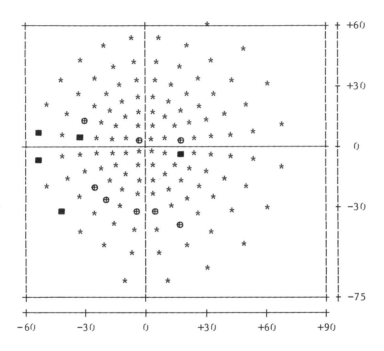

LEGEND: *   NORMAL
           ⊕   RELATIVE DEFECT
           ■   ABSOLUTE DEFECT

Fig. 7-10.   Screening program printout mode.

presented. Failure of the patient to respond is classified as a false negative response since the area had previously shown sensitivity during the same test session. The monitoring of these two parameters is very helpful in assessing patient reliability.

Special Programs

F-Program allows determination of threshold for a series of locations along any cord length in the visual field determined by identifying the X-Y coordinates of the starting and ending points. The spatial resolution of the points tested can be chosen down to 0.2 degrees if desired, and the number of test locations, the number of independent measurements per test location and the threshold determination strategy to be applied are all chosen prior to testing.

Sargon "User" program allows user to develop programs designed for specific clinical or research situations. The usual 4-2-1-bracketing is used for points tested but the location, sequence, and number of determinations are determined by the user in the elaboration of the program.

Sapro "spatial sensitivity" program is currently under development. This program will identify areas of abnormal values in standard testing and will automatically proceed to a fine grid intensive test of these areas to elaborate areas of abnormality.

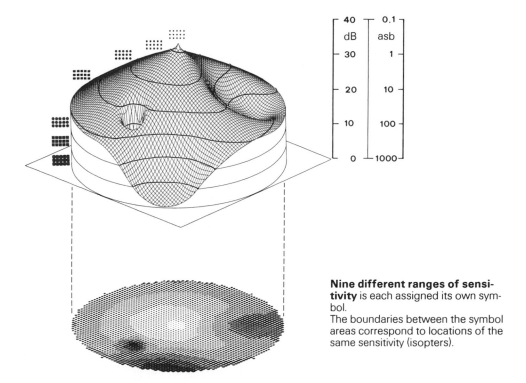

Nine different ranges of sensitivity is each assigned its own symbol.
The boundaries between the symbol areas correspond to locations of the same sensitivity (isopters).

Fig. 7-11. Grayscale relationship to island of vision.

PRINTOUT

There are several printout modes that are standard and available on the various Octopus models.

Screening Program

Normal values (suprathreshold target) are indicated by *, while absolute scotomas (1,000 asb target) are noted by ■. All points showing relative defects can be identified by symbol ⊕. (Fig. 7-10).

Quantitative Threshold Measurement

Several options are available to the examiner to review the data of a given examination. The "grayscale" is a graphic display of test results in nine different symbols according to the measured sensitivity. It is to be noted that while the actual measured points are separated on the X-Y axis by 6 degrees (programs 31, 32, 33, 34) or 12 degrees (programs 41, 42, 43, 44), the grayscale assigns a symbol value to points 1 degree apart by a linear interpolation of the values of the actually measured points. The grayscale therefore gives an overstatement of the data but is based on sound interpretive logic (Fig. 7-11).

Value tables give a very precise overview of the actual value of measured points displayed respecting the spatial orientation (X-Y coordinates) of the points tested. When a printout of values is chosen for programs 31, 32, 41, or 42, the ten points tested twice to determine the RMS are shown as are both values

obtained (Fig. 7-12). For programs 11 and 61 the value table shows the actual value with the triple determination plus the standard deviation for each point (Fig. 7-13).

Comparison value tables are also available and are found by many to be the most clinically useful print mode. In this instance we have access to the actual value table of examination, the normal values for each point and the difference (decibels) for each point (Fig. 7-14). These values are presented as values in decibels and also in symbols, all printed in a spatially related printout mode (Fig. 7-15, 7-16).

Special program printouts reflect the specific purpose of the program. In program F, the cord length starting and stopping points are shown graphically as are values of each point tested (Fig. 7-17). In SARGON programs, small areas of the field can be tested with high density (Fig. 7-18) or less dense (Fig. 7-19) grids.

DATA STORAGE

The Octopus system offers two possibilities for data storage and management, remote and internal.

Remote

All series of the system are equipped with an RS 232 port allowing direct link-up with micro-or mainframe computer systems. Several such hookups are currently in use and allow complete integration of data to a more complete data base as well as statistical

OCTOPUS®

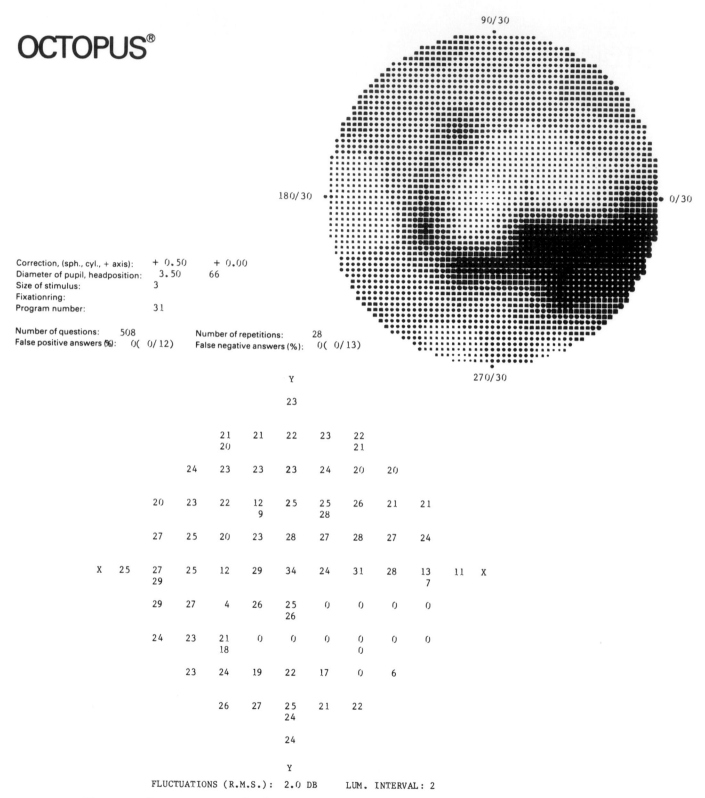

Correction, (sph., cyl., + axis): + 0.50   + 0.00
Diameter of pupil, headposition: 3.50   66
Size of stimulus: 3
Fixationring:
Program number: 31

Number of questions: 508 Number of repetitions: 28
False positive answers (%): 0(0/12) False negative answers (%): 0(0/13)

```
                                    Y

                                    23


                        21   21   22   23   22
                        20                  21

                   24   23   23   23   24   20   20


              20   23   22   12   25   25   26   21   21
                             9         28

              27   25   20   23   28   27   28   27   24


    X   25    27   25   12   29   34   24   31   28   13   11  X
              29                                       7

              29   27    4   26   25    0    0    0    0
                             26

              24   23   21    0    0    0    0    0    0
                        18                   0

                   23   24   19   22   17    0    6


                   26   27   25   21   22
                             24

                             24


                                    Y
```

FLUCTUATIONS (R.M.S.): 2.0 DB   LUM. INTERVAL: 2

Fig. 7-12. Program 31, actual value printout showing ten points tested twice to determine RMS.

OCTOPUS®

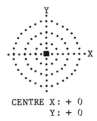

CENTRE X: + 0
         Y: + 0

Correction, (sph., cyl., + axis): − 2.50   + 0.00
Diameter of pupil, headposition: 4.00   71
Size of stimulus: 3
Fixationring: 0
Program number: 61

Number of questions: 274   Number of repetitions: 0
False positive answers (%):   0(0/ 11)   False negative answers (%): 0(0/ 2)

CENTRE X: + 0
         Y: + 0

```
   0.0  0.0      0.0  0.0      0.0  0.0      0.0  0.0      0.0  0.0
   0.0  0.0      0.0  0.0      0.0  0.0      0.0  0.0      0.0  0.0
   0.0           0.0           0.0           0.0           0.0


   0.5  0.7     11.5  7.5      0.5  1.8      0.5  0.8      0.0  0.0
   1.5  0.8      7.5  4.0      2.5  1.2      0.5  0.6      0.0  0.0
   0.0           3.5           2.5           1.5           0.0


  13.5 12.8     19.5 20.5     21.5 20.8     15.5 15.5      0.0  0.0
  13.5  1.2     22.5  1.7     21.5  1.2     16.5  1.0      0.0  0.0
  11.5          19.5          19.5          14.5           0.0


  15.5 16.2     11.5 14.5     14.5 14.5      4.5  3.2      0.0  0.0
  15.5  1.2     16.5  2.6     14.5  0.0      1.5  1.5      0.0  0.0
  17.5          15.5          14.5           3.5           0.0


   0.5  0.2      2.5  2.3      0.0  0.0      0.0  0.0      0.0  0.0
   0.0  0.3      4.5  2.3      0.0  0.0      0.0  0.0      0.0  0.0
   0.0           0.0           0.0           0.0           0.0
```

FLUCTUATIONS (R.M.S.): 1.7 DB   LUM. INTERVAL: 2

Fig. 7-13. Printout program 61 showing points tested three times mean and standard deviation.

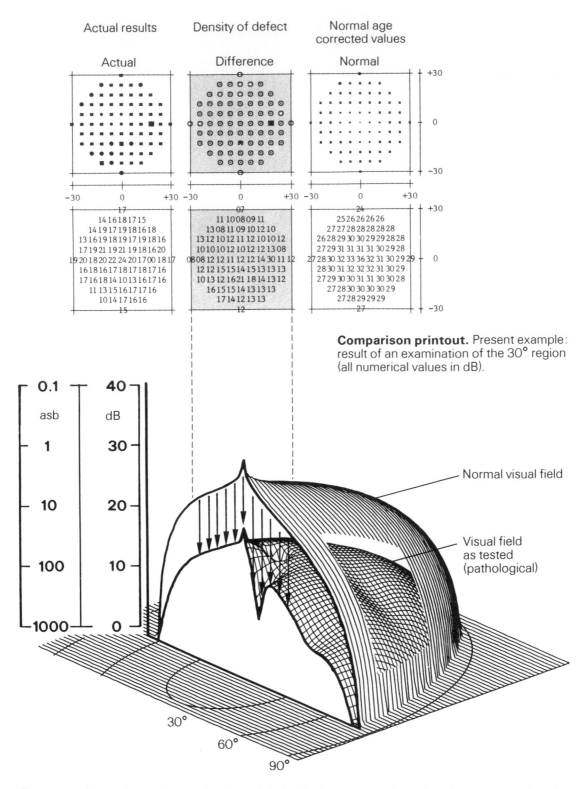

Actual results

Density of defect

Normal age corrected values

Actual

Difference

Normal

```
            17                        07                        24
     14 16 18 17 15          11 10 08 09 11          25 26 26 26 26
   14 19 17 19 18 16 18     13 08 11 09 10 12 10    27 27 28 28 28 28 28
  13 16 19 18 19 17 19 18 16  13 12 10 12 11 12 10 10 12  26 28 29 30 30 29 29 28 28
   17 19 21 19 21 19 18 16 20  10 10 10 12 10 12 12 13 08  27 29 31 31 31 31 30 29 28
 19 20 18 20 22 24 20 17 00 18 17  08 08 12 12 11 12 12 14 30 11 12  27 28 30 32 33 36 32 31 30 29 29
   16 18 16 17 18 17 18 17 16  12 12 15 15 14 15 13 13 13  28 30 31 32 32 32 31 30 29
   17 16 18 14 10 13 16 17 16  10 13 12 16 21 18 14 13 12  27 29 30 30 31 31 30 30 28
   11 13 15 16 17 17 16      16 15 15 14 13 13 13      27 28 30 30 30 30 29
     10 14 17 16 16            17 14 12 13 13            27 28 29 29 29
            15                        12                        27
```

Comparison printout. Present example: result of an examination of the 30° region (all numerical values in dB).

0.1	40
asb	dB
1	30
10	20
100	10
1000	0

Normal visual field

Visual field as tested (pathological)

30°

60°

90°

The comparison print mode permits the ophthalmologist to ascertain and evaluate the results of an examination immediately and without any further aids.

In the middle column, the depth of the disturbance is given quantitatively, and that is with respect to the age-corrected normal values.

Fig. 7-14. Comparative printout of actual tested values compared to age corrected normals.

OCTOPUS®

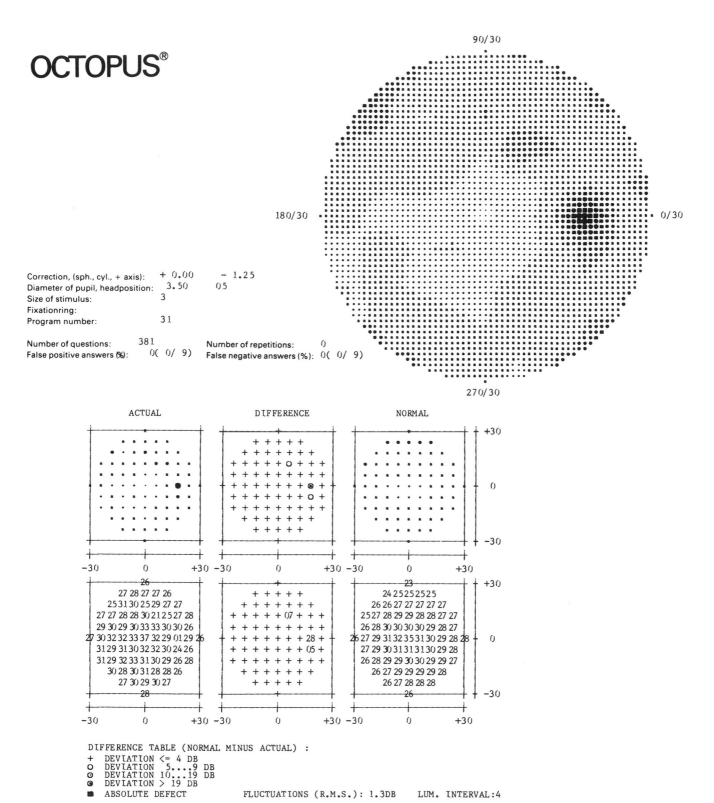

Correction, (sph., cyl., + axis):   + 0.00   − 1.25
Diameter of pupil, headposition: 3.50   05
Size of stimulus: 3
Fixationring:
Program number: 31

Number of questions: 381   Number of repetitions: 0
False positive answers (%): 0(0/ 9) False negative answers (%): 0(0/ 9)

DIFFERENCE TABLE (NORMAL MINUS ACTUAL) :
+   DEVIATION <= 4 DB
O   DEVIATION 5....9 DB
⊙   DEVIATION 10...19 DB
◉   DEVIATION > 19 DB
■   ABSOLUTE DEFECT   FLUCTUATIONS (R.M.S.): 1.3DB   LUM. INTERVAL:4

Fig. 7-15. Printout, program 31 showing comparison printout combined with grayscale.

79

OCTOPUS®

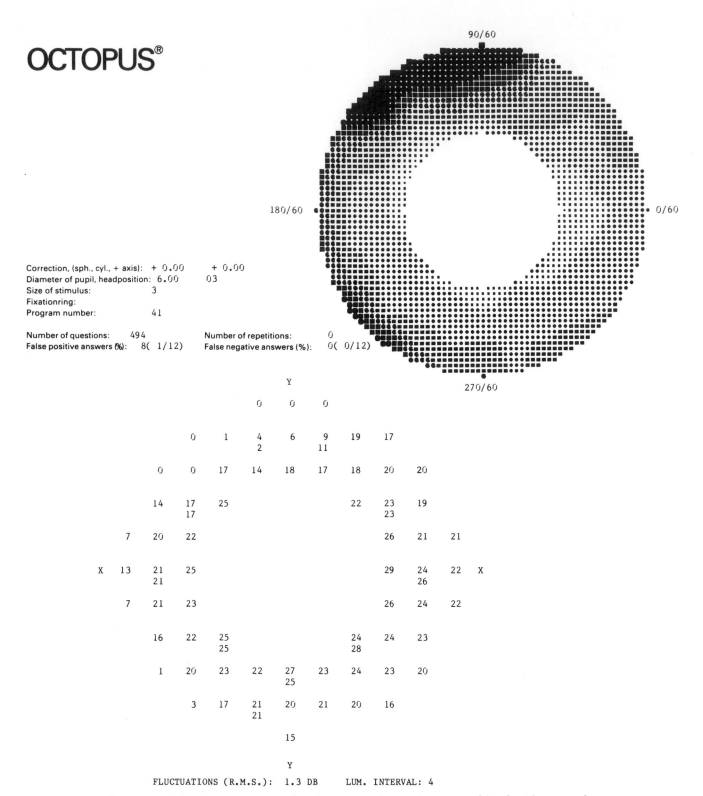

Correction, (sph., cyl., + axis): + 0.00   + 0.00
Diameter of pupil, headposition: 6.00   03
Size of stimulus: 3
Fixationring:
Program number: 41

Number of questions: 494
False positive answers (%):   8(1/12)

Number of repetitions: 0
False negative answers (%):   0(0/12)

```
                              Y

                       0     0     0

              0    1    4    6    9   19   17
                        2        11

         0    0   17   14   18   17   18   20   20

        14   17   25             22   23   19
             17                       23

     7   20   22                      26   21   21

X   13   21   25                      29   24   22   X
         21                                26

     7   21   23                      26   24   22

        16   22   25             24   24   23
                  25             28

         1   20   23   22   27   23   24   23   20
                            25

         3   17   21   20   21   20   16
                  21

                        15

                              Y
```

FLUCTUATIONS (R.M.S.): 1.3 DB   LUM. INTERVAL: 4

Fig. 7-16. Printout, program 41 showing comparison printout combined with grayscale.

OCTOPUS®

Correction, (sph., cyl., + axis): + 0.00   + 0.00
Diameter of pupil, headposition: 5.50   03
Size of stimulus: 3
Fixationring:
Program number: F2

Number of questions: 274
False positive answers (%):   0(0/ 6)

Number of repetitions: 0
False negative answers (%):   0(0/ 7)

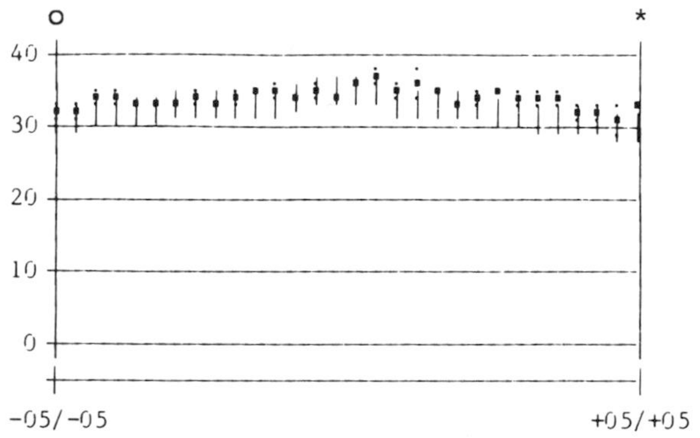

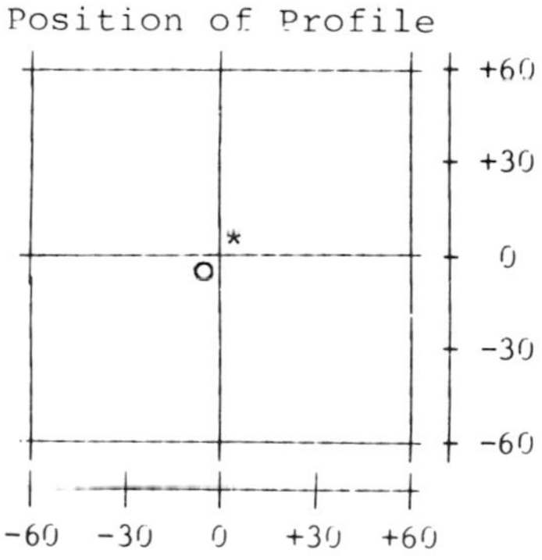

N	X	Y	V1	V2	MEAN	+-	S.D.	NORM
0	- 5.0	- 5.0	33	31	32.0	+-	1.4	31
1	- 4.7	- 4.6	33	31	32.0	+-	1.4	31
2	- 4.3	- 4.3	33	35	34.0	+-	1.4	32
3	- 4.0	- 3.9	35	33	34.0	+-	1.4	32
4	- 3.6	- 3.6	33	33	33.0	+-	0.0	32
5	- 3.3	- 3.3	33	33	33.0	+-	0.0	32
6	- 2.9	- 2.9	33	33	33.0	+-	0.0	33
7	- 2.6	- 2.6	35	33	34.0	+-	1.4	33
8	- 2.3	- 2.2	33	33	33.0	+-	0.0	33
9	- 1.9	- 1.9	35	33	34.0	+-	1.4	33
10	- 1.6	- 1.5	35	35	35.0	+-	0.0	33
11	- 1.2	- 1.2	36	34	35.0	+-	1.4	33
12	- 0.9	- 0.9	34	34	34.0	+-	0.0	34
13	- 0.5	- 0.5	36	34	35.0	+-	1.4	35
14	- 0.2	- 0.2	34	34	34.0	+-	0.0	35
15	0.2	0.2	36	36	36.0	+-	0.0	35
16	0.5	0.5	36	38	37.0	+-	1.4	35
17	0.9	0.9	36	34	35.0	+-	1.4	33
18	1.2	1.2	38	34	36.0	+-	2.8	33
19	1.5	1.6	35	35	35.0	+-	0.0	33
20	1.9	1.9	33	33	33.0	+-	0.0	33
21	2.2	2.3	35	33	34.0	+-	1.4	33
22	2.6	2.6	35	35	35.0	+-	0.0	32
23	2.9	2.9	33	35	34.0	+-	1.4	32
24	3.3	3.3	35	33	34.0	+-	1.4	31
25	3.6	3.6	35	33	34.0	+-	1.4	31
26	3.9	4.0	33	31	32.0	+-	1.4	31
27	4.3	4.3	33	31	32.0	+-	1.4	31
28	4.6	4.7	33	29	31.0	+-	2.8	30
29	5.0	5.0	33	33	33.0	+-	0.0	30

Position of Profile

STRATEGY : UP-DOWN (NORMAL)
LENGTH OF PROFILE (DEG)   : 14.1
NUMBER OF TEST LOCATIONS : 30
RESOLUTION (DEG)   : 00.5
NUMBER OF REPETITIONS   : 02
R.M.S. FLUCTUATION (DB)   : 01.3

• SINGLE DETERMINATION
■ LOCAL MEAN
| NORMAL

R.M.S. FLUCTUATION (WEIGHTED) : 1.3
STRATEGY: UP-DOWN (NORMAL)

Fig. 7-17.   Program F. Note illustration of starting and stopping points of cord tested, and printout of the values obtained.

OCTOPUS®

Correction, (sph., cyl., + axis): + 4.25   + 0.00
Diameter of pupil, headposition: 3.00   06
Size of stimulus: 3
Fixationring:
Program number: A1

Number of questions: 258   Number of repetitions: 3
False positive answers (%): 0(0/ 6)   False negative answers (%): 0(0/ 6)

USER-DEFINED PROGRAM. LABEL: S04

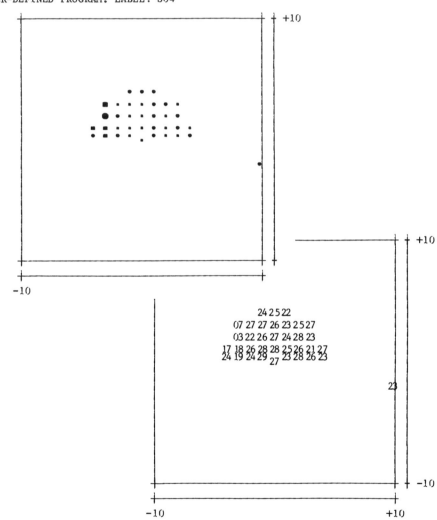

RMS FLUCTUATION : 01.6
STRATEGY: UP-DOWN (NORMAL)
NUMBER OF THRESHOLD DETERMINATIONS (TOTAL) : 45
NORMAL VALUES: SEE PRINTMODE "NL".

Fig. 7-18. SARGON program testing superior field within 4° of fixation with grid density of 1°.

OCTOPUS®

Correction, (sph., cyl., + axis):   + 4.25   + 0.00
Diameter of pupil, headposition: 3.00   06
Size of stimulus: 3
Fixationring:
Program number: A1

Number of questions: 270   Number of repetitions: 7
False positive answers (%):   0(0/ 6)   False negative answers (%):   0(0/ 7)

USER-DEFINED PROGRAM. LABEL: I08

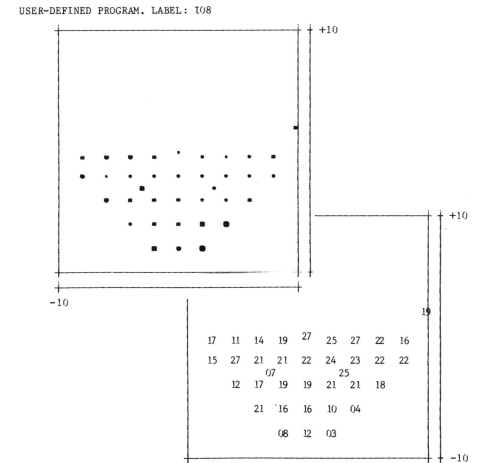

RMS FLUCTUATION : 01.8
STRATEGY: UP-DOWN (NORMAL)
NUMBER OF THRESHOLD DETERMINATIONS (TOTAL) : 45
NORMAL VALUES: SEE PRINTMODE "NL".

Fig. 7-19. SARGON program, inferior field tested with density of 2° out to 8° from fixation.

Correction, (sph., cyl., + axis):
Diameter of pupil, headposition:
Size of stimulus: 3
Fixationring:
Program number: 32

Number of questions: Number of repetitions:
False positive answers (%):   False negative answers (%):

	EX1	EX2	EX3	EX4	EX5	SUMMARY
DATE OF EXAM : DAY	20.07	23.11	22.03	13.09	10.04	
YEAR	1982	1982	1983	1983	1984	
PROGRAM / EXAMINATION	32/05	32/06	32/08	32/10	32/11	
TOTAL LOSS (WHOLE FIELD)	365	279	276	230	256	281 ± 22
MEAN LOSS (PER TEST LOC)						
WHOLE FIELD	4.9	3.8	3.7	3.1	3.5	3.8 ± 0.3
QUADRANT UPPER NASAL	5.1	4.2	4.1	3.5	4.1	4.2 ± 0.3
LOWER NASAL	4.1	2.0	2.2	1.7	2.4	2.5 ± 0.4
UPPER TEMP.	8.2	7.0	7.2	6.4	5.7	6.9 ± 0.4
LOWER TEMP.	2.3	1.9	1.6	0.9	1.7	1.7 ± 0.2
ECCENTRICITY 0 – 10	0.5	0.6	0.8	1.0	0.5	0.7 ± 0.1
10 – 20	7.3	4.8	6.3	4.3	5.1	5.6 ± 0.5
20 – 30	5.2	4.2	3.5	3.2	3.6	3.9 ± 0.4
MEAN SENSITIVITY						
WHOLE FIELD (N: 24.1)	18.0	19.5	19.6	20.3	19.5	19.4 ± 0.4
QUAD.UPP.NAS.(N: 23.4)	16.9	18.3	18.5	18.7	18.0	18.1 ± 0.3
LOW.NAS.(N: 24.4)	19.2	21.6	21.6	22.6	21.2	21.2 ± 0.6
UPP.TMP.(N: 23.5)	14.8	15.9	15.7	17.1	17.1	16.1 ± 0.4
LOW.TMP.(N: 25.1)	21.2	22.1	22.6	22.7	21.7	22.1 ± 0.3
ECC. 0 – 10 (N: 26.9)	24.8	25.8	26.3	25.7	24.9	25.5 ± 0.3
10 – 20 (N: 24.9)	17.1	19.5	17.9	19.4	19.0	18.6 ± 0.5
20 – 30 (N: 23.0)	16.6	17.8	18.5	19.1	18.2	18.1 ± 0.4
NO. OF DISTURBED POINTS	37	29	26	25	31	30 ± 2
R.M.S. FLUCTUATION	3.8	3.7	3.1	1.9	1.3	2.8
TOTAL FLUCTUATION						2.2

Fig. 7-20. Delta program, series mode showing the data of five examinations (05, 06, 08, 10, 11).

OCTOPUS®

Correction, (sph., cyl., + axis):
Diameter of pupil, headposition:
Size of stimulus: 3
Fixationring:
Program number: 32

Number of questions:
False positive answers (%):

Number of repetitions:
False negative answers (%):

	SUMMARY A	SUMMARY B	DIFF (B MIN A)
PROGRAM/EXAM/DATE	32/10/13.09.83	32/11/10.04.84	
TOTAL LOSS (WHOLE FIELD)	230 ± *	256 ± *	+ 26 ± *
MEAN LOSS (PER TEST LOC)			
WHOLE FIELD	3.1 ± *	3.5 ± *	+ 0.4 ± *
QUADRANT UPPER NASAL	3.5 ± *	4.1 ± *	+ 0.6 ± *
LOWER NASAL	1.7 ± *	2.4 ± *	+ 0.7 ± *
UPPER TEMP.	6.4 ± *	5.7 ± *	- 0.8 ± *
LOWER TEMP.	0.9 ± *	1.7 ± *	+ 0.8 ± *
ECCENTRICITY 0 - 10	1.0 ± *	0.5 ± *	- 0.5 ± *
10 - 20	4.3 ± *	5.1 ± *	+ 0.8 ± *
20 - 30	3.2 ± *	3.6 ± *	+ 0.4 ± *
MEAN SENSITIVITY			
WHOLE FIELD (N: 24.1)	20.3 ± *	19.5 ± *	- 0.8 ± *
QUAD.UPP.NAS.(N: 23.4)	18.7 ± *	18.0 ± *	- 0.7 ± *
LOW.NAS.(N: 24.4)	22.6 ± *	21.2 ± *	- 1.4 ± *
UPP.TMP.(N: 23.5)	17.1 ± *	17.1 ± *	+ 0.1 ± *
LOW.TMP.(N: 25.1)	22.7 ± *	21.7 ± *	- 0.9 ± *
ECC. 0 - 10 (N: 26.9)	25.7 ± *	24.9 ± *	- 0.8 ± *
10 - 20 (N: 24.9)	19.4 ± *	19.0 ± *	- 0.4 ± *
20 - 30 (N: 23.0)	19.1 ± *	18.2 ± *	- 0.9 ± *
NO. OF DISTURBED POINTS	25 ± *	31 ± *	+ 6 ± *
R.M.S. FLUCTUATION	1.9	1.3	
TOTAL FLUCTUATION	*	*	

			0	- 1:	- 1	- 2			
		- 2	5	2	0	0	3		
	0	- 5.	5.	- 3	- 1	0	3	2:	
1	- 1:	- 3:	1:	0:	2.	6	- 3:	- 2:	- 1:
- 7.	- 1:	- 3.	- 1:	0:	0:	- 3:		- 2:	0:
- 1	- 7.	- 4.	- 1:	- 2:	- 2:	- 1:		0:	- 1:
- 3:	- 6:	- 3.	- 1.	- 1:	0	- 3.	3.	0:	- 4:
	- 3:	4:	4.	1	- 2	- 1.	2:	0:	
		2:	- 1:	1	0:	- 1.	- 1:		
			- 4:	- 2:	- 2:	- 4:			

DIFFERENCE TABLE : MEAN B MINUS MEAN A (NEGATIVE VALUES: DECREASED SENSITIVITY)
0-0 ALL RESULTS ZERO <> LOW NORMAL VALUES
DOTS INDICATE THAT SOME (.) OR ALL (:) RESULTS ARE IN NORMAL RANGE (FULLY VALID)

CONFIDENCE INTERVAL FOR MEAN DIFFERENCE / T-TEST
(1) PATHOL. AREA (UNDOTTED) + 0.5 ± 1.0 (T-TEST: DATA DO NOT PROVE ALTERATION)
(2) WHOLE FIELD - 0.8 ± 0.6 (T-TEST: ALTERATION IS INDICATED)

Fig. 7-21. Delta program, change mode showing comparison of examination 10 and 11 in terms of the various data. Printout on right shows numerical difference (in db) of each point and result of positive test.

management of the visual field data according to one's needs.

Internal

The 201 series and 2000R series have internal data storage capacities that are integrated to the program software:

Master file.

Values for all points of the visual field are stored in age-corrected normals form to be used as the starting point for the first examination of each eye.

Patient file.

After initial examination, the values are stored to be used in all subsequent examinations (value of starting point).

Delta program.

This statistical program uses stored data from previous examinations and then compares to a current examination. The printout has two modes: series showing up to six examinations, including the current, and elaborating total field loss (in decibels), mean loss (per test location) and mean sensitivity (Fig. 7-20).

In the change mode, up to six previous test results can be averaged and compared with current test or a mean of several test results. A *t* test for each point determines statistical validity of differences (Fig. 7-21).

CLINICAL EXPERIENCE

Clinicians in all parts of the world have been gaining experience with the Octopus system of quantitative static assessment of the visual field. While the literature contains many references to studies carried out using suprathreshold static techniques, major experiences reported with thresholding techniques have been with the use of the Octopus system.

Early reports elaborated the programs used in determining normal values and those used in following glaucoma patients.[1] Efforts were centered on determining the range of short- and long-term fluctuations.[2-5] These parameters were then applied in developing a range of programs in an effort to provide precise information on field changes.[6-11]

Several studies have reported the value of the Octopus system in neurological disorders,[12,13] glaucoma,[5,6,9,14-16] and drug studies[17] and as a screener.[18] Studies presently under way are addressing the value of peripheral field examinations[11] and the correlation of the screening programs to the standard 30 series program.

The future of automated static perimetry in general and of the Octopus system in particular is very exciting. The facility with which data are objectively determined and then stored opens many new exciting areas of clinical and research application. Current mathematical models for data management allow small changes in the visual field to be detected and evaluated much more precisely than previously possible.[7,8,19]

REFERENCES

1. Fankhauser F, Spahr J, Bebie H: Three years experience with the Octopus Automatic Perimeter. Doc Ophthalmol Proc Series 14: 7–15, 1977
2. Gloor B, Schmied U, Faessler A: Changes of glaucomatous field defects: Degree of accuracy of measurements with the automatic perimeter Octopus. Int Ophthal 1, (3):5–10, 1980
3. Flammer J, Drance SM, Jenni A, et al: JO and STATJO: Programs for investigating the visual field with the Octopus automatic perimeter. Can J Ophthalmol 18: 1983
4. Flammer J, Drance SM, Schulzer M: The estimation and testing of the components of long-term fluctuation of the differential light threshold. Doc Ophthalmol Proc Ser 12, 5th Int Vis Field Symp, 1983
5. Flammer J, Drance SM, Zulauf M: The short- and long-term fluctuation of the differential light threshold in patients with glaucoma, normal controls and glaucoma suspects. Arch Ophthalmol 102: 704–706:1984
6. Flammer J, Drance SM, Augustiny L, et al: Quantification of glaucomatous visual field defects with automated perimetry. Invest Ophthalmol Vis Sci (In press)
7. Flammer J, Bebie H: The concept of visual field indices. Albrecht v. Graefes, Arch Ophthalmol (Submitted)
8. Jenni A, Flammer J, Funkhouser A, et al: Special Octopus software for clinical investigations. Doc Ophthalmol Proc Ser 35:351, 1983
9. LeBlanc RP: Abnormal Static Threshold Values in Computerized Visual Fields, Spaeth GL, Whalen WR (eds.), Charles Slack Publishers, 1984
10. Fankhauser F, Jenni A: Programs Sargon and delta: two new principles for the automated analysis of the visual field. Graefes Arch Klin Exp Ophthalmol 216: 41–48, 1901
11. Fankhauser F, Haeberlin H, Jenni A: Octopus programs SAPRO and F: two new principles for the analysis of the visual field. Graefes Arch Klin Exp Ophthalmol 216: 155–165, 1981
12. Younge BR: Computer-assisted perimetry results in neuro–ophthalmology problem cases. Doc Ophthalmol Proc Ser 35, 5th Int Vis Field Symp, Sacramento, 1982
13. Feldon SE: Octopus quantitative perimetry in the evaluation of chiasmal field defects. A.R.V.O. Annual Meeting, Sarasota, 1982
14. LeBlanc RP: Peripheral nasal field defects/automated perimetry. Doc Ophthalmol Proc of 6th Int Vis Field Symp, Genoa, 1984 Submitted
15. Heijl A, Drance SM: A clinical comparison of three computerized automated perimeters in the detection of glaucoma defects. Arch Ophthalmol 99: 832–836, 1981

16. Kriegelstein GK, Schrems W, Gramer E, et al: Detectability of early glaucomatous field defects. A controlled comparison of Goldmann versus Octopus perimetry. Doc. Ophthalmol. Proc Ser 26: 19–24, 1981

17. Flammer J, Drance SM: The effect of a number of glaucoma medications on the differential light threshold. Doc Ophthalmol Proc Ser 12, 5th Int Vis Field Symp, 1983

18. Fankhouser A, Wetterwald N, Fankhauser F: The accuracy of screening programs. Doc Ophthalmol Proc. Ser 35, 5th Int Vis Field Symp, Sacramento, 1982

19. Brechner RJ, Whalen WR: Creation of the transformed Q statistic probability distribution to aid in the detection of abnormal computerized visual fields. Ophthal Surg 15: 833—836, 1984

8

The Synemed "Fieldmaster" Perimeters

John L. Keltner   Chris A. Johnson

The family of Fieldmaster automated perimeters (Synemed, Inc., Berkeley, CA) includes the Fieldmaster 50, (a light emitting diode, LED, perimeter), Fieldmaster models 101PR, 200, and 225 (all fiberoptic perimeters), and the Fieldmaster 300 (SQUID, a projection perimeter). Since our major experience has been with the Fieldmaster 101PR and the SQUID, our discussion will concentrate on these two instruments. (For other models, see editor's note, page 98.)

DESCRIPTION OF FIELDMASTER 101PR

The Fieldmaster 101PR (Fig. 8-1) consists of a hemispherical cupola (30-cm radius) with 99 holes placed at strategic locations in the visual field. Fiberoptic elements positioned behind each hole provide the target illumination from a single central light source. During the examination, each spot lights up according to a random sequence. The patient depresses a button for each target seen, and the location of each response is recorded on heat-sensitive paper. Dark spots on the paper thus indicate visual field locations where the target is seen, whereas unfilled spots denote locations at which the target is not seen.

An adjustable head-and-chin rest keeps the patient securely positioned during testing. The examiner adjusts the position of the head-and-chinrest until the eye to be tested is aligned with a small red fixation cross presented in the center of the hemisphere. Accuracy of fixation is checked by an eye monitor located in approximately the central 6 degrees of the visual field (3 degree radius from fixation). The eye monitor continu-

ously compares the light reflections from the iris and cornea to a setting established during proper alignment. Changes in fixation will elicit a warning tone and stop the program until the patient resumes proper fixation. The sensitivity of the eye monitor can be adjusted to allow fixation error tolerance limits of any desired amount for each individual patient.

The most important features of the Fieldmaster pertain to the selection and control of various test conditions. Luminance of the background and test spots can be adjusted by independent controls. A calibrated photocell connected to a digital meter provides direct readout of either the background or test spot luminance (in apostilbs [asb]) by means of a selector switch. The background luminance may be varied between 1 and 45 asb, whereas test spot luminance levels from approximately 5 to 26,300 asb may be achieved. In addition to allowing precise calibration of test conditions, this process also permits direct compensation for changes due to bulb wear, room illumination, and other factors. Accurate comparison of results between examinations and/or among different machines is thereby possible with the Fieldmaster because of its standardized test conditions.

Additional stimulus controls allow variations in exposure duration of the test spot, time interval between successive presentations, and test spot color (Kodak Wratten filters No. 29 [red], No. 8 [yellow], No. 61 [green], and No. 38A [blue]. The Fieldmaster model 101PR also includes a lens holder for providing an appropriate refractive correction, an automatic recheck of all missed test spots on an individual run, and selection of programs for testing the full visual field, the central 30 degrees only, or the periphery only. As

AUTOMATIC PERIMETRY IN GLAUCOMA
ISBN 0-8089-1705-6

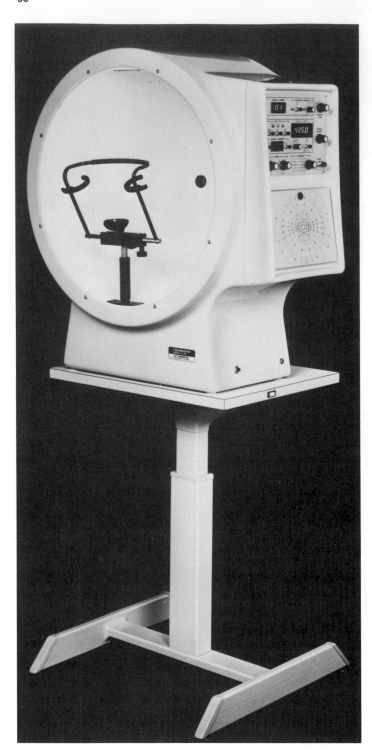

Fig. 8-1. The Fieldmaster 101PR automated perimeter.

presentation are checked a second time. Manual selection and presentation of individual test spots can also be performed. Details pertaining to the optimal test procedures and test conditions, as well as performance characteristics of the Fieldmaster model 101PR have been reported previously.[1-13]

The fieldmaster 101PR has a fixed set of target presentation patterns for evaluating the full visual field, the central 30 degrees alone, and the peripheral visual field alone. Additional target presentation patterns are available on the model 200 and 220 Fieldmaster perimeters for glaucoma, neuro-ophthalmologic and other screening modalities. Custom-designed patterns for the individual user are available on some models, as well as the option of several types of suprathreshold test strategies (fixed luminance for all targets or a two-zone, three zone, or multi-zone luminance profile for the entire visual field).

EXPERIENCE WITH THE FIELDMASTER 101PR

Our experience with the Fieldmaster model 101PR dates back to 1976, and includes testing in more than 30,000 eyes. For routine clinical visual field screening, we have reported standard test protocols and stimulus conditions that can be used in an effective manner.[1-13] We have additionally shown that the Fieldmaster 101PR can provide semiquantitative test results by using more extensive test protocols, and that it is capable of following glaucoma and neuro-ophthalmologic patients accurately and reliably.[1,4,9,12] Rapid screening of large populations has also been demonstrated for the Fieldmaster 101PR in a population of 10,000 drivers license applicants.[5,7,10,11] This combined experience with the Fieldmaster 101PR indicates that it has proven to be a useful clinical tool for many purposes.

A standard test protocol, consisting of a central 30-degree test at low suprathreshold luminances and a full visual field test at high suprathreshold luminances has been established for clinical visual field screening with the Fieldmaster 101PR.[1,6,13] In addition, a standardized set of test conditions and procedures for interpretation of test results have also been determined. Several clinical comparison studies in our laboratory (using these procedures) have demonstrated that detection rates of 96 percent and false alarm rates of less than 5 percent can be achieved with these procedures in patient populations with glaucoma, retinal disease and neuro-ophthalmologic disorders.[1,3,6,8,13] The test procedure requires approximately 6–8 minutes per eye to perform. Shorter screening procedures can be used,[11,13] but detection and false alarm rates will be somewhat poorer.

The ability to follow progression of visual field loss with the Fieldmaster 101PR has been reported for both

described in a later section, these features contribute significantly to the effective operation of this device. For the most commonly used time intervals (exposure duration, 0.8 seconds; time interval between presentations, 0.9 seconds), each test run of 99 spots takes approximately 2.5 min to complete (excluding rechecks of missed test spots). A digital display indicates which spot number is being presented in any given moment. All targets that are not detected on the first

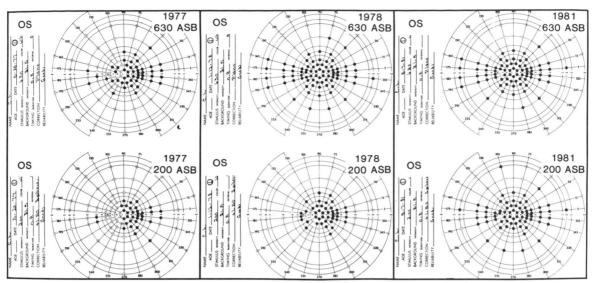

Fig. 8-2. Improvement in the visual field of a patient from 1977 through 1981 following removal of a craniopharyngioma. The "luminance sequencing" technique is illustrated (see text for explanation).(Reprinted by permission of the American Academy of Ophthalmology.)

glaucoma[6,9] and neuro-ophthalmic disorders.[1,12] These studies have shown that it is possible to follow patients accurately and reliably with ophthalmic or neurologic dysfunction and to monitor changes in the visual field using the Fieldmaster 101PR. However, it should be noted that this capability sometimes requires testing at three or four target luminances rather than the one or two target luminances typically used for screening. In addition, the interpretation of visual field information becomes more critical. It is necessary to make comparisons among different target luminances over different test dates. To assist interpretation of data over different test dates and luminance levels, we have used a procedure referred to as "luminance sequencing" to evaluate multiple visual fields from the Fieldmaster. The visual field data from different target luminances are ordered from top (highest luminance) to bottom (lowest luminance), and different test dates are ordered from left (earliest test date) to right (most recent test date). An example of this procedure, as used to evaluate a patient's visual field improvement following removal of a craniopharyngioma, is presented in Fig. 8-2.

The Fieldmaster 101PR can also be used to perform rapid screening populations.[5,7,10,11] In a study of 20,000 eyes, we used a 60–90-second screening test of the visual field in California driver's licence applicants.[5,7,10] Recommendations for appropriate stimulus conditions and test procedures for performing mass visual field screening have been previously reported.[11] Results of these studies indicate that the Fieldmaster 101PR can be used efficiently to perform visual field screening of large populations.

As the availability of low-cost quantitative threshold static perimeters becomes greater, devices such as the Fieldmaster 101PR may become obsolete. However,

the Fieldmaster 101PR currently serves as a useful clinical tool for many purposes, and has a documented track record of more than seven years of clinical trials and evaluations. It therefore remains as a viable alternative for many private practitioners whose needs can be adequately met by this device.

DESCRIPTION OF FIELDMASTER MODEL 300 (SQUID)

The Fieldmaster model 300, also known as the SQUID, represents the top of the line of automated perimeters manufactured by Synemed, Inc., Berkeley, CA (Fig. 8-3). Hardware components of the SQUID include a projection perimeter module and an operator's console that houses a microcomputer system and associated peripheral devices. The projection perimeter consists of a white hemispherical bowl (one half meter radius) with background illumination provided by two diffused light sources at the top of the perimeter bowl. Automatic adjustment of these two sources provides a uniform background luminance which can be varied between 4 and 300 asb. A calibrated photocell continuously monitors light reflected from the bowl surface to provide control of the background luminance. The standard background luminance level is 31.5 asb.

The stimulus target is projected onto the background by means of a servo motor-driven mirror located in front of and above the patient's forehead. Target size (Goldmann targets 0-V), luminance (0.1–5,000 asb), color (white, red, yellow, green, blue), stimulus duration (0.4 seconds minimum), average interval between stimuli (0.4 seconds minimum), target

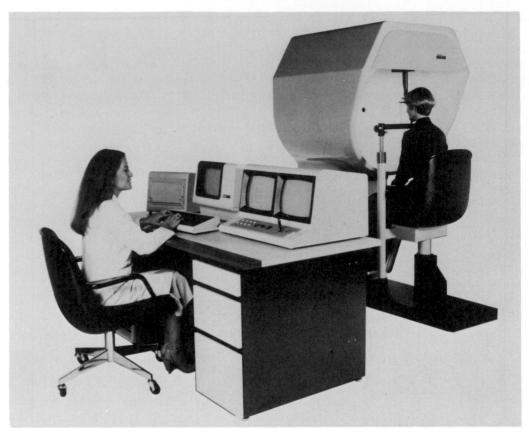

Fig. 8-3   The Fieldmaster model 300 (SQUID) automated perimeter.

location for both static and kinetic testing, and rate of movement for kinetic testing are all under control of the microcomputer system. The examiner can use the standard default values of these test parameters or can set them to any of the desired values within the range of the instrument. Calibration of target positioning by the servo motors and calibration of all target luminances are performed before testing by means of calibrated photocells.

Three different fixation targets can be presented by means of an additional projector at the top of the perimeter bowl. The fixation stimuli consist of a single red fixation point (15 minutes of arc in diameter), four red stimuli surrounding fixation in a 5-degree diamond pattern, and four red targets surrounding fixation in a 10-degree diamond pattern. These targets are projected 15 degrees to the left (for a right eye) or right (for the left eye) of center of the hemispherical bowl. This is done to place the eye movement television monitor, located at the center of the projection bowl, within the blind spot region for each eye. The presentation of target stimuli for static or kinetic testing with the SQUID are then performed relative to the fixation point.

A head and chin rest assembly with lens holder and transluscent occluders is attached to a moveable patient chair (see Fig. 8-3). The chair assembly can be moved back and forth, up and down, and rotated under motorized control to bring the patient's eye into alignment with the television eye movement monitoring system. An infrared television camera is used to provide both subjective and objective monitoring of eye and/or head movements during testing. The camera views the patient's eye through a 33-mm diameter hole located in the region occupied by the blind spot. A video display at the operator's console allows the examiner to view the patient's eye during testing and to examine its position relative to a projected reticle on the screen. Objective fixation monitoring is achieved by projecting the infrared reflection from the patient's eye onto a quadrant photodetector-like matrix, which is sensitive to changes in the reflections produced by eye and/or head movements. The sensitivity of the eye monitor can be adjusted by the operator before and during testing, with a standard 5-degree eye movement calibration performed at the beginning of each test. Depending upon the patient's cooperation, head movements and other factors, the sensitivity of the eye movement monitor can be made greater or smaller as the test proceeds.

In addition to the eye movement monitor display, the operator's console also has a video display terminal for communicating with the computer system and an additional video monitor for viewing the target pattern, progress of the test procedure, and response characteristics of the patient as the test is being performed. An additional joy stick control is present for control of the target during computer assisted kinetic testing. A good quality, high resolution printed copy of test results is available in several formats from a thermal printer.

The microcomputer system is housed in the lower portion of the operator's console and consists of an LSI-11 microprocessor with 64K memory, a 20 megabyte Winchester disc, two dual-sided, dual-density 8-inch floppy disc drives (1 megabyte storage for each) and the high resolution thermal printer for permanent copies of test results. This computer system comes complete with all of the SQUID software for performing perimetric testing, as well as the Digital Equipment Corporation (DEC) Maynard, MA RT-11 operating system, FORTRAN, and all additional software needed to use the SQUID as a separate LSI-11 computer system for nonperimetric purposes. In addition to the software provided by Synemed, Inc., a large variety of word processor, data base management, statistical packages, business, financial and billing programs, and other applications software packages are widely available. Also, the DECUS library of user programs, consisting of nearly 2,000 useful applications software packages, is available for use on this system through Digital Equipment Corporation.

The specialized SQUID software consists of several program modules. The first module incorporates a database management system for storing, retrieving, modifying, deleting, and comparing visual field test results and patient information. Because of the time and storage efficiency of this database management system, multiple visual fields for more than 5,000 patients can be stored and immediately retrieved by the operator from the Winchester disc without the need for changing floppy discs or accessing additional patient files. This feature makes the SQUID a very powerful and efficient clinical and research tool for evaluating and comparing large amounts of visual field information.

A second module is available for generating custom target patterns, and modifying, deleting, or merging existing test patterns. These test generation procedures can automatically generate grid patterns for a specified visual field region and spacing between target elements, or individual points can be entered for each visual field location. The automatic grid generation procedure is quite efficient; a specialized test pattern can be created, implemented as a permanent test, and initiated in less than 1 minute, thereby making it possible to design a test for further evaluation of a patient while seated at the perimeter.

A third module of static tests include a standard group of target patterns: two grids for the central 30 degrees with 6-degree spacing between elements, two tests for the region between 30- and 70-degrees with 12-degree spacing between elements in a grid pattern, one macula exam routine consisting of 9 points with three degree spacing between elements for the central 5 degrees, four blind spot evaluation routines with equal grid spacings of 16–57 points depending upon the exam, a standard glaucoma screening exam consisting of 66 points, a comprehensive glaucoma screening exam consisting of 83 points, a modified Heijl-Krakau glaucoma screening exam consisting of 54 test locations, and three square grids with 54 points separated by 2, 4, or 6 degrees, respectively. Each of these test patterns can be evaluated using a randomized staircase procedure for determining static thresholds to evaluate the test points. Initial target luminances for the static test procedures are derived from the average sensitivity values of 350 normal eyes, 50 in each of seven age groups between 5 and 20, 21 and 30, 31 and 40, 41 and 50, 51 and 60, 61 and 70, and over 70 years of age. These data are described by a mathematical function, which has been shown to provide a statistically significant "best fit" to the data. Targets are then randomly placed 4 db above or below these values as the starting point for testing.

Suprathreshold static test procedures currently use all of the standard target patterns plus any user defined target patterns. Targets are evaluated 6 db above the average normal sensitivity vlaues for the patient's age and a "yes" or "no" response is recorded. Missed spots are checked a second time and, if the target is missed, a third presentation at maximum intensity is presented for that point. Representation of the information is thus in terms of seen versus not seen for the 6-db suprathreshold luminance or the maximum intensity value.

Computer assisted kinetic test administration is also part of the standard test package. It consists of a routine in which various parameters of the target (size, shape, luminance) can be specified and an isopter can be determined by moving the stimulus with the joy stick control at the operator's console. The procedure is thus a semiautomated kinetic test under the control of the operator.

A report generation program allows test results to be displayed on the television monitor at the operator's console or printed in one of several formats (numerical display of data, grayscale representation of threshold values, or meridional profiles of sensitivity). The test comparison section of the report generator allows one to represent the data in the above format for differences between any particular pair of test results or differences from average normal values.

EXPERIENCE WITH THE SQUID

To date, we have performed over 700 visual field examinations on the SQUID for more than 250 patients. It has been a sensitive, accurate, and useful clinical tool that exhibits an acceptably high detection rate and a low false-positive rate.[14] Detailed clinical comparison studies with normal manual visual field testing and other automated perimeters are still ongoing, although our general experience indicates that the test results are similar to what one might expect with the Octopus or related automated perimeters of this type. The basic

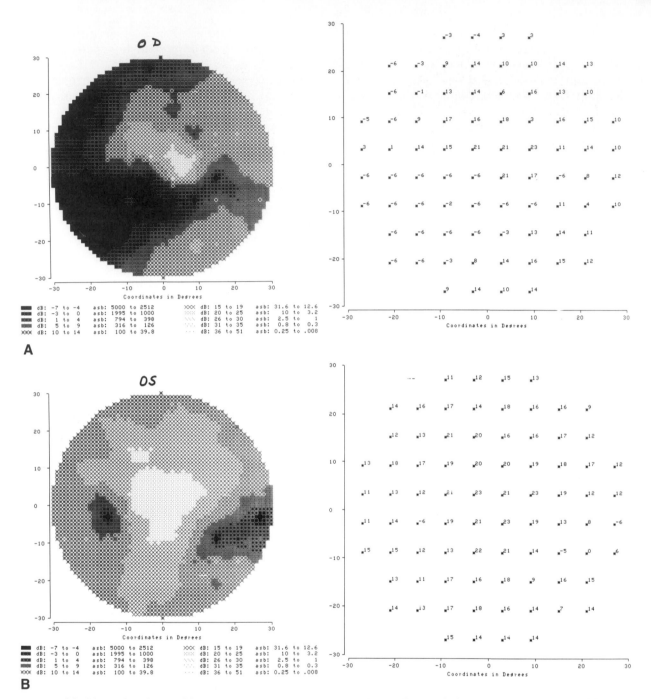

Fig. 8-4. Visual field results obtained by the SQUID from a patient with (a) advanced glaucomatous visual field loss OD and (b) early glaucomatous visual field loss OS. Both the grayscale and numeric decibel outputs are presented.

test strategies and examination protocols are quite similar to the Octopus and related devices.

Our standard static test procedure for the SQUID is program STD 320, which consists of 80 points in the central 30° using a size II test object and a background luminance of 31.5 asb. We have chosen a size II target and a 31.5-asb background luminance because it maximizes the liklihood of obtaining a clear photopic response function for all age groups, thereby providing the most stable conditions for responses over time. The use of lower backgrounds and/or larger targets will shift the response profile toward mesopic or scotopic val-

ues[15] (especially in older age groups) with less stable conditions over time.

An example of SQUID visual field results for a patient with advanced glaucomatous field loss in the right eye and early glaucomatous field loss in the left eye is shown in Figs. 8-4a and b, respectively. Both the grayscale representation and numeric decibel values are presented. We find it useful to evaluate the grayscale and the numeric decibel values together when attempting to interpret visual field abnormalities. An example of a patient with a right homonymous superior quadrant defect is shown in Fig. 8-5.

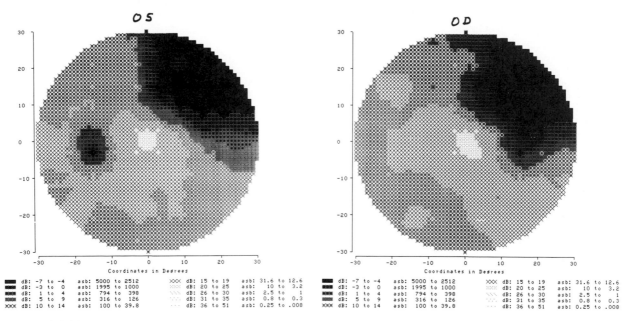

Fig. 8-5. Visual field results obtained by the SQUID from a patient with a right homonymous superior quadrant defect. Results for OS are on the left, OD on the right side of the figure.

In addition to the grayscale and numeric decibel output, data can also be represented in terms of static meridional profiles to better describe the size and intensity of localized visual field defects. An example is shown in Figs. 8-6a, b, and c. Grayscale and meridional profiles (120/300 degrees meridional cut) are presented for the right eye of a patient with thyroid optic neuropathy over a 2-month period. The meridional static profiles augment the grayscale representation by more clearly demonstrating the increase in depth of the scotomatous region.

When there is extensive visual field loss, the patient's sensitivity to smaller targets may be minimal or absent for large portions of the visual field. This makes it difficult to follow patients, since there will be little indication of progression of visual field loss (the grayscale representation will be predominantly black to begin with). Only for those cases in which the visual field improves will there be useful information obtained. In these cases, we use the maximum target size available on the SQUID (Goldmann size V) to obtain a greater sensitivity range over which to continue to follow the patient. Because target size influences the shape of the visual field profile,[15] we usually obtain one size II and one size V visual field determination on the same day to provide a basis for comparison between the two stimulus conditions. Examples of the extended range of sensitivity obtained with the size V target for extensive visual field loss are shown in Figs. 7 a and b for a patient with a progressive optic neuropathy.

As with most of these threshold devices, the greatest difficulty lies not in the ability to quantitatively define visual field defects, but rather in the length of time necessary to perform such testing. Two recent program developments have been implemented on the

SQUID to resolve this problem. The first consists of a sampling procedure whereby thresholds are initially evaluated for an inner and an outer point in each quadrant of a target presentation pattern (8 points total). These values are then used to estimate a local visual field slope for each quadrant of the pattern, and starting values for all other points in each quadrant are appropriately adjusted from the average normal values. This provides substantial reductions in time when the patient's overall visual field sensitivity is somewhat higher or lower than the average normal values, or when the patient has a large scotomatous area within one or more quadrants. Our experience with this procedure over the past eight months has been encouraging. The test time for a central 30-degree examination consisting of 80 points has been reduced from an average of 16 to 23 minutes to an average time of 10 to 14 minutes in most instances. This quadrant sampling technique thus has been useful in producing an average 30–40 percent reduction in the amount of time necessary for testing the central 30 degrees.

The second new program consists of automated kinetic testing of the peripheral visual field. The rationale for this test is based upon several factors. First, visual field defects that occur solely in the periphery are less common than central defects and are seldom small isolated scotomata. Secondly, the common types of peripheral field loss usually have distinct patterns reflecting the underlying anatomical relationships (e.g., nasal or vertical steps). Finally, there is considerably more area of the visual field beyond the central 30 degrees tobe evaluated, and responses typically exhibit greater variability outside the central 30 degrees than within.

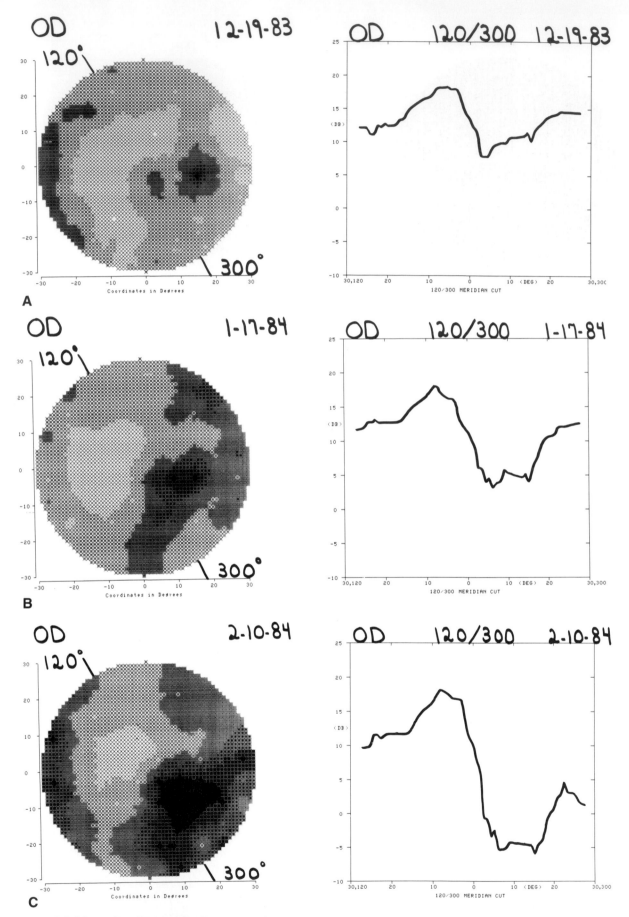

Fig. 8-6. Visual field results obtained by the SQUID from a patient with progressive thyroid optic neuropathy in the right eye on (a) 12/19/83, (b) 1/17/84, and (c) 2/10/84. Both grayscale and static meridional profiles are presented to illustrate progression of both the size and depth of the scotoma.

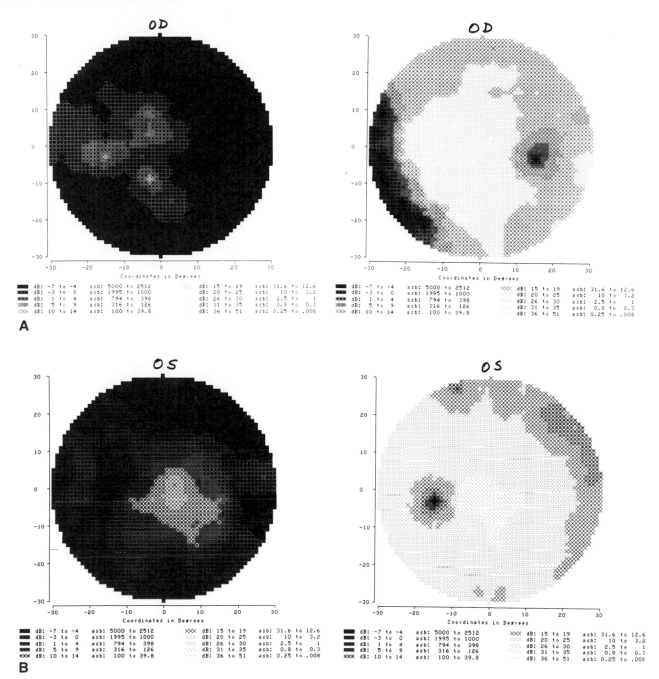

Fig. 8-7. Visual field results obtained by the SQUID from a patient with extensive visual field loss (a) OD and (b) OS due to bilateral optic neuropathy. Results for the size II and size V targets are shown, illustrating the utility of using a larger target to follow patients with severe, extensive visual field loss.

With these factors in mind, a kinetic test procedure for evaluating the peripheral visual field beyond 30 degrees was developed. The basic procedure consists of kinetic testing of two isopters beyond 30 degrees. The algorithm performs decision-making based on the results of preliminary kinetic scans to determine which target values are optimal for providing the most uniform coverage of the peripheral visual field for a two isopter determination (greater than 30 degrees and less than 70 degrees, with approximately equal spacing of

isopters in normal visual field regions). For a normal visual field, each isopter consists of kinetic scans along 12 half-meridians (every 30 degrees, with bracketing of the horizontal and vertical meridians). Kinetic scans that depart from normal values are rechecked. Normal isopter values are based on curvature characteristics of isopters in 350 normal eyes (50 in each of 7 age groups: 5–20, 21–30, 31–40, 41–50, 51–60, 61–70 and over 70 yr).

Kinetic scans are rechecked if they differ from one

or more neighboring scans by an amount greater than the range of normal isopter curvature values. If they are still outside of the normal range, then additional kinetic scans are performed to define the abnormal area. If the transition from normal to potentially abnormal sensitivity crosses the vertical meridian, horizontal kinetic scans are directed toward the presumed vertical border at intermediate locations between the isopter end points. In a similar fashion, intermediate vertical scans are directed to the presumed horizontal boundary. Isopter depressions that are between the vertical and horizontal meridians are evaluated by linearly interpolating between the two isopter points defining the abnormal region, and directing kinetic scans toward the presumed border. For a normal peripheral visual field, approximately 2 to 2.5 min are required to complete the kinetic testing. Abnormal peripheral visual fields require an additional .5 to 1.5 min to complete. Preliminary clinical trials to establish the efficacy of this procedure are currently being conducted.

At the present time, the SQUID represents a flexible and powerful tool for performing automated perimetric testing, especially for clinical research purposes. In addition to our laboratory at University of California, Davis, several other institutions with SQUID perimeters are developing their own custom software for clinical and research purposes. This is perhaps the single biggest advantage of a SQUID perimeter in an academic research environment. Although the SQUID is also a valuable clinical tool, it is likely that smaller, less expensive versions of this device will be of greatest interest to the private practitioner.

EDITOR'S NOTE

The authors properly did not review the Synemed models with which they had no experience, but for completeness' sake the other models should be mentioned.

The Fieldmaster model 200, is like model 101, but instead of 99 points has 133 points available, sets of which can be used in several suprathreshold screening programs that are neither threshold-related nor eccentricity-compensated.

The more advanced Fieldmaster model 225 has 149 sitmulus locations, which are served by fiber-optic cables as in the other models. This instrument is also primarily designed for suprathreshold testing, but has the ability for using threshold-related stimuli (which they call "prethresholding") and also can use stimuli that in two to four steps are compensated for eccentrically (which they call "contour" strategy). Model 225 also has partial threshold capabilities along four meridional profile cuts with spatial resolution limited to the available stimulus locations.

More recently, model 50 has been introduced, with 362 LEDs with standard suprathreshold screening programs (including "prethresholding" and up to seven steps of contour adjustment for eccentricity) and optional full threshold programs, controlled through a cathode ray tube (CRT).

Finally, model 275 is under development to be a smaller version of the projection perimeter 300 (SQUID).

REFERENCES

1. Johnson CA, Keltner JL: Automated suprathreshold static perimetry. Am J Ophthalmol 89:731–741, 1980
2. Johnson CA, Keltner JL: Comparison of manual and automated perimetry in 1,000 eyes, in Greenfield RH, Colenbrander A (eds): Computers in Ophthalmology, Sponsored by IEEE Computer Society, 5-6 April, 1978, St. Louis, Missouri. New York, Institute of Electrical and Electronic Engineers, 1979, pp. 178–181
3. Johnson CA, Keltner JL: Comparative evaluation of the Autofield-I®, CFA-120®, and Fieldmaster Model 101-PR® automated perimeters. Ophthalmology 87:777–783, 1980
4. Johnson CA, Keltner JL: Computer analysis of visual field loss and optimization of automated perimetric test strategies. Ophthalmology 88:1058–1064, 1981
5. Johnson CA, Keltner JL: Incidence of visual field loss in 20,000 eyes and its relationship to driving performance. Arch Ophthalmol 101:371–375, 1983
6. Johnson CA, Keltner JL, Balestrery FG: Suprathreshold static perimetry in glaucoma and other optic nerve disease. Ophthalmology 88:1278–1286, 1979
7. Keltner JL, Johnson CA: Mass visual field screening in a driving population. Ophthalmology 87:785–790, 1980
8. Keltner JL, Johnson CA: Capabilities and limitations of automated suprathreshold static perimetry. Doc Ophthalmol Proc Ser 26:49–55, 1981
9. Keltner JL, Johnson CA: Effectiveness of automated perimetry in following glaucomatous visual field progression. Ophthalmology 89:247–254, 1982
10. Keltner JL, Johnson CA: Correlations between peripheral visual function and driving performance. Doc Ophthalmol Proc Ser 35:211–216, 1983
11. Keltner JL, Johnson CA: Screening for visual field abnormalities with automated perimetry. Surv Ophthalmol 28:175–183, 1983
12. Keltner JL, Johnson CA: Automated and manual perimetry—a six-year overview; special emphasis on neuro-ophthalmic problems. Ophthalmology 91:68–85, 1984
13. Keltner JL, Johnson CA, Balestrery FG: Suprathreshold static perimetry; initial clinical trials with the Fieldmaster automated perimeter. Arch Ophthalmol 97:260–272, 1979
14. Keltner JL, Johnson CA: Preliminary examination of the Squid automated perimeter. Doc Ophthalmol Proc Ser 35:371–377, 1983
15. Johnson CA, Keltner JL, Balestrery FG: Static and acuity profile perimetry at various adaptation levels. Doc Ophthalmol 50:371–388, 1981

9

Quantitative Perimetry:Dicon

Richard P. Mills

DICON HARDWARE

Coopervision Diagnostics (San Diego, CA) markets a small family of Dicon automated perimeters (Table 9-1), which use light-emitting diodes (LEDs) as stimuli and a Heijl-Krakau method of fixation monitoring by periodic blind spot checks. The table-mounted AP200 has 196 test loci and a limited array of screening programs. It is intended for use exclusively as a screening device and possesses only limited diagnostic or quantitative capabilities.

The AP2000 has 372 test loci (Fig. 9-1) arranged along 36 radials in 10-degree increments. Significantly, no test loci are located on the horizontal or vertical meridians, so detection of "steps" across those meridians is facilitated. Stimulus density within the central 30 degrees is enhanced by the placement of LEDs at separations of 2.5 degrees for the first 10 degrees of eccentricity, then every 5 degrees out to 30 degrees, and every 10 degrees until the far periphery is reached. An array of 21 LEDs is placed on each side of the perimeter bowl near the expected location of the physiologic blind spot. As in most perimeters, the viewing periscope and patient fixation target occupy the exact center of the bowl. Testing within the central 2 degrees is therefore done with eccentric fixation, and the dense array of 21 "blind spot" targets is used for macular testing.

Bowl radius for the AP2000 is 33 cm. (Table 9-2), so the standard Goldmann table for choosing suitable corrective lenses for testing within the central 30 degrees may be used. Background illumination is provided by a white fluorescent tube, and is adjustable to 0, 10, 31.5 (standard), and 45 asb. Even at low levels, the color of the background stays white. Luminance at different areas of the bowl varies less than 0.8 dB from

nominal value,[1] and a potentiometer is used for continuous automatic calibration.

The LEDs are mounted in precision drilled holes at the loci described above, and approximate a Goldmann size II (1.00 mm²) target.[1] Stimulus luminance is adjustable from 0 to 10000 asb by means of varying the duty cycle of the LED. An LED can be switched on and off many times per second, faster than the eye can see. The brightness perceived by an observer is related to the percentage of time the LED is on (the LED duty cycle). Diffusing covers for the LEDs are not provided because they would reduce maximum stimulus luminance to 1,000 asb and lower the testing range of the instrument.

Two major technical problems with LED perimeters have been solved in the Dicon AP2000. All LEDs are not alike, and their brightness may vary up to 40 percent within a single manufacturing lot. Furthermore, because of highly sensitive directional characteristics of their light emission, mounting them perfectly in the bowl is nearly impossible. The solution lies in the factory calibration of each perimeter. A fish-eye lens is placed inside a light tight bowl cover at the location of the patient's eye, focused on a photomultiplier tube. The intensity characteristics of each LED are measured and the results are stored at the factory and in the memory module of the perimeter. These intensity characteristics are unique to each perimeter. Before any stimulus location is illuminated, the computer references the intensity characteristics of that LED and makes the necessary adjustments to achieve the chosen luminance. Using this method, all stimuli are within 2.2 percent (0.1 dB) of one another.[2]

The LEDs produce light with a peak emission of 570 nm (yellow-green), corresponding to the peak photopic sensitivity of the retina. Because the LEDs are not

AUTOMATIC PERIMETRY IN GLAUCOMA
ISBN 0–8089–1705–6

Table 9-1
Dicon Perimeters

Dicon Model	Type of Stimuli	Fixation Monitor	Test Number Loci	Standard Software	Print Modes	Disk Drive	Price ($ U.S.)
AP200	LEDs	Heijl-Krakau	196	Suprathreshold	Symbols	None	$5,200
AP2000D	LEDs	Heijl-Krakau	372	Suprathreshold	Symbols	None	$9,000
AP2000T	LEDs	Heijl-Krakau	372	Suprathreshold Threshold-related Static threshold	Symbols Profiles Numeric Grayscale	None	$11,500
AP2000Z	LEDs	Heijl-Krakau	372	Suprathreshold Threshold-related Static threshold	Symbols Profiles Numeric Grayscale	One	$15,500
AP3000	LEDs	Heijl-Krakau	512	Suprathreshold Threshold-related Static threshold	Symbols Profiles Numeric Grayscale	Two	$25,000

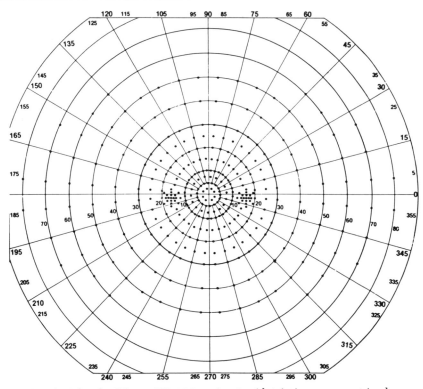

Fig. 9-1. Test loci for the Dicon AP2000 perimeter (dots). Arrangement is along radials from 5 to 355 degrees, at eccentricity increments of 2.5 degrees within the central 10 degrees, of 5 degrees within the 10 to 30-degree circles, and of 10 degrees peripheral to that.

Table 9-2
Dicon AP2000

Bowl radius = 33 cm
Background intensity = 31.5 asb
  (adjusts to 0, 10, or 45 asb)

Stimulus size (Goldmann I target)	1/4 mm²
Stimulus intensity	0–10,000 asb
Stimulus duration	0–12 sec
Interstimulus interval	0–10 sec

Two corrective lens holders
Motorized chinrest and stand
Wheelchair access
Periscope to watch fixation
CRT screen with light pen
Interrupt by operator and patient
80 column impact printer
Plug-in memory module

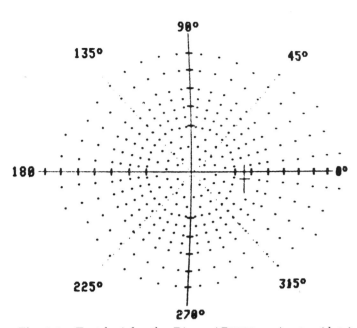

Fig. 9-2. Test loci for the Dicon AP3000 perimeter (dots). Arrangement is along radials from 5 to 355 degrees, at eccentricity increments of 2.5 degrees within the central 30 degrees, and 10 degrees peripheral to that.

illuminated continuously, their aging is minimal. After eight visual field examinations per day for 15 yr, LED aging might account for a 5 percent (0.2 dB) variation from stated luminance.[2] Stimulus duration and interstimulus intervals are adjustable from 0 to 10 seconds.

Corrective lens holders are mounted on telescoping rods that extend from both sides of the bowl (to avoid conflict with the nose when testing the contralateral eye). The molded plastic patient chinrest, while marginally comfortable for some patients, is motorized. Horizontal and vertical readjustments in position are easy to make as the test proceeds. An integral motorized stand designed for wheelchair access obviates the need to purchase a table for the AP 2000. An adjustable patient stool is still advisable however, to accommodate comfortably unusually short or tall patients. A periscope with an infinite depth of field allows the operator to monitor manually patient fixation while standing well back from the eyepiece. A cathode ray tube (CRT) screen displays the menu options and shows test results as the test progresses, including location, intensity, and duration of each stimulus, as well as patient response. Operator commands are given by a light pen contacting the CRT screen. An exceptionally convenient feature is the ability of the operator to suspend testing briefly by pressure on the tip of the light pen. Like most perimeters, the AP 2000 allows the patient to suspend testing by continuous depression of the patient response button.

Early models of the AP2000 had a thermal dot matrix printer that produced small charts that were difficult to read and faded with time. Currently the instrument features an 80-column impact printer that produces high quality permanent charts, albeit somewhat slowly. The plug-in memory module can be changed by the operator without a service call, allowing software updates to be promptly implemented.

The Dicon AP2000 is available in three models, all with the hardware described. The AP2000 is the basic model, the AP2000T contained additional software capable of threshold static determinations and grayscale printouts, and the AP2000Z is enhanced by a floppy disk drive for data storage and manipulation.

The Dicon AP3000 entered production in April, 1984. It features 512 test loci (Fig. 9-2), 379 of which are located within the central 30-degrees at 2.5-degree separations. The enhanced central density allows meridional threshold determinations at 2.5-degree resolution, and better scotoma delineation with interactive software. A video fixation monitor, dual disk drives, full color CRT, RS-232 interface to personal or office computers, and faster impact printer are standard equipment.

Table 9-3
Dicon AP2000 SOFTWARE

Methods of Testing	Stimulus test	Patients
Suprathreshold	72 Point	Blindspot
Threshold-related	120 point	Neurologic
suprathreshold	171 point	Hemianopic
"Two-zone threshold"	239 point	Esterman
"Hill-of-vision"	333 point	Meridional static
	Central	Arc (circular) threshold
	Peripheral	Central 30 grid
	Central	Macular threshold
	Glaucoma	

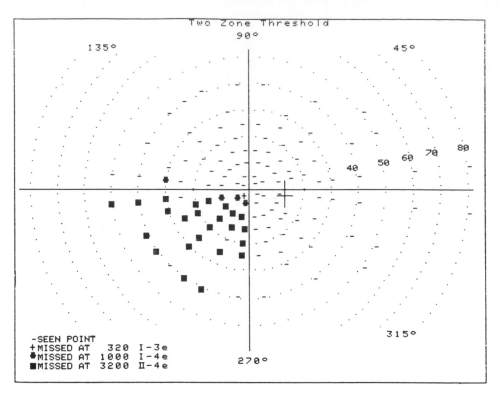

Fig. 9-3. The "two-zone threshold" testing method showing inferonasal quadrantic defect. Points seen at the threshold-related stimulus intensity (320 asb) are indicated by dashes. Those missed twice at the initial stimulus intensity (320 asb) are recorded as fine crosses, those missed at 0.5 log units stronger (1,000 asb) are recorded as broad crosses, and those missed at 1.0 log units stronger (3200 asb) are recorded as squares. The blind spot is denoted by a large cross.

DICON SOFTWARE

Fixation Monitoring

Automatic fixation monitoring using the Heijl-Krakau method is under software control in the Dicon perimeters. At the beginning of a test (or series of tests), 21 closely spaced points centered at the normal location of the physiologic blind spot are tested at maximum luminance. The computer locates the center of the blind spot defined by the missed points. In the normal mode of operation of the monitor during field testing, a maximum luminance stimulus is presented at the center of the blind spot every 7–10 seconds. In common with monitors of other perimeters using the Heijl-Krakau method, if the patient responds to that stimulus, a fixation loss is recorded. The number of fixation losses serves as an index of fixation quality. Unlike most instruments, however, which use the Heijl-Krakau method of monitoring, the Dicon perimeters also recapture all stimuli presented during the 7–10 seconds preceding the fixation loss, returning them to the pool of untested points. The recapture provision is of particular value in patients whose fixation is generally good with occasional lapses. Patients with poor fixation cause frequent recaptures, prolonging the test time. Once fixation has been deter-

mined to be irreparably poor, it is best to disable the automatic monitor and proceed manually.

In patients with large blind spots, fixation errors of several degrees will go undetected when fixation is monitored by use of stimuli at the center of the blind spot. The operator therefore has the option of enhancing the sensitivity moderately, by using the central one third of missed points in the blind spot, or maximally, by using the central two thirds for the periodic blind spot checks.

In patients with extensive field loss, fixation may wander during periods when several points are missed and the patient becomes apprehensive. Consequently, after four consecutive missed stimuli, a location at which the patient previously responded is illuminated. This patient interest stimulus is not considered in the final results.

Software for the Dicon AP2000 (May, 1984)

Program selection is achieved through light pen contact on a CRT screen that displays the menu options. The menus displayed have evolved through multiple software additions and revisions. While they are easy to use given minimal practice, the available software is easier to describe in a different format.

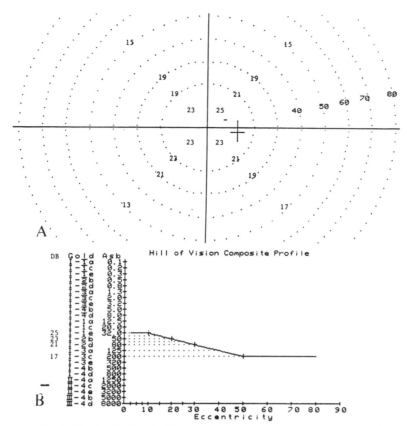

Fig. 9-4. (A) Individual threshold determinations at 10, 20, 30, and 50 degrees eccentricity in four diagonal meridians are shown in decibels (10 times the number of log units that the stimulus is dimmer than the maximum intensity of the instrument). The best sensitivity at each eccentricity is represented by the highest number among the four diagonals. When stimuli are simultaneously presented at the same eccentricity in all four diagonals, a patient response should indicate the "best" sensitivity at that eccentricity. (B) The graph of stimulus intensity against eccentricity (hill-of-vision) obtained by patient responses to simultaneous stimuli in the four diagonals. The points indicated by vertical slashes correlate with the values obtained from the best threshold value at each eccentricity shown in the top part of the figure.

Basically, two strategic choices are made by the operator: the testing method to use and the pattern of points to be tested (Table 9-3).

A full range of testing methods compatible with an LED perimeter are available on the Dicon AP2000. Suprathreshold testing, available since the instrument was released in 1980, threshold-related suprathreshold testing, available since 1983, and threshold static testing, released in 1984, may be selected.

With the suprathreshold method, a single intensity stimulus is chosen by the operator and all points are tested at that level. All missed points are automatically retested once before a miss is recorded.

The threshold-related methods utilize a unique four-point multiple stimulus presentation technique. Equal intensity stimuli are simultaneously presented in each of the four quadrants at the same eccentricity. Since a patient is instructed to respond when he sees one or more lights, the threshold determination is actually performed on the point with the greatest sensitivity. The bracketing algorithm operates with 2-dB resolution, but requires that two consecutive miss-hit pairs occur at the same level before accepting a threshold value. While this double determination improves accuracy, it can be time consuming if fluctuation (scatter) is pronounced. This problem may be overcome by future refinements in the algorithm planned by the manufacturer.

The multiple stimulus presentation technique is used once at 25 degree eccentricity to determine stimulus strength for testing within the central 25 or 30 degrees in several Dicon programs. The stimulus can be set either at the determined threshold or 4 dB brighter. If peripheral field testing is desired, peripheral stimuli are presented 5 dB brighter than the central stimuli. When combined with logic that allows missed points to be retested with stimuli 5 dB, then 10 dB stronger than the base level, the Dicon "two-zone threshold" package results (Fig. 9-3).

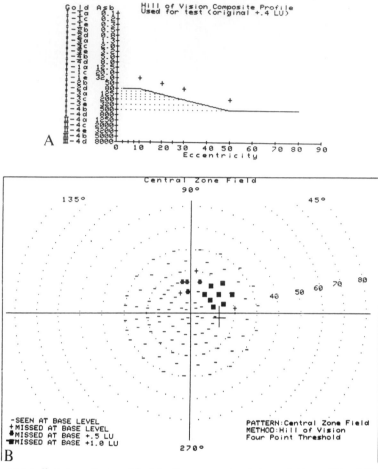

Fig. 9-5. (A) 4 db intensity is added to the computer interpolation of the hill-of-vision plot from Fig. 9-4. For each eccentricity, test stimulus intensity can be determined by reference to the graph. (B) Arcuate scotoma appearing on hill-of vision plot. Base stimulus intensity for each location can be determined by reference to the graph above. Points seen at base intensity are indicated by dashes, those missed twice at base intensity are indicated by crosses, those missed at 0.5 log units stronger than base intensity are indicated by broad crosses, and those missed at 1.0 log units stronger than base intensity are indicated by squares. Blind spot location is denoted by the large cross.

If the multiple stimulus presentation technique is used at several eccentricities, the slope of the sensitivity reduction with increasing eccentricity can be determined in an individual patient (Fig. 9-4). This "hill-of-vision" plot is derived from the most sensitive points among the four quadrants, and is therefore an idealized representation of the slope of the visual island. Using computer interpolations, each of the test points in a chosen pattern can be assigned an expected threshold based on its eccentricity. Testing then proceeds by setting stimulus luminance 4 dB above the expected threshold at each point. Missed points are retested 5 and 10 dB brighter, and recorded with different symbols (Fig. 9-5), so as to provide some information about depth of scotomas discovered on screening.

True static threshold determinations can also be selected as a testing method for several patterns of test points. Threshold is determined according to an algorithm that requires no patient response to stimuli presented at intensities of 4 and 2 dB below the threshold response. The level at which testing begins at each point is presently determined by the eccentricity of the point. The manufacturer intends to introduce logic refinements that use previously determined thresholds at neighbor points to determine initial stimulus intensity for new points.

A large selection of patterns of test points are available to combine with a chosen testing method to perform visual field examination. The 72-point field locates stimuli in the central 10 degrees, arcuate areas, and along the horizontal meridian. The 120-, 171-, 239-, and 333-point fields are graded enhancements thereof (Fig. 9-6). The central 30 degree field of 70 points is intended to combine with a peripheral field pattern of 74 points to perform screening in a manner similar to that suggested by Johnson and Keltner for the Fieldmaster (Synened, Inc) 101PR.[3] Other options include a 120-point pattern designed for glaucoma screening,

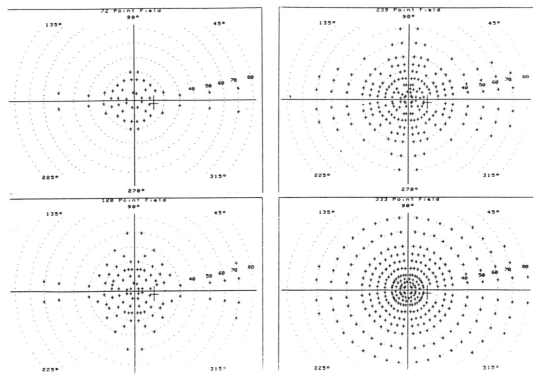

Fig. 9-6. Standard visual field patterns available on the Dicon AP2000 perimeter. (upper left) 72 point, (lower left) 120 point, 171 point (not shown), (upper right) 239 point, (lower left) 333 point.

patterns limited to the macula or blind spots, a neurologic screening pattern, patterns that ignore testing in one or another hemifield if hemianopia is known to exist, and an Esterman pattern for binocular disability testing.

The light pen may be used to circle areas of the field where the operator wishes maximal point density. Use of this diagnostic option can be selected as a separate test or as an enhancement of another test pattern. When implemented while a test is running, the additional points are added to the pool of untested points, from which random selections are made.

In the static threshold testing mode, four patterns are currently available. Any of the 36 LED meridians may be selected for testing a threshold profile of 11 to 13 points. An arc straddling a suspected step may be defined by the operator. A grid of 84 points within the central 30 degrees can be tested, with numeric threshold or grayscale printouts. Finally, foveal and parafoveal thresholds of 14 points along the vertical and horizontal axes can be performed during eccentric fixation at one of the blind spot arrays.

Software for the Dicon AP3000

The AP3000, released in April, 1984, has all the capabilities of the AP2000, with further additions. Its enhanced point density within the central 30 degrees will allow 2.5-degree resolution for meridional threshold determinations. Its dual disk drives will allow

previous patient data to be used in choosing initial stimuli and performing computer-generated comparisons between fields. It will be user-programmable so special field protocols can be designed for special needs. Upon discovery of a scotoma on screening, an automatic "smart scotoma mapping" program will add additional stimuli in the area of the scotoma to determine size and test at different intensities to determine depth. The AP3000 has been designed to fulfill research requirements for LED perimeters. The hope is that worthwhile software designed on the AP3000 can later be "downloaded" to the less expensive AP2000, if desired.

Table 9-4

Performance of Screening Perimeters (Manual quantitative Standard)

Instrument	False Alarm Rate	Detection Rate
	(False Positive/No. Eyes)	(True Positive/No. Eyes)
Goldmann	9% (3/33)	92% (79/86)
Fieldmaster	6% (2/33)	90% (77/86)
Dicon	9% (3/33)	94% (81/86)

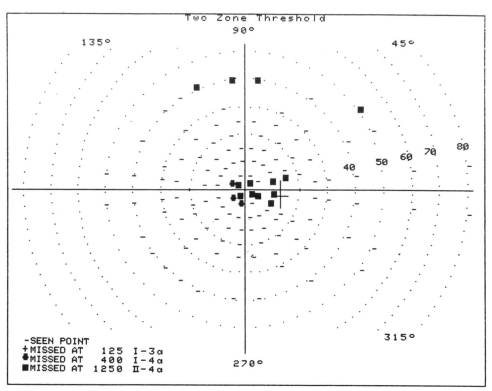

Fig. 9-7. Cecocentral scotoma as shown on two-zone threshold plot of Dicon AP2000. Central 30 degrees are tested 0.4 log units stronger than threshold determination 25 degrees eccentric to fixation using simultaneous four point stimulus technique. Seen points at base intensity of 125 asb are depicted as dashes, points missed twice at base intensity are depicted as crosses (none), points missed at intensity 0.5 log units stronger than base intensity are depicted as broad crosses, and points missed 1.0 log units stronger than base intensity are depicted as squares. Locations peripheral to 30 degrees eccentricity are tested at 0.5 log units stronger than base intensity; seen points are depicted as dashes, points missed twice are depicted as broad crosses (none), and points missed 1.0 log units stronger than base intensity are depicted as squares. The large cross is the physiologic blind spot.

QUANTITATIVE CAPABILITIES OF DICON

A quantitative device is one that can be used to detect significant changes in the visual field between two separate examinations. To do this the instrument must be capable of showing changes in size and depth of scotomas and changes in overall sensitivity in the visual field. While static threshold perimetry is useful in determining scotoma depth and overall differential sensitivity of the field, scotoma size can probably be determined more efficiently by other methods, including multilevel suprathreshold static perimetry.

The Dicon AP2000 is capable of both threshold static and suprathreshold static perimetry. My experience with the Dicon using suprathreshold strategies spans 2 yr. Static threshold strategies have just been released, and I have used them for some 6 wk.

The author's initial studies with the Dicon compared its performance with the Fieldmaster 200 and Goldmann perimeters used in a simple screening mode. A similar strategy was used with the three perimeters, featuring testing of the central 30 degrees at one intensity and testing of the periphery with stimuli 1 log unit stronger. The central stimulus was chosen after threshold determination on each perimeter of a single point temporal to the blind spot at 25 degrees eccentricity. Classification of the 33 normal and 86 abnormal fields, comprising all degrees of severity of field loss from various causes, was made on the basis of a subsequent multiple isopter Goldmann quantitative field done during the same testing session. Details of the methods used have been published elsewhere.[4]

The automated Dicon and Fieldmaster acheived detection rates and false alarm rates essentially equivalent to the Goldmann manual perimetry, performed according to a modified Armaly-Drance screening method (Table 9-4). These rates are in the range of those found by Keltner and Johnson in their studies with the Fieldmaster 101PR,[3] those of Trobe et al. using trained technicians performing manual perimetry[5] and, considering differences in patient populations, those found by Heijl and Drance using the Competer, Octopus, and Perimetron.[6]

The validation of the Dicon's ability to perform acceptably as a screener is important and will be reassuring to the 2,500 current owners of the instrument. Users of automated perimeters are interested not only in determining whether a field is normal or abnormal, but also in being able to assign the screening field into a diagnostic category. The simple suprathreshold screening strategy used in this study had serious deficiencies in diagnostic capability. There was often insufficient data on examination of the field charts to make a confident diagnosis of the character of the defect without further field testing. The author would have required further testing for diagnosis in 42 percent of the eyes after Dicon screening and 56 percent of the

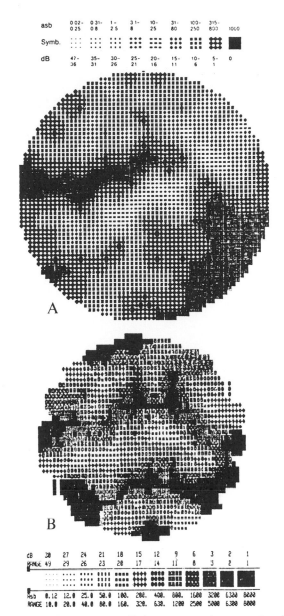

Fig. 9-8. (A) Octopus 2000R (program 32) grayscale plot of glaucomatous field defect, right eye. (B) Dicon AP2000 grayscale plot of same patient. Reference to legends demonstrates differences in grayscales that explain the different appearance of the printouts, which actually are quite similar.

eyes after Fieldmaster screening, if the automated screening field had been the only information available. A second complete run at a different stimulus intensity represents one approach to further testing. It is relatively time-consuming and produces a separate sheet of paper that is inconvenient to handle and store.

Other approaches on the Dicon are the two-zone threshold and hill-of-vision methodologies described. The screening field is performed with stimuli related to threshold determination(s) and each missed point is automatically tested with stimuli 5 and 10 dB brighter than the base level. These more complex interactive

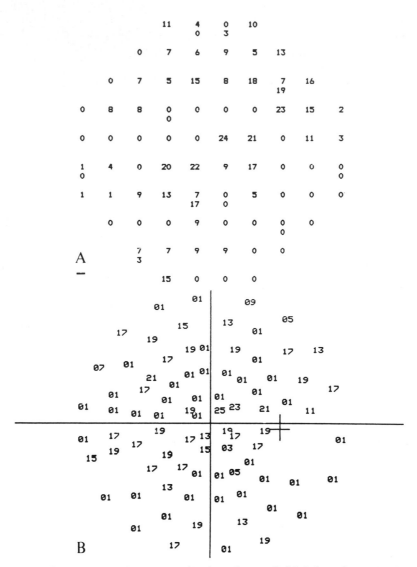

Fig. 9-9. (A) Octopus 2000R numeric display of same field defect shown in Fig. 9-8. O refers to an absolute defect. (B) Dicon AP2000 numeric display of same defect. 01 refers to an absolute defect.

strategies are being currently evaluated. Preliminary results indicate that with these strategies considerable improvement in diagnostic capability can be achieved at the cost of a minor increase in test time and false alarm rate. Some quantitative information is also available, and the results are printed on a single sheet of paper (Fig. 9-7). Whether these strategies or variants thereof can safely be used to follow chronic glaucoma is yet to be investigated, but they may represent an alternative to purely static threshold methods.

The Dicon AP2000 has four programs using static threshold determinations. When a grid pattern of 84 points within the central 30 degrees is tested, a numeric or grayscale printout can be produced. In a small group of glaucoma patients, good correlation was found between such Dicon fields and program 32 on the Octopus 2000R run consecutively (Figs. 9-8 through 9-11).

In several other patients, an arc of points straddling the horizontal meridian was used to define a nasal step, again correlating well with results obtained on the Octopus, Goldmann, and Oculus perimeters (Fig. 9-12).

Meridional threshold cuts have limited resolutions of 2.5–5 degrees, but can be helpful in determining whether isolated scotomas found on screening are real or artefactual.

Finally, the Dicon can perform foveal and parafoveal threshold determinations at 13 locations along vertical and horizontal meridians. The author ran this program eight consecutive times on a few normal persons and calculated means and standard deviations for each point, with an overall root mean square (RMS) value. The same people were tested with an F8 program at similar test locations on the Octopus 201. The eight repetitions in the F8 program yielded similar data, and similar RMS values (Fig. 9-13). It is encouraging that overall scatter or short-term fluctuation as reflected by the RMS in those few normal individuals appears to be no worse on the Dicon LED perimeter than on the projection Octopus system. Further work using a series of normals and patients with field defects will have to be done.

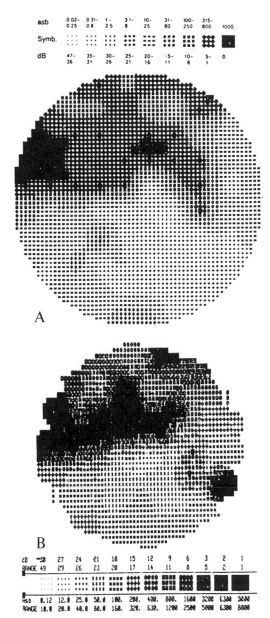

Fig. 9-10.   (A) Octopus 2000R (program 32) grayscale display of glaucomatous field defect, right eye. (B) Dicon AP2000 grayscale display of same defect. Reference to legends demonstrates grayscale differences that explain the different appearance of the printouts, which actually are quite similar.

STORAGE AND COMPARISON OF VISUAL FIELDS

This function requires a disk drive, which has just become available as a single drive option for the AP2000, or the double disk drive, standard on the AP3000. Software to accomplish automatic visual field comparison has recently been released for the AP2000 with disk drive. An asterisk is printed if the field is better at a point, while a number reflecting the threshold decrease in decibels indicates worsening of a point. The author has not personally had an opportunity to evaluate this software.

METHOD OF PRINTOUT

The original Dicon AP2000 had a thermal 40-column dot matrix printer that produced small charts whose quality decreased with storage. The new models have an impact 80-column printer capable of graphic, numeric, or grayscale printing. Older models can be upgraded with a free-standing printer. The slow speed of the new printer is a drawback when doing multiple field examinations on the same patient, but with a disk drive, all printing can be performed at a later time. The

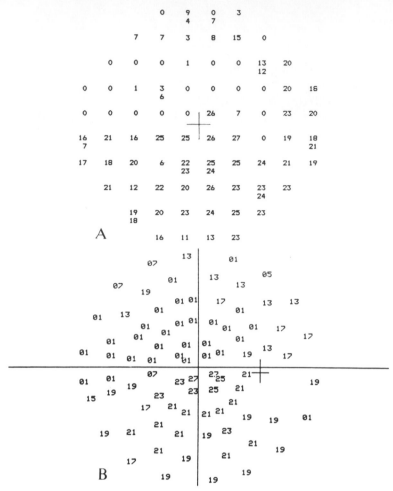

Fig. 9-11. (A) Octopus 2000R numeric display of same field defect shown in Fig. 9-10. 0 refers to an absolute defect. (B) Dicon AP2000 numeric display of same defect. 01 refers to an absolute defect.

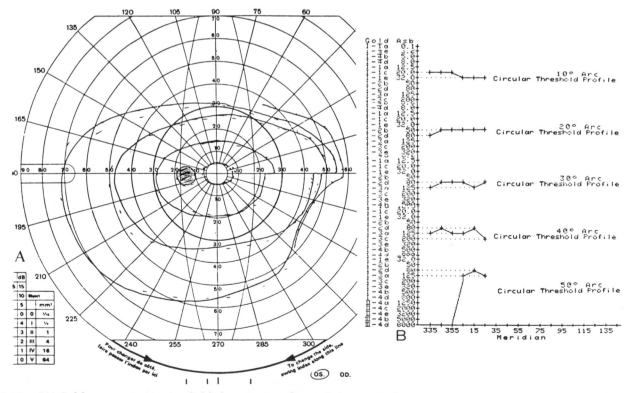

Fig. 9-12. (A) Goldmann quantitative field showing nasal step, left eye. (B) Dicon AP2000, series of short arc profiles across the horizontal meridian at five eccentricities. Step shown at 25 degrees on Goldmann plot is barely significant, and probably represents less than 2 db, the resolution of the threshold used by the threshold technique.

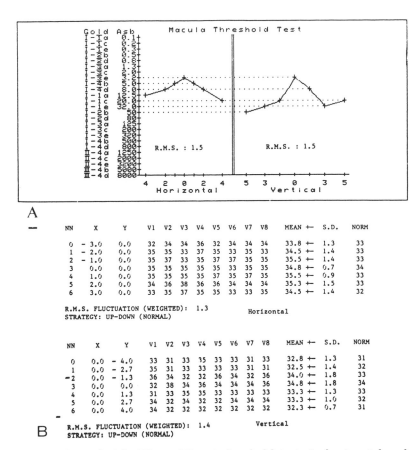

Fig. 9-13. (A) One of eight Dicon AP2000 threshold tests in horizontal and vertical meridians within central 5 degrees performed on normal patient. RMS is an indication of the variance of the individual threshold determinations about the mean for all points tested. (B) Octopus 201 (program F8) numeric printout of similar threshold test. NN, stimulus number; X and Y are horizontal and vertical coordinates; V1-V8 are individual thresholds (decibels) in each of eight determinations; and Norm is the normal threshold for that eccentricity. RMS fluctuation is an indication of the variance of individual threshold determinations about the mean for all points tested.

Dicon AP3000 has a printer that operates more quickly in a bidirectional mode.

ADVANTAGES AND DISADVANTAGES

The primary advantage of the Dicon AP2000 is the relatively lower cost when compared to other automated perimeters with similar features, but with a complete array of options that enable quantitative testing. it is not inexpensive. Another advantage is its excellent reliability, probably because it has no moving parts except in the printer. Software support by the company has been good, and modifications are easily installed by the user.

The primary disadvantage of the Dicon AP2000 is the fixed stimulus locations, which cannot be varied as in projection devices. With the good stimulus density

of the AP2000, however, this has not proven to be a clinically important problem. Another disadvantage is the uncovered holes in which the LEDs lie, which disrupt the uniform background on which the stimuli appear. Whether this "black hole" effect is clinically significant is yet to be investigated.

SUMMARY

The Dicon perimeters have only recently been enhanced with software that enable quantitative visual field testing and storage and comparison of fields. Already clinically validated as a screening device, the AP2000 appears to have surprisingly good quantitative capabilities. Further clinical testing will determine whether or not it can function on a par with its more expensive competitors.

REFERENCES

1. Hart WM Jr, Gordon MO: Calibration of the Dicon Auto Perimeter 2000 compared with that of the Goldmann perimeter. Am J Ophthalmol 96:744–750, 1983
2. Technical data provided by the manufacturer, Coopervision Diagnostics, 9449 Carroll Park Drive, San Diego, California 92121
3. Johnson CA, Keltner JL: Automated suprathreshold static perimetry. Am J Ophthalmol 89:731–741, 1980
4. Mills RP: A comparison of Goldmann, Fieldmaster 200, and Dicon AP2000 perimeters used in a screening mode. Ophthalmology 91:347–353, 1984
5. Trobe JD, Acosta PC, Shuster JJ, et al: An evaluation of the accuracy of community-based perimetry. Am J Ophthalmol 90:654–660, 1980
6. Heijl A, Drance SM: A clinical comparison of three computerized automatic perimeters in the detection of glaucoma defects. Arch Ophthalmol 99:832–836, 1981

10

The Competer

Anders Heijl

The Competer perimeter was developed at the Department of Experimental Ophthalmology at the University of Lund, Sweden. The prototype was constructed in 1974 using experience gathered with an earlier, simpler computerized perimeter in which several different approaches for automatic measurements of increment thresholds had been tested.[1] At that time the primary aim was to analyze the prerequisites for fully automatic computerized perimetry in order to find out whether such a procedure was feasible and how it should be carried out. Nevertheless, the basic theoretical and clinical research that was carried out resulted in an instrument that later became commercially available. The Competer perimeter is produced by Bara Elektronik AB (Lund, Sweden). A modified version is distributed by Digilab (Cambridge, MA).

HARDWARE

The Competer has been produced in several different models. Most of the clinical data gathered with the instrument has been obtained with the original model[2] (Fig. 10-1a). Later modifications have included a model for high resolution profile perimetry[3] and the standard model during the last few years (Competer 350), which uses a larger test point pattern that covers the central field out to 35°.[4] The present chapter will mainly deal with these models, but the new Competer 750 (Fig. 10-1b) which is just now becoming available will also be briefly described.

Stimulus Generator

The Competer was the first perimeter to use light emitting diodes (LEDs) for the generation of stimuli.

Several other computerized perimeters now also use LEDs. LEDs can easily be controlled over a very high intensity range and they therefore make it possible to produce perimetric stimuli with very variable intensities without the use of neutral density filters. A perimeter using LEDs can therefore be constructed without any moving parts. The light output from LEDs is almost constant during the entire life-span of a diode. LEDs have two shortcomings: The light output differs even between LEDs from the same production line. Each diode must therefore be individually calibrated. High-output LEDs emit a narrow beam of light and since the position of the light emitting part of the diode varies between diodes, even from the same production line, the use of LEDs is rather problematic unless the surface behind which they are mounted is covered by a diffusor.

The LEDs of the Competer are therefore individually calibrated and covered by a thin, translucent highly diffusing film that eliminates these problems. The film hides the LEDs, which cannot be seen except when lit. The LEDs of the Competer can be lit at 15 intensity levels, the ratio between consecutive levels being 2:1 (0.3 log units). Stimulus duration and interstimulus interval may be varied.

The earlier Competer models used a test point pattern of 64 points covering the central 20° of the visual field (Fig. 10-2a). This design is reminiscent of some of the features of the Armaly selective perimetry pattern. The Competer 350 has the same test point pattern with the addition of some stimuli at 2.5° and 20°–35° from fixation (Fig. 10-2b). The new 750 model has 188 targets (plus 24 extra targets in the blind spot areas) arranged in concentric circles from 2.5° to 75° (Fig. 10-2c).

AUTOMATIC PERIMETRY IN GLAUCOMA
ISBN 0–8089–1705–6

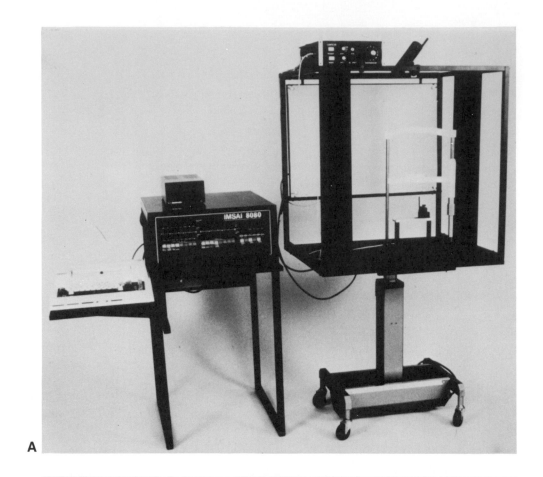

A

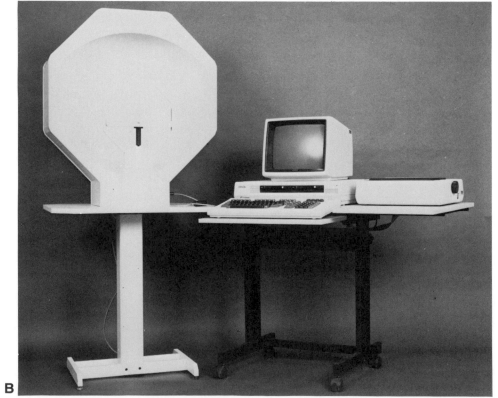

B

Fig. 10-1. (a) The original Competer. (b) Competer 750.

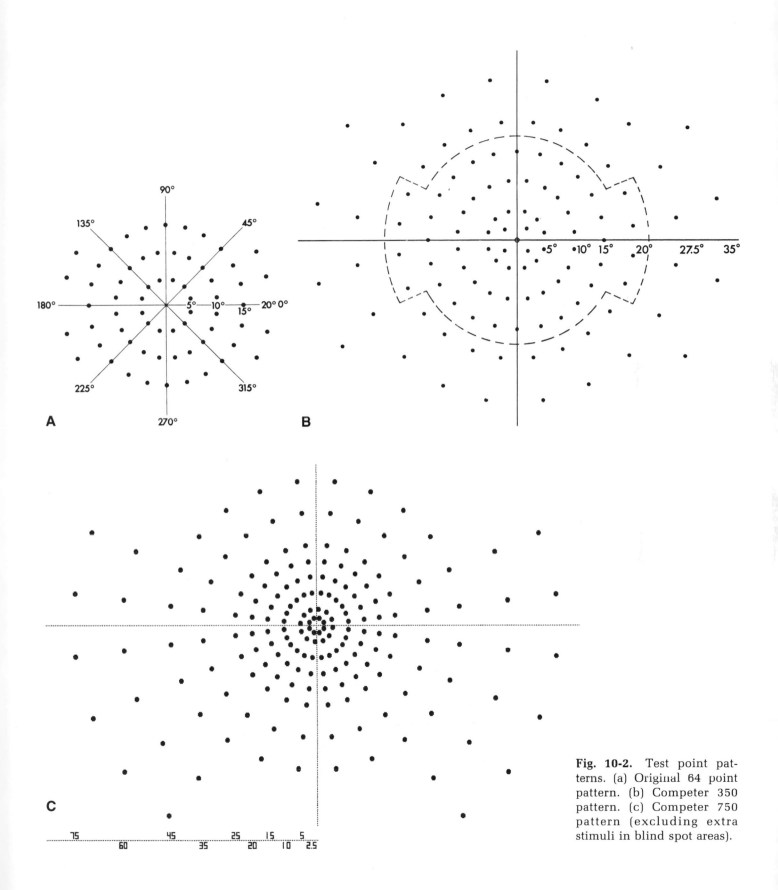

Fig. 10-2. Test point patterns. (a) Original 64 point pattern. (b) Competer 350 pattern. (c) Competer 750 pattern (excluding extra stimuli in blind spot areas).

115

Computer

The early Competers used external mini- and micro-computers programmed in Basic. In the 350 model the external computer was replaced by a built-in microprocessor with the test programs stored in PROMs. With the introduction of the new 750 model this system was abandoned in favor of the original concept with an external customer-programmable advanced computer, programmed in high-level computer language (in the 750 an Epson QX10 with 256 kilobytes RAM memory). This computer may also be used for office routines, word processing and other tasks.

Fixation Control

The blind spot fixation monitoring technique was originally developed for the Competer and is now used in several other automatic perimeters. Stimuli are exposed in the blind spot of the test eye at random intervals. If a blind spot stimulus is perceived this indicates that the patient did not maintain fixation when the stimulus was shown. The score of exposed and perceived blind spot stimuli indicates the patient's fixation reliability and is printed out on the field chart as a fixation quotient. In the 750 model this score is continuously displayed on the TV monitor. This system for fixation monitoring is quite sensitive to deviations of fixation and unlike electronic monitoring it is not disturbed by unimportant head movements. Its disadvantage, of course, is that it is a sampling method, which cannot separate between answers given when proper fixation is maintained and those given when fixation was poor.

Printer

All Competer instruments use conventional 80-column printers producing field charts on standard width paper.

Disk System

Earlier Competers used floppy disk systems only in the more advanced research versions. A dual disk drive using 5.25 in. double sided, double density floppy disks (2 × 320 kilobytes storage capacity) is standard in the new 750 model.

SOFTWARE

Test Strategies

All Competers use the same basic strategies for threshold determination and supraliminal screening.

Threshold determinations are performed using a repetitive up-and-down staircase technique with constant step size. (Test logic I[5]). The test starts in four primary points 10° from the point of fixation. These primary stimuli are first shown at intensity levels, which are definitely supraliminal for normal subjects. The testing at these four points continues until three changes of sign (from seen to not seen or vice versa) have taken place at each point. By continuing the test until the third reversal, instead of stopping after the first change of sign, one false positive or false negative answer at each tested point will not disturb the threshold determination. The threshold levels at the first four points are then transferred to and used as starting levels for the test process in surrounding secondary points. Each of these secondary points is tested until the first change of sign. After this the last perceived level is compared to the measured threshold of the neighbor point from which the starting level was derived. If this difference is equal to or less than one intensity step (0.3 log units) the test process is finished and the last perceived level is accepted as the threshold. If the difference is greater the testing is continued until two more changes of sign have taken place. As soon as the threshold has been determined, it is transferred to and used as starting level in a new tertiary test point and the test continues until the threshold has been determined at all points. This type of testing where the visual field is allowed to grow from primary points saves time by using the knowledge that neighboring points in the visual field usually have similar increment thresholds.

The screening strategy of the Competer perimeter (Fig. 10-3)[6] is a threshold related, eccentricity compensated supraliminal screening with quantification of all defects. It starts by determining threshold in four primary points at 10° from fixation (using same test strategy as in the threshold-measuring strategy already described). The supraliminal screening intensity levels are based on the results at the two most sensitive (or sometimes the most sensitive) of these initial points.[6] The screening levels are thus adjusted to the general sensitivity level of the field being tested. They are also adjusted to compensate for the normal decay of sensitivity with increasing distance from the point of fixation. The stimuli are then exposed at these intensity levels in all points tested. If the first supraliminal screening stimulus is seen, no further testing is performed and the point is accepted as normal. If not seen it is reexposed at the next higher intensity level (0.3 log units above the first stimulus intensity level). If it is seen at this level, the testing of that point is completed. If, on the other hand, it is not seen at this second exposure, the instrument will go to the maximum intensity level to determine whether the identified defect is absolute or not. If it is not an absolute defect the depth of the relative defect will be determined using a staircase procedure.

In both the threshold and the screening strategies the stimuli are shown in a randomized sequence facilitating the patient's fixation.[7] The combination of test

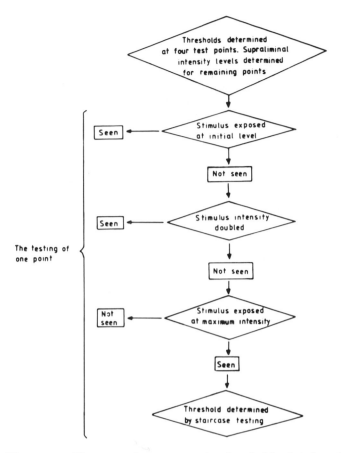

Fig. 10-3. The screening strategy in threshold-related and eccentricity compensated. The defect depth is measured in all points missed twice. (Reproduced with permission from Dyster-Aas K, Heijl A and Lundqvist L. Acta Ophthalmol 1980; 58:918–928

Table 10-1
Combinations of Test Point Patterns and Strategies of the Various Competer Models

	Supraliminal screening	Threshold determination
The original Competer		
64 point 0–20° pattern	+	+
Research model		
64 point 0–20° pattern	+	+
0–30 high resolution profiles	−	+
Custom programs	+	+
Competer 350		
68 point 0–20° pattern	+	+
44 point 20–35° pattern	+	−
Competer 750		
76 point 0–20° pattern	+	+
112 point 20–75° pattern	+	−
188 point full field test	+	−
Profiles	−	+
Custom programs	+	+

strategies and test point patterns of the various Competer models are shown in Table 10-1.

Output Formats

The main output format of the Competer is a numerical printout (Fig. 10-4). The sensitivity levels are numbered 1 to 15, where 1 is the highest intensity level and each consecutive level is 0.3 log units weaker. A higher number thus corresponds to lower intensity threshold stimulus, that is a higher sensitivity. To facilitate interpretation the computer defines a Q value (mostly the modal value), which is a normal sensitivity level in the test field. All points with a threshold equal to the Q value is printed out as 0 in the field chart. The threshold values of all other test points are printed out in relation to the Q value. Points with lower sensitivity than the Q value are thus printed out as negative numbers (−1 if 0.3 log units below Q, −2 if 0.6 log units below Q). Zeroes are added to negative values to make defects stand out more clearly.[8]

The printout format of the Competer profiles is very similar to that of conventional manual profile perimetry (Fig. 10-5).

In the Competer 750 the user has the option of using the traditional Competer numeric representation or a symbol printout (Fig. 10-6).

STORING AND COMPARISON OF VISUAL FIELDS

In earlier Competers only the research models were capable of storing visual fields, thus making it possible to perform comparisons and statistical analyses of measured results. The research instruments have used retrieval of stored fields for subsequent evaluation in several of the studies which will be discussed later. With the introduction of the 750 model disk storage will become standard enabling e.g., linear regression analyses of consecutive fields from the same eye, averaging and comparisons of test results.

EXPERIENCE WITH THE UNIT AS A QUANTITATIVE DEVICE

The Competer has been used in many published scientific studies, some of which were among the first clinical studies in which automated perimetry was clinically tested. Its reliability in detecting field loss has been compared with different methods of manual perimetry and with other automated perimeters. The original 64-test point Competer was used in most of

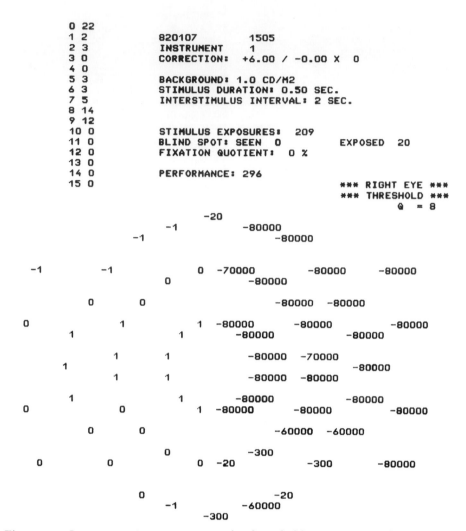

Fig. 10-4. Competer printout in a case of right-sided hemianopia. Defective points are indicated by negative numbers, the first figure showing the depth of the defect in intensity levels (each level corresponding to 0.3 log units). Zeroes are added to negative numbers in order to make defect stand out more clearly.

NAME J.C.
DATE OF TEST 20 MARCH 79
LEFT/RIGHT EYE
BACKGROUND 1.0 CD/M^2
NO OF STIMULUS EXPOSURES   215
BLIND SPOT: SEEN   1

DATE OF BIRTH   12 DEC 25
HOUR 1510
MERIDIAN 135-315°
CORRECTION 0
EXPOSED   24   FIXATION QUOTIENT   .0416667

```
13
12
11
10
 9                              XXXX X X
 8             XXX   XX X  XXXXX XXXXX XX
 7             X XXX XXXXXXXXXXX XXXXXXXXXXX   X XXXXXXX X
 6   X X    XXX XXXXXXXXXXXXXXXX  XXXXXXXXXXX X XXXXXXXXX XXX X
 5   XXXXXXXXXXXXXXXXXXXXXXXXXXXXX XXXXXXXXXXXX XXXXXXXXXXXXXXX
 4   XXXXXXXXXXXXXXXXXXXXXXXXXXXXX XXXXXXXXXXXX XXXXXXXXXXXXXXX
 3   XXXXXXXXXXXXXXXXXXXXXXXXXXXXX XXXXXXXXXXXX XXXXXXXXXXXXXXX
 2   XXXXXXXXXXXXXXXXXXXXXXXXXXXXX XXXXXXXXXXXX XXXXXXXXXXXXXXX
 1   XXXXXXXXXXXXXXXXXXXXXXXXXXXXX XXXXXXXXXXXX XXXXXXXXXXXXXXX
 0   XXXXXXXXXXXXXXXXXXXXXXXXXXXXX XXXXXXXXXXXX XXXXXXXXXXXXXXX
     3   •   2   •   1   •   0   •   1   •   2   •   3
OK
```

Fig. 10-5. Competer profile.

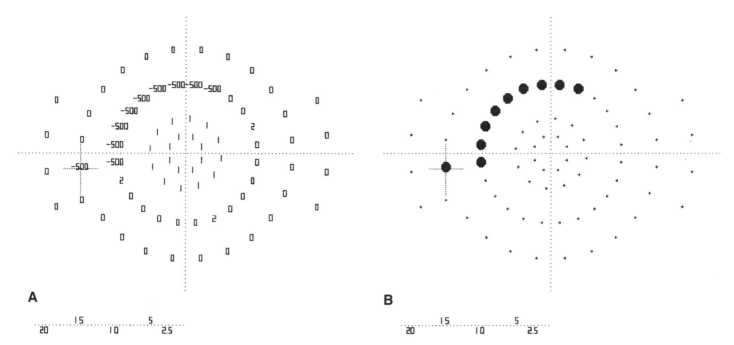

Fig. 10-6. In the 750 model, fields may be printed out in the traditional way (a) or as a symbol printout (b).

these studies. This instrument, in its supraliminal screening mode, has been shown to detect glaucomatous field loss as effectively as manual Armaly screening on the Goldman perimeter, performed under laboratory conditions.[6] The detection rate of the screening program surpasses that of manual kinetic perimetry with sparse static testing[9] and Armaly screening performed in a clinical setting.[6] Using the threshold mode the results are very similar to those obtained with very time-consuming manual perimetry with both numerous isopters and abundant static testing including meridional profiles.[10] The results are very similar to those obtained with the Octopus and Perimetron instruments.[11] Gramer et al.[12] have found that while the standard pattern of 64 points is very efficient in detecting field loss situated in the area covered by the central Competer pattern, this area is not large enough for the detection of early glaucomatous field defects. They found 12 percent of the field defects to be located peripherally to the central Competer pattern, but still within the central 30 field. Some early glaucomatous field defects occur 20° to 30° from the point of fixation, but it is likely that some of the defects found by Gramer et al. were false positive defects due to lens rim artefacts or a drooping lid. If not, the sensitivity figures of some of the studies mentioned here[10,11] would have been much lower.

The ability of the Competer threshold program to detect and follow neurological field defects has also been studied. The original 64-point pattern is more effective in detecting this type of field loss than manual kinetic perimetry.[13,14] It may replace manual perimetry

in the follow-up of small and medium-sized defects, but it is not suitable for large defects.[14] The enlarged test point pattern of the 350 model facilitates topical diagnosis.[4] The original Competer has been used to detect glaucomatous visual field loss in a large-scale study, where all persons were subjected to automated perimetry, and where even the classification of the fields was computerized.[15,16]

The reproducibility of threshold values measured by the instrument has been studied. The standard threshold measuring logic (test logic I[5]) achieves the same reproducibility[5] as the standard threshold measuring strategy of the Octopus perimeter for example with programs 31 and 32 of that instrument.[17] Using averaging procedures even better reproducibility can be achieved, but at the cost of increased test time.[5] The reproducibility of the findings otained with the Competer are better than that obtained by manual, kinetic perimetry.[18,19]

The Competer has been used in a number of studies where it was used as a means in elucidating changes in the visual field over time.[20–22] Krakau has defined a P (performance) value, which summarizes the total increment sensitivity of the tested field into one figure.[23,24] Linear regression analyses may be performed on performance values demonstrating statistically significant deterioration, or improvement, of individual fields over time. The performance value has been used in numerous scientific studies using the Competer instrument (25–28). In several of these studies the disk storage system was used to facilitate handling of the data involved. Other investigations have

dealt with differences between the right and left hemifields for diagnosis of hemianopias[29] and with identification of areas with increased local threshold variation.[30]

CONCLUSION

The Competer automatic perimeter was one of the
first threshold-measuring computerized perimeters and
has been in clinical use for ten years. The basic concepts of the device have been left unchanged in later
models, the main differences between early and later
models being that the test point pattern of later models
covers a larger area than the original pattern.

Some of the advantages and disadvantages with
the device may be summarized:

Disadvantages:
1. Fixed stimuli, limiting flexibility.
2. Some training required to efficiently interpret
   the standard type of printout.
3. Earlier models cover only the central field.

Advantages
1. Time-effective and precise threshold strategy.
2. Fast threshold related, eccentricity compensated supraliminal screening strategy.
3. Mechanically uncomplicated, reliable construction.
4. Easy to operate; no supervision required during test.
5. Research models and the new 750 model are
   completely customer programmable. Test programs written in high level computer language,
   accessible for modification, including creation
   of custom point patterns or completely new
   research tests.
6. Effectiveness documented in a large number of
   clinical studies.

REFERENCES

1. Heijl A, Krakau CET: An automatic static perimeter,
   design and pilot study. Acta Ophthalmol 53:293–310,
   1975
2. Heijl A, Krakau CET: An automatic perimeter for glaucoma visual field screening and control; construction
   and clinical cases. Albrecht von Graefes Arch Klin Exp
   Ophthalmol 197:13–23, 1975
3. Heijl A, Drance SM: Computerized profile perimetry in
   glaucoma. Arch Ophthalmol 98:2199–2201, 1980
4. Bynke H, Krakau CET: A modified computerized perimeter and its use in neuro-ophthalmic patients. Neuro-
   Ophthalmol 2:105–115, 1981
5. Heijl A: Computer test logics for automatic perimetry.
   Acta Ophthalmol 55:837–853, 1977

6. Heijl A: Automatic perimetry in glaucoma visual field
   screening; a clinical study. Albrecht von Graefes Arch
   Klin Exp Ophthalmol 200:21–37, 1976
7. Heijl A, Krakau CET: A note on fixation during perimetry. Acta Ophthalmol 55:854–861, 1977
8. Krakau CET: Aspects on the design of an automatic
   perimeter. Acta Ophthalmol 56:389–405, 1978
9. Dyster-Aas K, Heijl A, Lundqvist L: Computerized visual
   field screening in the management of patients with
   ocular hypertension. Acta Ophthalmol 58:918–928,
   1980
10. Heijl A, Drance SM, Douglas GR: Automatic perimetry
    (COMPETER); ability to detect early glaucomatous field
    defects. Arch Ophthalmol 98:1560–1563, 1980
11. Heijl A, Drance SM: A clinical comparison of three
    computerized automatic perimeters in the detection of
    glaucoma defects. Arch Ophthalmol 99:832–836, 1981
12. Gramer E, Gerlach R, Krieglstein GK: Zur Sensitivität
    des Computerperimeters Competer® bei frühen glau-
    komatösen Gesichtsfeldausfällen; Eine Kontrollierte
    Studie. Klin Monatsbl Augenheilkd 180:203–209, 1982
13. Bynke H, Heijl A: Automatic computerized perimetry in
    the detection of neurological visual field defects; a pilot
    study. Albrecht von Graefes Arch Klin Exp Ophthalmol
    206:11–15, 1978
14. Bynke H, Heijl A, Holmin C: Automatic computerized
    perimetry in neuro-ophthalmology. Doc Ophthalmol
    Proc Ser 19:319–325, 1979
15. Bengtsson B, Krakau CET: Automatic perimetry in a
    population survey. Acta Ophthalmol 57:929–937, 1979
16. Bengtsson B: Aspects of the epidemiology of chronic
    glaucoma. Acta Ophthalmol Suppl 146:1–48, 1981
17. Bebie H, Fankhauser F, Spahr J: Static perimetry: accu-
    racy and fluctuations. Acta Ophthalmol 54:339–348,
    1976
18. Gramer E, Pröll M, Krieglstein GK: Die Reproduzierbark-
    eit zentraler Gesichtsfeldbefunde bei der kinetischen
    und der computergesteuerten statischen Perimetrie.
    Klin Monatsbl Augenheilkd 176:374–384, 1980
19. Gramer E, Pröll M, Krieglstein GK: Die Perimetrie des
    blinden Flecks. Ein Vergleich zwischen kinetischer und
    computergesteuerter statischer Perimetrie. Ophthalmo-
    logica 179:201–208, 1979
20. Heijl A: Time changes of contrast thresholds during
    automatic perimetry. Acta Ophthalmol 55:696–708,
    1977
21. Holmin C, Krakau CET: Variability of glaucomatous
    visual field defects in computerized perimetry. Albrecht
    von Graefes Arch Klin Exp Ophthalmol 210:235–250,
    1979
22. Heijl A, Drance SM: Changes in differential threshold in
    patients with glaucoma during prolonged perimetry. Br
    J Ophthalmol 67:512–516, 1983
23. Holmin C, Krakau CET: Automatic perimetry in the
    control of glaucoma. Glaucoma 3:154–159, 1981
24. Krakau CET: A feasible development of computerized
    perimetry. Acta Ophthalmol 59:485–494, 1981
25. Holmin C, Krakau CET: Visual field decay in normal
    subjects and in cases of chronic glaucoma. Albrecht von
    Graefes Arch Klin Exp Ophthalmol 213:291–298, 1980
26. Holmin C, Krakau CET: Regression analysis of the cen-

tral visual field in chronic glaucoma cases; a follow-up study using automatic perimetry. Acta Ophthalmol 60:267–274, 1982

27. Holmin C, Krakau CET: Short term effects of timolol in chronic glaucoma. A double blind study using computerized perimetry. Acta Ophthalmol 60:337–346, 1982

28. Heijl A, Bengtsson B: The short-term effect of laser trabeculoplasty on the glaucomatous visual field. A prospective study using computerized perimetry. Acta Ophthalmol 62:705–714, 1984

29. Bynke H: A statistical analysis of normal visual fields and hemianopsias recorded by the computerized perimeter 'Competer'. Neuro-Ophthalmol 3:129–137, 1983

30. Heijl A: A simple routine for demonstrating increased threshold scatter by comparing stored computer fields. Doc Ophthalmol Proc Ser, in press

11

Peritest and Perimat 206

Erik L. Greve

The Peritest (804) automatic and semiautomatic perimeter has been introduced in 1980 and has been used in our department for three years. Several publications on the Peritest have appeared.[1-6] The Perimat (206) is in many respects comparable to the Peritest[6a] but does not have some of the semi-automatic functions of the Peritest. The Perimat became commercially available in September 1984. Both instruments are shown in Fig. 11-1.

The technical data on both types of instruments are given in Table 11-1. I shall discuss a few special features. The dynamic luminance range of 3.0 log units is extremely useful in cases with cataract. The instruments have two automatic operation modes, both using single stimulus static presentations. The automatic mode may be called fully automatic if the instruments determines itself whether all or only some of the positions are examined. In the second automatic mode the examiner may choose the positions (phases).

A special feature of both Peritest and Perimat is the possibility of using multiple stimulus presentation. In the new software the multiple stimulus presentation can be used in an almost automatic way. If all stimuli of a group are seen all positions of the group are considered normal by the computer; if, however, only part of the stimulus of a group is seen this group is stored and retested in a single stimulus mode later on. In the author's opinion this combined multiple-single stimulus presentation is the most efficient present screening technique.

The Peritest can also be operated in a manual semiautomated mode in which position, luminance and timing are directed by the examiner, using the computer memory to facilitate the examination. These different operation-possibilities make the Peritest-Perimat an extremely flexible automated perimeter.

The Peritest-Perimat both have an optical fixation-control device. The new software also includes a blind spot check type of fixation control. The manufacturer has stated that an infrared fixation control has been developed and will be made available if there is sufficient demand from the users.

The total number and distribution of stimuli is illustrated in Fig. 11-2. The choice of stimulus positions is presented in Table 11-2. Most of the choices speak for themselves. The neurological and glaucoma programs measure thresholds along meridians at each side of the vertical and horizontal meridians, respectively. The profiles will measure thresholds along vertical or horizontal cuts.

The Peritest and Perimat have a number of strategies that can be used in combination with the different stimulus presentation possibilities. The total of present and near future programs is presented in Table 11-3.

The standard program uses a threshold-related suprathreshold gradient-adapted strategy.[5,7] The general threshold level is measured accurately and repeatedly at a few representative positions (the center being the most important one). All other positions are tested at a 0.6 suprathreshold level. Positions not seen at this slightly suprathreshold luminance level are further assessed (with either 0.2 or 0.6 luminance steps). Separate areas selected by the examiner can be retested.

In the new software-programs threshold techniques comparable to those in the Scoperimeter[7,8] with fluctuation analysis will be incorporated. The programs on defect volume and an comparison are being developed.

The defect-intensity (depth) measurements provide information on relative intensity of the defects, i.e., relative to normal general sensitivity. The changes in the visual field are expressed as general reductions of

AUTOMATIC PERIMETRY IN GLAUCOMA
ISBN 0-8089-1705-6

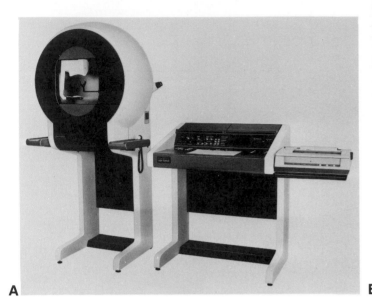

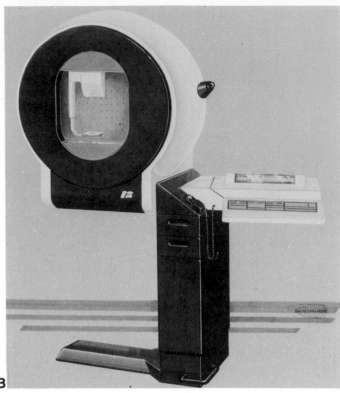

Fig. 11-1. (A) Peritest. (B) Perimat.

sensitivity and local reductions of sensitivity. The author prefers this system to absolute values. It allows an intensity description that is comparable at all eccentricities. It is important to separate local from general reduction of sensitivity. In glaucomatous disease the general reduction of sensitivity is either caused by cataract (major cause) or by a diffuse affection of the

visual field (minor cause). Both should be separated from the well known local nerve fiber bundle defects.

The defect volume program describes the total defect intensity for separate areas and the whole visual field. Fluctuation measurements provide a basis for comparison. The statistics involved will be described elsewhere. The type of strategy used in the Peritest/

Table 11-1
Technical Data of Peritest and Perimat

	Peritest	Perimat
Type	Separate operation desk	Built in operation panel
	Hemispherical perimeter; radius 30 cm	idem
	Separate operation desk	
Background L. stimuli	1 candela/m²	idem
L-source	Light emitting diodes, LED	idem
L-steps	02. log units	idem
L-range	3.0 log units (25°-eccentricity)	idem
Color	Peak at 560 mm	
Size	30 ft	idem
Duration	0.2 sec	idem
Presentation		
Automatic	Static, single	idem
Semiautomatic 1.	Static combined single-multiple	idem
Semiautomatic 2.	Static, single or multiple	
Fixation		
Optical	+	+
Blind spot	+	+
Infrared	Developed for both types, but not commercially available at this stage	idem

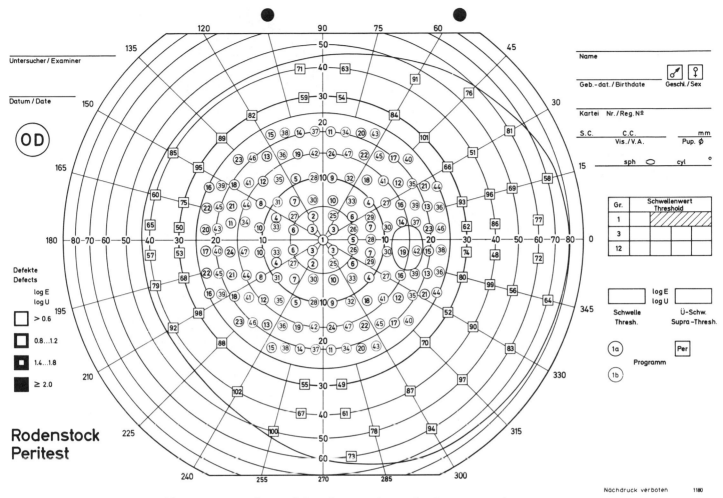

Fig. 11-2. Number and distribution of stimuli of Peritest and Perimat.

Perimat allow for a direct and single measurement of defect volume after a single examination. These measurements depend on a correct estimation of the individual general threshold (INSC). A special chart was developed which reflects the relative importance of the central visual field. This chart allows a representation of the whole visual field on one chart without loosing detailed information on the central part (Fig. 11-3). In this way the extension of visual field defects into the

Table 11-2
Choice of Stimulus Distribution of the Peritest and Perimat

	1983	1984	1985
1ᵃ	+		
1ᵇ	+		
1ᵃ + 1ᵇ	+		
10°	+		
Periphery	+		
Quadrant		+	
Blind Spot		+	
Quick Test		+	
Neurological-Vertical Meridians*			+
Glaucoma-Horizontal Meridians*			+
Profiles*			+

The three columns indicate the time of availability of the programs.
* Only with threshold program.

Table 11-3
Programs of the Peritest and Perimat

Threshold-related Suprathreshold	1983	1984	1985
Two classes (Normal-defect)	+		
Four classes (0.6 Step)	+		
0.2 Step	+		
Threshold		+	
Threshold + fluctuation		+	
Additional Programs			
Defect volume			+
Comparison			+

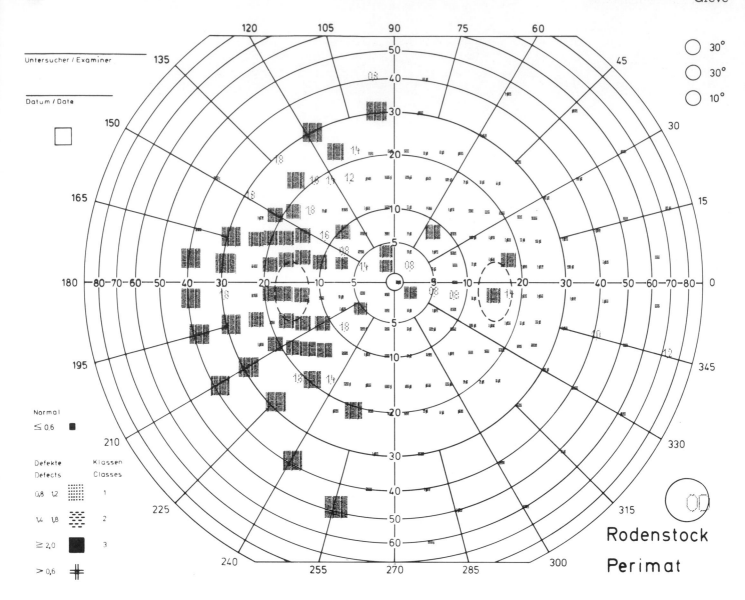

Fig. 11-3. The noninterpolated grayscale printout on the special chart of the Peritest in case of a glaucomatous nerve fiber bundle defect.

peripheral field can be well demonstrated. The printout deliberately gives noninterpolated grayscales. After a comparison between interpolated and noninterpolated grayscales we came to the conclusion that the latter is to be preferred, the main reason being that one gets a better impression of the results at individual positions without having to go to another type of presentation (e.g., numbers).

The new printout has a very attractive new possibility; defects for maximum luminance and normal positions can be expressed by symbols while relative defects appear in number (Fig. 11-4). This type of printout provides easy readability of the results. The printout also presents data on general reduction of sensitivity (INSC), on the fluctuation of the central measurements, on the actual paracentral thresholds, on

fixation shifts (blind spot check), and on false-positive and false-negative responses.

SENSITIVITY AND SPECIFICITY

The sensitivity and specificity of the Peritest suprathreshold threshold related strategy has been evaluated in three investigations. Douglas[2] described a comparison between the Peritest, automatic mode, phase IA, IB and periphery, suprathreshold, threshold related strategy on the one hand and manual perimetry with the Goldmann perimeter (Armaly-Drance screening technique) and the Tübingen perimeter on the other hand. His results regarding sensitivity are shown in Table 11-4. In those cases where he found a discrep-

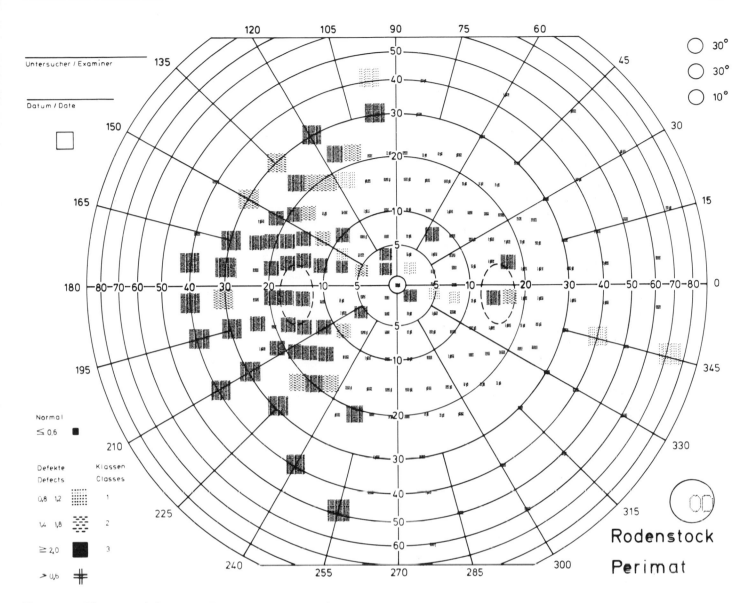

Fig. 11-4. The same defect as in Fig. 11-3 now using the printout mode with maximal defects and normal positions indicated by symbols (similar to the grayscale printout) and the intensity of the relative defects expressed in numbers (0.2 steps).

ancy between the Peritest results and manual perimetry, the Peritest showed a more extensive loss in 73 percent of cases. In this study 46 eyes showed no defects on manual perimetry. Of these 36 (78 percent) also showed no defect on Peritest examination. The remaining 10 (22 percent) were called false-positives. Douglas also mentioned that two visual fields, which were originally classified as false-positives (defect on Peritest and normal on manual perimetry) were on subsequent examinations found to have defects. This implies that at least some of the so-called false-positives of the Peritest may really be false-negatives of classical manual perimetry. In this respect a study of Hotchkiss et al.[6] is interesting. This group described a comparison between the Peritest, phase IA and periphery, with the Goldmann perimeter results (modified Armaly-Drance screening technique). The patients were subdivided in three groups: glaucoma, suspect

(no visual field defect but suspect disc or raised intra-ocular pressure [IOP]) and normal. Of the 81 eyes with glaucoma the Peritest detected 80, i.e., 98.8 percent. However, in the 47 patients with suspect glaucoma the Peritest detected defects in 23 cases, i.e., 48.9 percent. These could be called either false-positives of the Peritest or false-negatives of the manual Goldmann

Table 11-4

Results of Comparative Examinations Between Peritest and Manual Perimetry (Douglas-3)

	Detected	Percent
Total 69 Eyes with defects	62	90
Of which 22 Eyes with dense defects	21	95
50 Eyes with relative defects	39	75
18 Eyes with soft defects	11	61

perimeter technique. The authors studied 20 cases of the suspect group in which disc photographs were available. They found signs of damage to the optic nerve in 11 cases. This suggests that in at least some of the cases in which the Peritest demonstrated visual field defects in the suspect-group the Peritest result was correct. Out of 19 normal cases the Peritest showed one false-positive (5.3 percent).

Greve et al.[5] compared the Peritest results, phase IA, IB and periphery, suprathreshold, threshold related strategy, with manual perimetry with a modified visual field analyzer and the Tübingen perimeter. It was found that the Peritest detects all stage II defects.[9] Small defects for maximal luminance were detected in 70 percent of cases and so were small relative defects. These figures are comparable to those of Douglas. Greve et al.[10] also found that nasal and temporal peripheral defects were better detected with the Peritest than with manual perimetry.

The overall conclusion from these studies is that the Peritest will detect close to 100 percent of stage II defects (defects for maximal luminance larger than the size of the blind spot). Smaller and/or relative defects, which are hardly detected by routine kinetic techniques, will be detected in about 70 percent of cases. It should be noted that such defects are usually only found by careful, degree by degree meridional static perimetry.

PSYCHOLOGICAL FACTORS

The Peritest is the only instrument that allows an automatic procedure as well as a semiautomatic procedure. The major difference between the two procedures is the psychological effect of the active presence of the examiner.

To study the psychological effects we compared two sets of automatic fields with two sets of semiautomatic fields of the same patient, all made in one day.[11] It was found that in 10 of 19 patients there was a significant difference between the automated and semi-automated procedure.

The defect volume in the automated procedure was usually smaller. The intra-automatic defect volume-difference was found to be larger than the intra-semiautomatic defect volume difference. The major causes for the larger variation in the automatic proce-

dure were reaction and judgement problems. Psychological support in a semiautomatic procedure of visual field examination may be necessary in at least part of the glaucoma patients.

In conclusion, major desirable features of the Peritest-Perimat are flexible examination possible with automatic or semi-automatic procedures; efficient strategy, specially in combination with multiple stimulus presentation; large luminance range; special chart with noninterpolated automated grayscale numbers in addition; and solid opticoelectromechanical construction.

REFERENCES

1. Dannheim F: Zur Anwender-Software für die neuen Rodenstock-Perimeter. b) Klinische Erfahrungen. Der Augenspiegel 28:60–74, 1982

2. Douglas GR: The Peritest automatic perimeter in screening for glaucomatous visual field defects. Can J Ophthalmol 18:318–320, 1983

3. Greve EL: The Peritest. Doc Ophthalmol Proc Ser 26:17–18, 1981

4. Greve EL: Peritest. Doc Ophthalmol Proc Ser 22:71–74, 1980

5. Greve EL, Dannheim F, Bakker D: The Peritest, a new automatic and semi-automatic perimeter. Int Ophthalmol 5:201–214, 1982

6. Hotchkiss ML, Robin AL, Pollack IP, et al: A comparison of Peritest (automated) and Goldmann perimetry. In press

6a. Krieglstein GK, Mochnac E: Zur Sensitivität und Specifizität des automatischen Perimeters Peritest in der Glaukom diagnostik. Z Prakt Augenheilk 5:17–28, 1984

7. de Boer RW, van den Berg TJTP, Greve EL, et al: Concepts for automatic perimetry, as applied to the Scoperimeter, an experimental automatic perimeter. Int Ophthalmol 5:181–191, 1982

8. de Jong DGMM, Greve EL, Bakker D, et al: Psychological factors in computer assisted perimetry; automatic and semiautomatic perimetry. Doc Ophthalmol Proc Ser 1985. In press

9. Greve EL: Performance of computer assisted perimeters. Doc Ophthalmol 53:343–380, 1982

10. Greve EL, Groothuyse MT, Verduin WM: Automation of perimetry. Doc Ophthalmol 40:243–254, 1976

11. Greve EL, de Boer RW, Bakker D, et al: Clinical evaluation of the Scoperimeter, an experimental automatic perimeter. Int Ophthalmol 5:193–200, 1982

Humphrey Field Analyzer

Anders Heijl

The Humphrey field analyzer is a new computerized projection-type automatic perimeter manufactured by Humphrey Instruments Inc., San Leandro, Calif. The concept behind the instrument is to provide a fully automatic projection perimeter with a wide variety of standard and customized static field tests, including both threshold-measuring and various types of suprathreshold logics, several different printout modes, and disk storage capability in an instrument using standard Goldmann stimuli and background.

HARDWARE

The Humphrey field analyzer (Fig. 12-1) is a single-unit instrument consisting of a stimulus generating system, a computer, a cathode ray tube (CRT) unit for display and communication, an impact printer, and a double floppy disk drive.

Stimulus Generator

The instrument uses projected stimuli the intensity of which can be varied over a range of 5.1 log units (51 db) between 0.08 and 10,000 asb through a set of fixed neutral density filters and a filter wedge. Each time the instrument is turned on, stimulus intensities are calibrated over the whole intensity range by means of a photocell. The instrument is equipped with a set of color filters (red, blue, and green) and can thus be used for color perimetry. There are five sizes of stimuli corresponding to the Goldmann perimeter stimuli V to I.

The stimuli are projected on to the surface of a white hemispherical bowl (330-mm radius) by means of a mirror system placed inside the bowl. The mirror and hence the stimuli are moved by two stepper motors. Mirror position is automatically checked and adjusted before each test and rechecked each time the mirror passes the positions corresponding to the horizontal and vertical meridians of the visual field.

The bowl is uniformly illuminated by two diffused light sources. The background luminance is adjusted to 31.5 asb when the instrument is switched on and is checked at the beginning of each test with the patient in position for testing. Furthermore, local background intensity is checked prior to each stimulus presentation. If necessary the stimulus intensity is adjusted prior to exposure to compensate for any local variation of background level.

Computer

The perimeter is equipped with a built-in computer system consisting of an Intel 8088 microprocessor and 64 kilobytes RAM memory plus 64 kilobytes ROM memory (in PROMs). All test programs, input and output routines are stored in the PROMs, which can easily be changed when the software is modified or expanded.

Fixation Control

The instrument uses the blind spot fixation monitoring technique originally used in the Competer computerized perimeter.[1] At the beginning of a test the instrument locates the blind spot. During the remaining part of the test the stimulus is presented in the blind spot at random intervals. If the patient perceives such a stimulus this indicates that he did not maintain proper fixation when the stimulus was shown. The score of exposed and perceived blind spot stimuli is displayed

AUTOMATIC PERIMETRY IN GLAUCOMA
ISBN 0–8089–1705–6

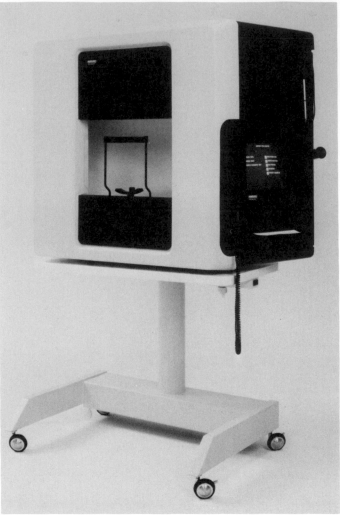

Fig. 12-1. The Humphrey field analyzer.

therefore aware among other things of the patient's reaction to blind spot catch stimuli and the approximate remaining test time.

Printer

The built-in printer is a high resolution (70 lines/in.) impact printer producing permanent records on conventional paper.

Disk System

The Humphrey field analyzer is equipped with a dual disk drive (optional) using 5.25 in. double sided, double density floppy disks. The disks are used to store results of field tests and can supply earlier patient data required for fast threshold-measuring strategies or for analysis of consecutive tests which will be described. Each disk has a capacity of 400 kilobytes or 150 to 200 field charts. Each test is written on two disks, and therefore a back-up is automatically provided every time a field is stored.

SOFTWARE

The software may be divided into test strategies, output and disk handling routines.

TEST STRATEGIES

There are three different types of test strategies: screening programs, threshold measuring programs (including custom tests) and the automatic diagnostic program, which is a space adaptive strategy.

Screening Strategies

The instrument has three glaucoma screening programs, three central field patterns and three full field patterns with different test point densities (Table 12-1). Custom points may be added to these basic patterns. Not only test point patterns may be selected but there is also a choice of four different screening test strategies. One of these is a simple single intensity suprathreshold test. The other three of these are threshold-related supraliminal tests (Fig. 12-4). where the stimulus intensities used for the screening are based on actual threshold determinations in four primary points. The target intensities are adjusted not only to the general level of the tested field thus determined, but also to the normal slope of the visual field. In tests involving not only the central but also the peripheral field separate sets of primary points are used in the two parts of the field in order to increase accuracy. In the basic threshold-related strategy all missed points are automatically retested and the results will divide the tested points

on the CRT during the test and the final score is printed on the field chart. If, blind spot stimuli are perceived with a high frequency, an alarm is sounded alerting the operator to reinstruct the patient. A conventional telescope is also available enabling the operator to check fixation. The telescope is normally used to align the eye.

CRT Unit

The CRT unit of the Humphrey Field Analyzer serves the double purpose of input unit and display. A number of different "menus" can be displayed on the video screen. The operator can choose test programs and parameters, start and interrupt tests and demonstration subroutines, and operate the disk system by touching various pads on the screens with a light pen (Fig. 12-2). The screens are arranged in a hierarchical system. One of the screens resembles a conventional typewriter keyboard (Fig. 12-3). It is used to enter alphanumerical data like names of patients. During actual field testing the operator can follow the progress of the examination on the video screen. The operator is

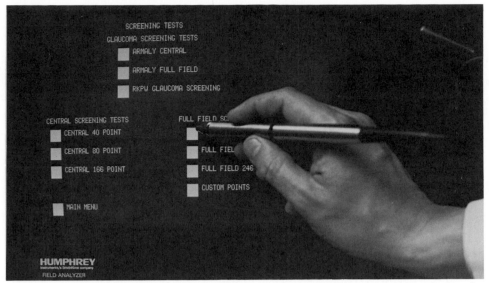

Fig. 12-2. CRT/light-pen unit. The instrument is operated by touching pads on the screen with the light-pen.

into two categories, normal and pathological. There are also two other threshold related strategies. These are (1) the three zone strategy in which all points missed twice are tested at the maximum intensity level, thus permitting separation of the missed points into relative and absolute defects, and (2) the quantify defect strategy where the depth of the field defect is measured in all pathological points.

Output Formats

Printout modes for screening tests naturally differ somewhat between the different test strategies. The standard threshold-related and the single-intensity tests simply indicate seen and missed points (Fig. 12-5) while the three-zone tests indicate normal points, rel-

ative defects and absolute defects. The most advanced screening with quantification will indicate seen points as such and point out the defect depths in tenths of log units in all pathological points (Fig. 12-5).

Threshold Strategies

The Humphrey field analyzer has eight standard test point patterns for threshold tests. Five of these cover the central 30°, the 30–60° area, and the temporal crescent (Table 12-2). In the two 30° programs the interstimulus distance is 6° and the test point patterns of the two programs are interlocking. Thus, if both tests are performed, the resulting interstimulus distance will be 4.2°. The interstimulus distance in the 30–60° programs (30/60-1 and 30/60-2) is 12°.

There are also two neurological programs testing pairs of points on each side of the vertical meridian and a macula program that tests a 16-point square grid centered around the fovea with an interstimulus distance of 2°.

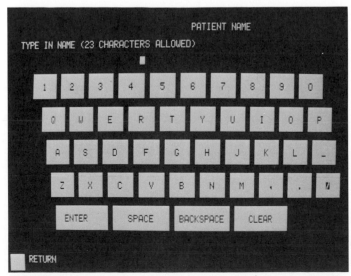

Fig. 12-3. One of the screens is very similar to a conventional typewriter keyboard. It is used to enter patient names.

Table 12-1
Humphrey Field Analyzer Screening Programs

	Defect type	No. of points
Armaly central	Glaucoma	84
Armaly full field	Glaucoma	98
RKPW points glaucoma screen	Glaucoma	15–20
Central 40 point	General	40
Central 80 point	General	80
Central 166 point	General	166
Full field 81 point	General	81
Full field 120 point	General	120
Full field 246 point	General	246
Custom	N/A	

The RKPW screening is described.[2]

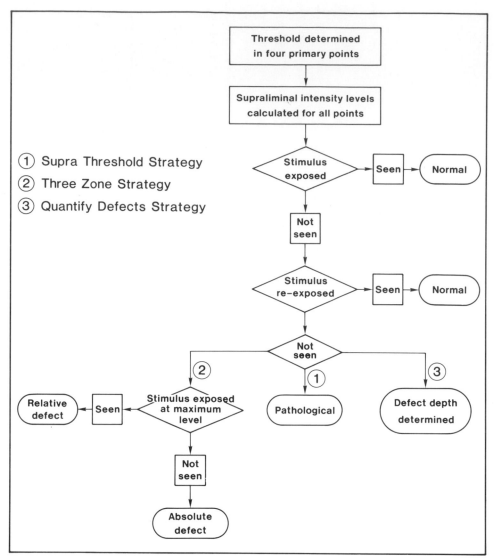

Fig. 12-4. Flow diagram for the three different threshold related suprathreshold tests.

The basic threshold strategy (full threshold) starts by determining the threshold in four primary points. The stimuli are initially presented at supposedly supraliminal intensity levels and the intensities are decreased in 4-db steps until they are no longer perceived. The test process then reverses and moves in 2-db steps until the stimulus is seen again. The procedure is performed twice at each primary point. The results of these four points are then used to determine the starting levels of the test process in neighboring secondary points (the starting levels are also adjusted according to the location of the tested point in the visual field). As with the primary points, test process for the secondary points first moves in 4-db steps until the reversal (from seen to not seen or vice versa), then in 2-db steps until the second reversal occurs. If at this stage the measured threshold is within N 4-db of the expected threshold (the threshold of the neighboring point from which the starting level was determined to which is added the correction for location in the field) the test is completed. If the measured threshold differs by more than 4

db from the expected, the threshold is measured once again in 4- and 2-dB steps. The measured thresholds in secondary points are used to determine starting levels for tertiary points and so forth. The visual field therefore grows gradually from the initial four points (Fig. 12-6).

Table 12-2
Humphrey Field Analyzer Threshold Programs

	Point density	No. of points
Central 30-1	6°	71
Central 30-2	6°	76
Peripheral 30/60-1	12°	63
Peripheral 30/60-2	12°	68
Temporal crescent	8.5ᵃ	37
Neurological 20	N/A	16 tested 2× each
Neurological 50	N/A	22 tested 2× each
Macula	2°	16 tested 2× each
Custom	N/A	

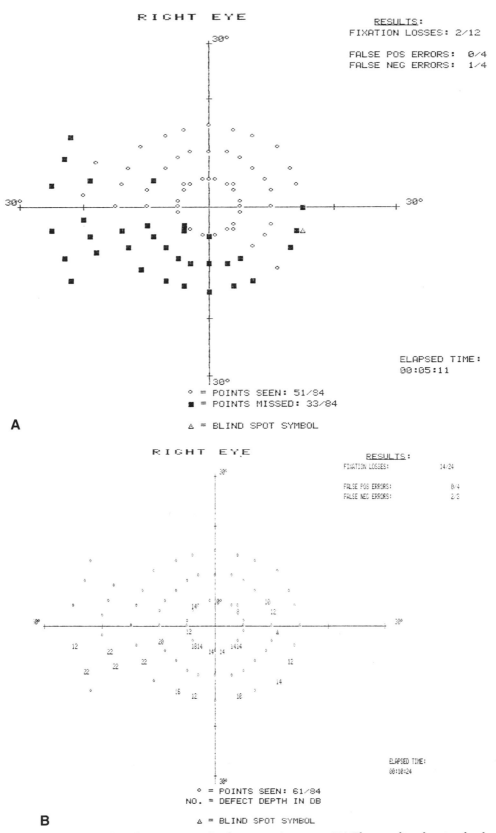

Fig. 12-5. Examples of printout modes for screening tests. (A) The results of a standard threshold-related test. The points are divided into two categories: seen (circles) and not seen (black boxes). (B) The results of a quantify defects screening. Normal points are indicated by circles, while in missed points the depth of the defect is printed out (in tenths of log units = decibels).

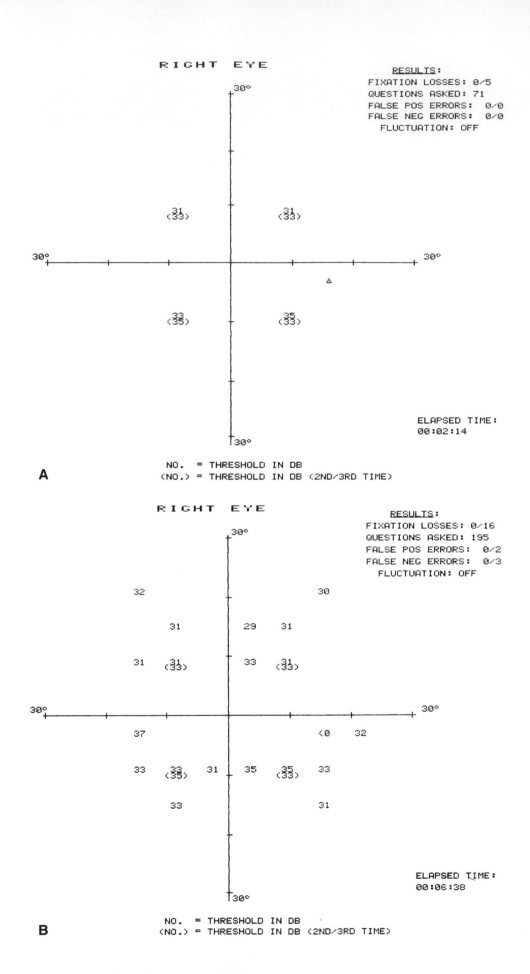

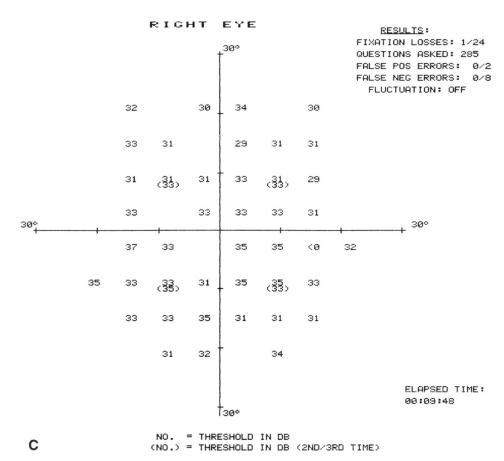

C

NO.   = THRESHOLD IN DB
⟨NO.⟩ = THRESHOLD IN DB ⟨2ND/3RD TIME⟩

Fig. 12-6. The threshold strategies start by measuring the threshold in four primary points (a). The results obtained in these points are used to define starting levels for the test process in neighboring points. The results from these points determine starting levels in tertiary points, etcetera. The field will therefore gradually grow from the initial four points (b, c).

If previous threshold data are available from a disk, two other threshold techniques may be used: (1) In the full threshold from prior data strategy, the most recent test results from the same test and eye are used to determine the initial intensity levels used for the threshold bracketing at each test point. The bracketing strategy is identical to that of the regular full threshold strategy, but since the starting levels will be close to threshold the test will require less time than the first test, performed with the standard strategy. (2) The fast threshold strategy also uses stored results from previous tests of the same eye. This is a much faster test logic where each point is tested with a stimulus 2 db brighter than the stored values. If this stimulus is seen, no attempt is made to determine the threshold. Only points missed twice at that level are subjected to a new threshold determination. This strategy then can be regarded as an individually tailored slightly supraliminal screening, the objective of which is only to see if the field has deteriorated since the previous examination. It can of course be used both in normal and in pathologic visual fields.

Output Formats

There are three different output formats for the standard threshold tests (Fig. 12-7): (1) A numeric representation of measured thresholds. (2) A grayscale printout. (3) A numeric printout of the defect depth. (The defect depth shows departures from the expected threshold levels of the tested eye based on the threshold levels of the four primary points. This means that localized field loss is clearly indicated as such while mild general depressions of sensitivity, corresponding to a foveal threshold > 25 db, are shown only as a depression of the test level—the expected foveal threshold. This has the advantage that this type of mild general depression, which is nonspecific and often encountered in elderly patients with media opacities and/or miosis is not highlighted in the printout. The disadvantage, of course, is that even if the mild general depression due to diffuse glaucomatous damage, it is indicated only as a depression of the test level).

Profiles through any meridian of the field may also be printed out (Fig. 12-7d), but one should be aware of the fact that these profiles are based only on the results of those few points that happen to be situated along the meridian plus interpolated values and this type of profile does not yield nearly the same detailed information as a true profile test (see below).

Custom Tests

One of the most attractive features of the Humphrey field analyzer is its fairly comprehensive package of custom threshold tests. Five different custom tests are available: meridional profiles, circular profiles, grids, point clusters, and single points. These tests greatly increase the versatility of the instrument. Meridional profiles and arcs may be tested anywhere within the central 30° field at interstimulus intervals of 1–12°. Grids and point clusters may be placed anywhere in the field using interstimulus intervals of 2° to 12°. The numbers of tested points may vary up to 60. Examples of these tests are shown in Fig. 12-8. The custom tests may also be used as screening tests.

Option Measurements

Two optional measurements may be appended to the standard tests, foveal threshold determination and fluctuation evaluation. The individual threshold fluctuation is estimated by performing duplicate threshold measurements at 10 points and calculating the root mean square of the differences between measurements.

AUTOMATIC DIAGNOSTIC STRATEGY

The automatic diagnostic strategy is an improved screening strategy with space adaptive properties. The first phase of this strategy consists of an 80-point threshold related supraliminal screening of the central 30° field. In the second phase the depth in any detected defects is measured as in the quantify defects suprathreshold screening strategy. Additional points are then added around the pathological points and these are tested supraliminally. If in the first phase no points are missed, or more than 40 points are missed twice, the test will end after that phase. This strategy is very useful especially in cases with small or questionable defects where the space adaptive approach will facilitate interpretation of the test result and help to delineate any scotoma found (Fig. 12-9). If the field defects are small this approach requires only little added test time. The automatic diagnostic strategy bears some resemblance to the SAPRO program of the Octopus instrument,[3] but there are important differences since it uses a supraliminal test for the initial phase of testing, since it covers a much larger area of the field, and since it uses a lower density of extra points than SAPRO. It is therefore more suited as a general examination program and less suited for very detailed analyses than SAPRO.

STORING AND COMPARISON OF VISUAL FIELDS

The double disk drive system makes it possible to store the results of field tests. Data from stored fields may be used in the two different strategies previously mentioned under threshold strategies. The stored re-

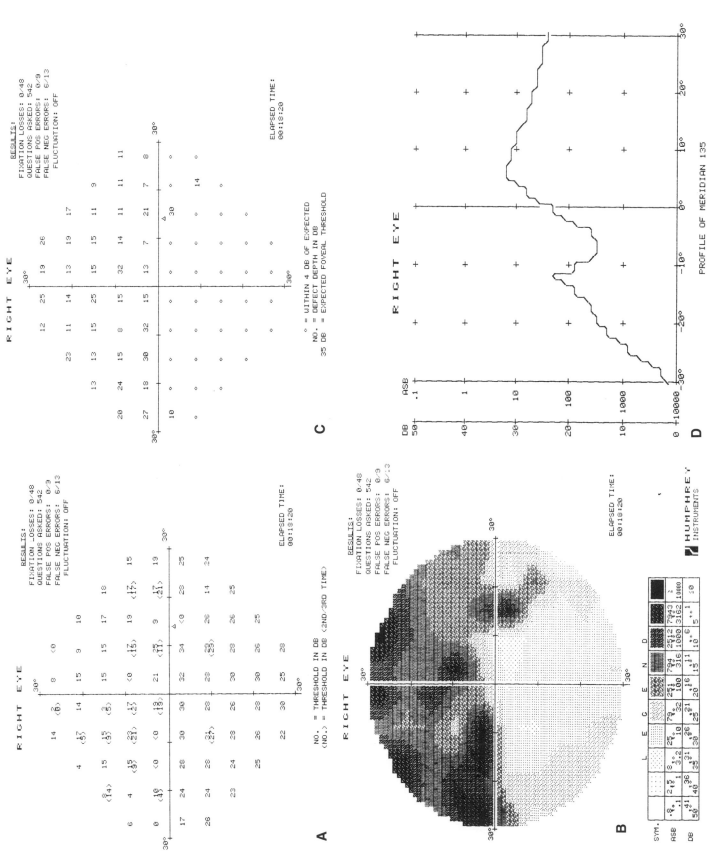

Fig. 12-7. Output formats for threshold tests. The result from a 30-2 test in a glaucomatous eye displayed in four different ways: (a) Numeric representation of the thresholds in all measured points. (b) Grayscale representation. (c) Defect depth representation. (d) Interpolated profile through 135°–315° meridian.

137

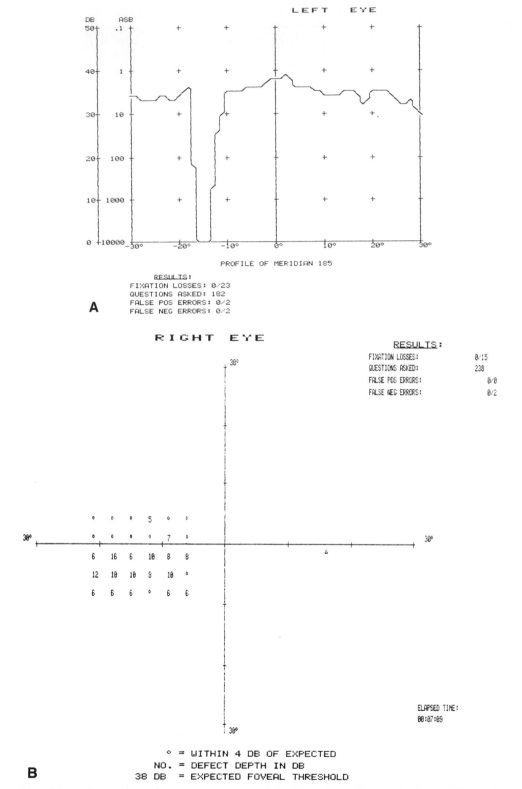

Fig. 12-8. Examples of custom tests: (a) Meridional profile (185–5° meridian, 2° resolution) through blind spot of a normal eye. (b) Forty-two point 10 × 12° grid (2° interstimulus distance) in blind spot area of the same eye.

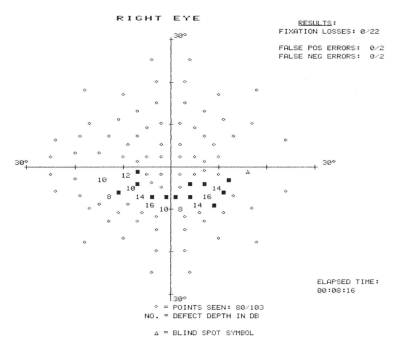

Fig. 12-9. Field chart of an automatic diagnostic strategy test. Of the 80 points 11 of the primarty test point pattern have been identified as pathological. In these points, on the 10° and 15° circles, the defect depth is printed out. The instrument has then automatically added extra points around the missed points resulting in a higher resolution in the defective area than elsewhere in the field. These extra points, printed out as black boxes if missed and as circles if seen, help delineate the arcuate defect.

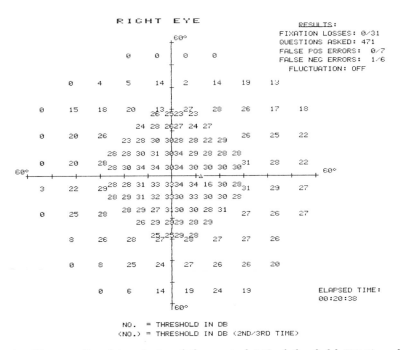

Fig. 12-10. The results of two tests, of the central 30° of the field (30-2) and of the 30–60° area (30/60-2), merged into one printout.

sults make it possible to recall and print out new copies of all previous tests and to merge results from several tests into one common printout (Fig. 12-10). The disk drive system also allows consecutive fields from the same eye to be subjected to automated comparisons. Currently, the automatic comparison routines are limited to algebraic operations on the available data including averaging of tests and a "compare mode" where the findings from an earlier threshold test are subtracted from those of a more recent test, the result being a subtraction field where changes are graphically represented. The software for analysis is expected to grow considerably in the near future and include programs for the identification of areas with high threshold variability and programs analyzing statistically progression and regression in consecutive fields.

CLINICAL EXPERIENCE WITH THE DEVICE

Since the field analyzer is such a new device no validation studies have yet been published. In our department it has been used for nine months and it has performed reliably without hardware problems. It is presently used in several scientific studies. Results obtained mainly with the central threshold and the Armaly screening programs have shown good correspondance with results from threshold and screening programs performed with the Competer computerized perimeter and with Goldmann fields. The custom tests have proved particularly valuable in examination of subtle defects. The quantifying mode of screening test is often helpful in interpretation of results since deep nuclei may be identified, thus increasing the diagnostic value of test. The space adaptive automatic diagnostic test is theoretically sound and seems very useful.

ADVANTAGES AND DISADVANTAGES OF THE INSTRUMENT.

Some of the particularly attractive features and disadvantages may be summarized.

Disadvantages:
1. Slow printer.

2. Statistical package still small, but being developed.
3. The standard thresholding strategies rather slow, but yield high quality results.
4. The customer cannot permanently store his very own test protocols.

Advantages:
1. Efficient threshold-related, eccentricity-compensated screening tests, where the possibilities of quantification and space adaptive screening increases the clinical usefulness even further.
2. Large choice of thresholding programs including fast threshold strategies, which take advantage of patient's prior test results.
3. Very large flexibility due to the custom test package and projection system.
4. Specific glaucoma screening patterns.
5. Easy to operate; no supervision required during test.
6. Complete selection of stimulus sizes and colors; large range of stimulus intensities.
7. Large selection of output formats including defect depth, which compares test results with the patient's expected normal threshold level.

REFERENCES

1. Heijl A, Krakau CET: An automatic perimeter for glaucoma visual field screening and control; construction and clinical cases. Albrecht von Graefes Arch Klin Exp Ophthalmol 197:13–23, 1975
2. Rabin S, Kolesar P, Podos SM, et al: A visual field screening protocol for glaucoma. Am J Ophthalmol 92:530–535, 1981
3. Fankhauser F, Haeberlin H, Jenni A: Octopus programs SAPRO and F. Two new principles for the analysis of the visual field. Albrecht von Graefes Arch Klin Exp Ophthalmol 216:155–165, 1981

13

Interpretation of Automatically Plotted Visual Fields

Douglas R. Anderson

The interpretation of visual fields can be divided into three aspects. The first is to decide if the field is normal or abnormal. The second is to categorize the nature of the defect. The third is to decide if the field has changed from a previous occasion. These three aspects need to be considered for both suprathreshold spot-checking and for thresholding methods.

SCREENING WITH SUPRATHRESHOLD TESTING

The Negative Test

If an individual has a negative test (all points were seen), the likelihood that he truly has a field defect depends in part on the sensitivity of the test: what percentage of those with a defect will be detected, or inversely how often will a defect remain undetected? The predictability of a negative test also depends on the prevalence of normal individuals in the population tested. In other words, how many truly normal people with negative tests are there compared with the number of false negatives (people with field defects that were undetected)? If an 80 percent sensitive test thus is applied to a population of 1,000 people of whom 1 percent have glaucoma, 8 of the 10 glaucomas will be detected. There will be two glaucoma patients with negative tests, and 990 nonglaucomatous patients with a negative test (or perhaps a few less if there are some false positives). The odds approach 990:2 that a person with a negative test is indeed normal.

The result would be different if the same test is applied to a mixture of 120 office patients, some who have glaucoma and others who are glaucoma suspects. Suppose there are 20 patients who do not have a defect and that they all have a negative test. Of the 100 who truly have a defect, 80 percent will be detected, but 20 percent will have a negative test. Thus, of the 40 with a negative test, half will have an undetected defect. If the sensitivity of the test were higher than 80 percent, there would be fewer false negatives, and in this situation the sensitivity of the test becomes important.

Simply put, if the group tested has a vast majority of normal individuals, it is unlikely that a negative test will be a false negative. If however there are few normals in the group, one must be more concerned about the sensitivity of the test and about whether or not a negative test represents a person with a defect that was undetected. In an office patient in whom there is special reason to be suspicious, one can thus be less confident that a person with a negative test truly has a normal field.* When a negative suprathreshold test result is obtained on a person who is highly suspect, it is important to evaluate whether or not the test was sensitive enough to have picked up the type of defect under consideration. The negative test is more reliable when a large number of points is tested, when the stimulus is not excessively suprathreshold, and preferably when the stimulus is adjusted for eccentricity from fixation. This extra effort to achieve higher sensitivity

---

* Recall that in screening a population to find the few with a defect, specificity of the test is very important, in order to maximize the meaningfulness of a positive test (see Chapter 5), even if some sensitivity has to be sacrificed. However, when visual field tests are done on a group of individuals with a moderate or high suspicion of abnormality, a high sensitivity is more important, both to improve the detection of those who have defects and to improve the confidence in a negative results.

AUTOMATIC PERIMETRY IN GLAUCOMA
ISBN 0–8089–1705–6

may be worthwhile in an office or research setting, but not cost effective in a population screen.

In a sense, the "sensitivity" of a test depends on the type of defect under consideration. Most tests would be 100 percent sensitive in detecting an absolute defect occupying an entire quadrant of the field. The chance that spot-checking a given number of locations with a certain suprathreshold stimulus will detect an existing abnormality depends on the size and depth of the defect. It also depends on the defect's location. A peripheral defect is not detected if only the central field is tested, but the risk that the field will falsely be called normal depends on the proportion of peripheral defects that are accompanied by detectable defects in the central field (see Chapter 4).

Therefore, another way of thinking about the negative test result is to consider how minimal a defect could be present and have at least a 99 percent chance of detection. Where and how large could a defect be and still fit between the locations that were checked? How deep must a defect be for detection to be almost certain with the stimulus used? The negative result is then considered to mean with 99 percent confidence simply that if a defect is present, it is in an untested location, it is smaller than the space between locations tested, or it is of insufficient depth to be detected with 99 percent likelihood. Seen this way, the negative test puts a limit on how severe a defect might be present.

Missed Responses

It is not unusual for a person with a normal field to fail to respond to one or several stimulus presentations. If the test were repeated, the person may again fail to respond to one or several stimulus presentations, but not necessarily in the same locations. Therefore, missed responses are not to be interpreted to mean that the stimulus is infrathreshold at the missed locations, unless the missed responses are each confirmed. Such confirmation is almost routinely sought by presenting the stimulus a second time at any location where the initial stimulus presentation does not elicit a response. The stimulus is judged invisible at a location where it is not seen on two separate opportunities. In principle, points in a cluster serve to confirm each other, and the points in such grouping do not need retesting, but existing programs retest all missed points indiscriminately. In some testing strategies, the points with the missed response are tested with one or two stronger stimuli. A low visual sensation is more than confirmed if a stronger stimulus is also missed, and a rough quantitation of the abnormal points is also achieved. In any test method, the underlying rule is that a missed response is not to be considered meaningful unless there is some confirmation.

If on repeat testing of the entire field one or a group of points are inconsistent (sometimes seen and sometimes not) while other locations are consistently seen, it may be interpreted that the spot-checking stimulus is close to threshold in the involved area, whereas other regions of the field have a greater sensitivity. Alternatively, the affected region may simply have a higher degree of response variability ("short term fluctuation"), which may occur as an early defect before there is frank development of an abnormal threshold.

The Candidate Abnormal Field

Once the validity of missed responses is confirmed, the next step is to decide if the test result represents a defect in the visual system. For example, if the central 30-degree region is spot-checked with a stimulus that is not seen at one or several peripheral-most points, such a result means that the isopter for that stimulus is just inside 30 degrees. This result is not necessarily abnormal if the stimulus was selected to be one thought to threshold near 30 degrees. A more extreme finding would be if the stimulus is seen at all points inside 12.5 degrees and not at any points outside 12.5 degrees. Such a result may be taken as representing a depression or contraction of the field, if the stimulus was selected on the basis that its isopter should be at 30 degrees and 12.5 degrees is an abnormal isopter position for that stimulus. (The criterion for judging depression of the field is different if a threshold-related strategy is used that begins with thresholding a selected point in that individual, for example, at 25 or 30 degrees. In that case generalized depression is likely present if the threshold determined is a stronger stimulus than usual for the person's age, even if the stimulus is seen at all test points.)

Suprathreshold spot-checking is more specifically aimed at detecting localized defects. A wedge of missed points extending to the edge of the tested area represents a localized depression or part of a scotoma that bridges the boundary of the tested area (see Chapter 2, Fig. 2-4). One or several adjacent points at which the stimulus is not seen, surrounded by points at which the test stimulus is seen, represents a scotoma. A single missed point may deserve attention if the missed response is confirmed by a repeat presentation of the stimulus, and even more if a stronger stimulus is also not seen. However, the clinical significance of such a scotoma must be interpreted in light of the rest of the clinical findings.

SCREENING WITH STATIC THRESHOLDS

The Individual Point

The threshold value at each point can be compared to the average normal threshold for age at that point. To be judged abnormal, the measured threshold must be outside an acceptable range surrounding the average value, taking into account both the range of normal and the error or variability in the threshold measurement (short term fluctuation). Experience with each of the automated instruments will be necessary to teach us in the next few years what is the acceptable range, but a typical Octopus printout will call attention to points at which the sensitivity is 5 dB (0.5 log units) less than the average for age at that location. Especially when the individual shows a high variability of the retested thresholds (expressed as the root mean square of the short term fluctuation), a normal field may contain one or several scattered points that exceed the 5-dB reduction in sensitivity, but the majority of normal fields do not.

Scotomas and Localized Depressions

The judgment of whether or not a visual field is normal rarely, if ever, depends on whether or not a single point has a depressed sensitivity compared to normal. Instead generalized depression is recognized when all points are subsensitive, and a localized defect is judged to be present if one point or a group of several points has a depressed sensitivity compared to other points in the field.

For example, a scotoma is judged to be present if one or several adjacent points are less sensitive than surrounding ones. Although four randomly scattered points with slightly reduced threshold is likely to be normal (unless the exact same points show reduced threshold on repeat examination), it seems that four adjacent points with sensitivities 5 dB less than surrounding points is likely to be a true shallow scotoma. The depressed value of four points that are adjacent serve to confirm each other. This qualitative principle of considering the spatial correlation of defective points can be quantified as the calculatable index SC, which one day may be used to calculate the statistical probability of abnormality (Chapter 14). A single point with only 5 dB of depression compared to surrounding points is not an abnormal finding, but especially if other clinical findings suggest that there might well be a shallow scotoma in that location, the clinician might be suspicious. With any suspicious finding the clinician may decide to confirm his suspicion by a static cut through the region, by testing a fine grid of points in the region, or simply by repeating the original test again. The defect may be judged real if the slightly abnormal threshold is again found in that location on retesting with the same or a different program. If the judgment is not urgent, or if the clinical circumstance make it unlikely that the defect is real, he may defer judgment until the next regular time that the patient has a field examination. In general, any finding that could have resulted from one or two faulty or failed responses during testing is not likely by itself to be a real defect. However, the clinician has a right to be suspicious of such a soft finding and seek to reproduce it by retesting if it fits the clinical circumstance.

Localized depressions are judged by comparing the suspect points with those in an equivalent position elsewhere in the field. Points above and below the horizontal meridian thus are compared to look for a nasal step. A temporal wedge is represented as the sector within which abnormal points have a reduced sensitivity compared to other points of the same eccentricity in adjacent sectors. An altitudinal depression is detected by comparing equivalent positions of equal eccentricity above and below the horizontal, in this case also taking into account the fact that there is normally some depression superiorly; this may be done by comparing loss (difference of actual threshold from the normal value) at equivalent positions instead of comparing actual threshold values. Again, as with scotomas, mildly abnormal threshold values may be safely ignored if they could have resulted from one or two faulty patient responses, but otherwise such findings deserve attention.

Slight localized depression and shallow scotomas may be difficult to recognize among the normally present variability of measurement. However, several shallow scotomas and irregular diffuse depression of the field will make the contour of the hill of vision slightly irregular. Statistical methods are under development to measure unevenness of the contour of the hill of vision to a greater degree than can be expected from the measurement variability. Indices such as loss variance (LV) and corrected loss variance (CLV) (Chapter 14) may find diffuse shallow defects while they are quite shallow. More localized defects affecting fewer test locations may be detectible while still shallow with the M3 and Q indices. It is hoped that these approaches will prove to be reliable indicators of very early localized defects (see Chapter 14).

Generalized Depression

There are three approaches to recognizing mild generalized depression of the field. Comparison of threshold measurements to normal value is the usual approach. Although the average normal values and the range of normal are known, at least for the Octopus, there is no well-established rule that exists for what constitutes a pathologic degree of depression; but it may be usually considered that attention should be paid to a 4- or 5-dB (0.4 or 0.5 log units) depression of most or all points in the field from the average normal sensitivity. Unfortunately, if the person originally had a threshold of 5 dB better than average sensitivity, he must loose 10 dB in sensitivity before the field is judged abnormal by this criterion, and this represents considerable change of visual function. Moreover, given that there is a measurement variability of several decibels in measuring each point, a generalized depression of 4 or 5 dB may be difficult to recognize by casual scanning of the numerical printout. Statistical calculation of the average loss compared to normal values ("mean defect," see Chapter 14) should prove helpful in recognizing slight degrees of depression. If, as seems likely to occur often, the generalized depression is somewhat uneven in amount, the irregularity of the surface of the hill of vision may also show up in the LV and CLV indices already mentioned.

The second approach is to make a comparison with opposite eye. Though not well documented with good scientific data, the two eyes normally seem very closely matched, and perhaps a consistent difference of 2 or 3 dB between the two eyes should at least arouse suspicion.

Finally, a generalized depression can be documented by comparing the field to a previous baseline on that individual. The criterion is that change must greater than can be attributed to long-term fluctuation, which is the day-to-day variation of visual function that depends on daily variation of physiologic status (see Chapter 15). The principles are the same as judging progression of the field (see below).

DIAGNOSTIC EVALUATION

Once an abnormality is detected, its nature is appreciated principally by the contour of the defect. An arcuate defect that crosses the vertical meridian, a temporal wedge with its apex pointed at the blind spot, and a nasal step thus may each represent a nerve-fiber-bundle defect from a lesion in the optic nerve or retinal nerve fiberlayer. Paracentral scotomas, as well as localized peripheral depressions and scotomas, may represent nerve fiber bundle loss or localized retinal disease. Defects that strictly respect the vertical meridian are hemianopias from chiasmal or postchiasmal lesions. Central scotomas may represent macular or optic nerve lesions. Generalized depressions represent diffuse optic nerve or retinal disease, or else preretinal factors (media, refraction, etc.).

With suprathreshold spot-checking, often the nature of the defect (for example an arcuate scotoma or a dense hemianopia) is perfectly obvious. However, spot-checking with a single stimulus intensity is equivalent to plotting one isopter, and it may not always be apparent whether a cluster of missed points in the upper nasal quadrant represents a nasal step or a hemianopia. Likewise, if a standard stimulus-for-age was used and was seen only at points within 10 degrees of fixation, further testing would be needed to say if this is a nonspecific generalized depression or a field that is contracted to a small central island by a dense double arcuate defect. In such cases, it is necessary to outline the defect with one or more additional stimuli, or to perform a more quantitative visual field examination. If the need for additional testing is anticipated a program can be selected that will classify or quantify any missed points. One program on the Humphrey instrument (if fewer than 40 points are defective) will not only quantify the missed points, but also spot-check with a finer grid of points in the abnormal area.

The degree of additional evaluation may depend on the purpose for testing the visual field in the first place. In a general community screening project, it may be sufficient to know with reasonable certainty (high specificity) that the field is abnormal and that the individual needs to be referred for a complete ocular evaluation that includes more definitive visual field testing. If the field is done in order to determine the cause for a complaint of poor vision, one may be trying to make a distinction between generalized depression on the one hand, and a central scotoma (perhaps with temporal hemianopia in the other eye) on the other hand.

Sometimes the examiner has a particular diagnosis in mind before the visual field test is performed, for example when the field test is performed because of elevated intraocular pressure. One must be careful not to assume that the field defect is due to the disease under consideration, unless it is quite typical. Although such coincidences are very infrequent, in a lifetime of practice one may well encounter an unusual combination such as a large physiologic cup, a mildly elevated intraocular pressure, and a progressive central scotoma due to a meningioma pressing the optic nerve.

One must also be careful not to dismiss too lightly a generalized depression as a nonspecific type of defect. Generalized depression can be diagnosed as glaucomatous when for example, asymmetric generalized depression, asymmetric cupping, and perhaps asymmetric pupil reactions correspond to an asymmetric intraocular pressure. In cases in which generalized depression is to be dismissed as nonglaucomatous, it is best to identify specifically the cause and to determine that an appropriate degree of cataract, high refractive error, retinal disease, or other cause is present as an explanation for the depression.

Even in the case of more typical defects, the interpretation of the visual field is never done in isolation, but must take into account the pupil reactions, biomicroscopic observations with the slit lamp, and especially ophthalmoscopy. A defect in the inferior arcuate region of the field may be due to glaucoma, anterior ischemic optic neuropathy, branch retinal vein occlusion, or toxoplasmic retinitis. The distinction is best made by observation of the fundus.

PROGRESSION

Progression may occur continuously or in episodes and be manifest in any of several ways (see Chapter 3). There may be enlargement of a previously existing defect, such that an increasing number of points have thresholds outside the normal range (or an increasing number of points deviate from the person's baseline threshold determination). There may be deepening of a defect, with the threshold values worsening in an already defective region. New defects may appear in new locations, with the freshly abnormal points not contiguous with the previously abnormal points. Finally, there may be a generalized depression, with the threshold worsening rather diffusely at all points, both those that were previously abnormal and those that were previously normal.

The basis for judgment of progression is the comparison of results of the recent field with the previous. When looking at one or a limited number of points, the minimally detectable progression is that which exceeds the magnitude of variable responsiveness (short-term fluctuation) and the natural day-to-day variation in the visual status (long-term fluctuation). A rule of thumb might be to look for changes greater than 5 dB, moderating the judgment according to the measured variability of responsiveness in that particular patient.

As a larger number of points is taken into account, or indeed if the field as a whole is judged, a field that has not progressed may have as many points with an improved threshold measurement as it has points with a worsened measured threshold. The average "change in threshold" will be statistically close to zero. A computerized calculation (program Delta of the Octopus perimeter) of the average change in threshold from one examination to another, as well as and a statistical calculation with a t test to determine if the average change is statistically different from zero, is often helpful in deciding if there is a slight change that deserves attention (see Chapter 14). The analysis can be performed separately on normal and abnormal regions of the field. By averaging the change over many points, the statistical comparison overcomes the effect of response variability (short-term fluctuation), and even a mean threshold change of 1 dB can be quite significant. The confounding effect of long-term fluctuation, which is a small genuine change in the threshold values, can be reduced in such statistical testing by combining the results of two or three fields done on different occasions as a baseline and comparing it to the combined result of two or three recent field examinations.

In an already defective area, a greater degree of change should be demanded before concluding that there is progression of the nerve damage, because the variability in a defective area is greater than for normal points. A 5-dB change in threshold in a defective area thus is not as worrisome as a 5-dB change in a previously normal area.

When progression is apparent, it is wise to pause and consider whether the progression is due to glaucoma or not. A new scotoma, or deepening and widening of a previous defect (unaccompanied by a change in the more normal regions of the field) is likely a result of the glaucoma, especially if the pressure has been under marginal control. However, such things as a branch retinal vascular occlusion could produce a new scotoma that mimics a new glaucomatous defect. A miotic pupil may diminish the threshold, and some drugs may affect visual threshold.

Perhaps the most difficult interpretation is a slowly progressive generalized depression. This can be produced either by a slowly developing cataract or by slowly progressive optic nerve damage, and sometimes the distinction can be difficult to make. The dilemma is that one doesn't want to proceed with filtration surgery if the cause for declining vision is a developing cataract, which would be aggravated by surgery. It is equally unacceptable to attribute the decline to cataract, later to remove the cataract, and to discover in retrospect that progressive optic nerve damage accounted for a significant portion of the usual decline. A clinical evaluation of the media opacity and a judgment about the adequacy of pressure control are sometimes misleading, but remain as the only basis for judging the significance of such changes.

14

Computerized Techniques of Visual Field Analysis

Hans Bebie

When interpreting the results of a visual field examination, whether it is automated or manual, kinetic or static, we are faced with two types of problems: for a first examination emphasis is on the detection of any disturbances, evaluation of their clinical significance and the classification of the defect; in follow-up examinations we concentrate on whether visual sensitivity has changed or not. In both situations it is the marginal case that attracts most attention. Not only do minor deviations from normality or slight changes with time occur quite frequently, but it is exactly in these cases that a sound judgment is most difficult to achieve and most urgently needed.

This chapter analyzes some of the existing schemes of visual field data processing that assist the decision-making process in individual cases, (for different approaches not described here[1–7]). Usually, a computer is used for the purpose of delivering us from some tedious numerical work. It has to follow a predefined program however, and cannot go beyond what a very well-informed perimetrist may have instructed the computer programmer to accomplish. We should like to stress at the outset that the efficiency and reliability of computer-assisted evaluation of the visual field data relies on our own insight into the behavior of normal and pathological visual fields. In other words, the topic is perimetry, and not the computer.

It is not accidental that computerized evaluation of visual field data has been stimulated by the rise of automated perimetry. Automated perimetry is predominantly carried out by means of static examination procedures. The results are numerical and lend themselves more naturally to further processing than the results of kinetic perimetry. Automated perimeters are usually controlled by some programmable computer. The results of examinations are available in memory (or even stored permanently, as is the case with the Octopus models 201 and 2000), so can be made available for further processing. The provision of supplementary programs aimed at assisting the evaluation of data is a most tempting expansion of the system's capabilities. Automated perimetry has stimulated visual field research. Our knowledge of the behavior of normal fields (or categories of pathologic fields) has increased considerably and it has been described with more precise mathematical formulations. A large amount of material has been analyzed, and the results are available in terms of statistical descriptions. Again, it is tempting to put this knowledge to practical work in individual cases.

STATIC PERIMETRY: DATA STRUCTURE

Results of an Examination

Static perimetry determines quantitatively the differential light sensitivity at a set of about 70 test locations. At each location sensitivity is determined with an up and down bracketing procedure involving about four to six stimuli per test location. The results are expressed numerically, for example in terms of the threshold stimulus luminance (in apostilbs) or an appropriate logarithmic scale (in decibels) (see Fig. 14-1). Threshold values are valid only for the fixed examination conditions used, which in Octopus perimetry are a background luminance of 4 asb and a test spot diameter

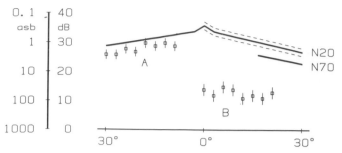

Fig. 14-1. Scale and order of magnitudes in static perimetry. Abscissa: test locations along a profile. Ordinate: contrast sensitivity; threshold stimulus luminance scale (in apostilbs) and decibel scale. N20: mean normal thresholds (subjects 20 yr of age) as obtained under OCTOPUS examination conditions. N70: same, 70 yr. Dashed lines: + − 1 SD of interindividual variance. (A) Marginally normal results; vertical bars indicate accuracy of single threshold determination (1 SD), typical for Octopus examinations. (B) Very advanced defects.

of 0.43 degrees, a stimulus duration of 0.1 second, and a white stimulus. All numerical statements (like current threshold, normal values, defect depth) will be presented throughout this chapter in terms of "decibel values" (dB) of the light sensitivity. As seen in Fig. 14-1, each threshold stimulus luminance value between 1,000 asb and 0.1 asb is arbitrarily assigned a decibel value between 0 and 40. Note that 1 dB is 0.1 log unit of the threshold stimulus luminance.

Fluctuations

In the following explanation, the so-called "threshold fluctuations" will play a decisive role.[8–10] This topic is treated in detail in Chapter 15. To summarize, if a visual field examination is repeated, the results are never exactly reproducible, and there are two types of fluctuations.

Short-term Fluctuation

Short term fluctuation is essentially the error of the threshold determination. It is due to the fact that dim stimuli near threshold are sometimes seen and sometimes not according to the "frequency of seeing curve" described in previous chapters. Because of short term fluctuations an immediate repetition of the examination usually does not produce exactly the same threshold value. The magnitude of scatter may be diminished by using more stimuli for any given threshold determination, but this increases the examination time. In the procedure applied in the Octopus system (crossing the threshold twice, and taking about five stimulus presentations per threshold determination), short-term fluctuations amount to about 1.2 to 1.8 dB (root mean square, RMS, ± 1 SD) for normal visual fields and they tend to be larger for pathologic fields. To some extent, a correction for the effect of short-term fluctuations may be accomplished by averaging the results of measurements from many test locations, but at the cost of losing possibly important information. This straightforward procedure will be taken up in later sections. Another, more time-consuming method consists of performing many examinations and averaging the several values obtained for each location, thus, in principle, defining the "true individual local thresholds" to any desired accuracy. When dealing with the results of only one or two examinations, short-term fluctuations limit the detectability of defects and of a local change between examinations.

Long-term Fluctuations

These are true but reversible changes of the thresholds between examinations that are days, weeks, or months apart. For normal visual fields this effect is almost negligible. However, long-term fluctuations may easily reach an order of magnitude of 1 to 2 dB or even more for pathological fields. In glaucomatous fields they are known to be predominantly homogeneous,[10] which means that they affect all the points in the visual field in the same way within one examination. Therefore, long-term fluctuations cannot be attenuated by averaging the results at different test locations within one exam. A pathologic change between two examinations must be greater than this physiologic long-term fluctuation to be recognized as a genuine pathologic change.[11]

Normal Thresholds

The normal threshold at a given location of the visual field is defined as the mean of thresholds measured in disease-free visual fields within a given age group at that test location. (In the Octopus perimeter the average normal values are stored in the systems software for all test locations, approximate age corrections being taken into account automatically. See Fig. 14-1 and 14-2.).

The average normal values serve as a reference when it comes to deciding whether or not the results of an examination correspond to a normal field. However, in critical applications normal distribution of true thresholds from one individual to another (at the same test location and within the same age group) cannot be neglected. The standard deviation of the interindividual variation is about 1.2 dB. In other words, the normal visual field is not described by precise average values, but only in statistical terms, with 96 percent of the population falling within 2 SD (i.e.; within 2.4 dB) of the stored average value.

Data Structure in Typical Situations

To accomplish mathematical analysis each location in the visual field can be assigned a number, represented as the symbol i. The symbol n represents the normal value and the normal value at a particular

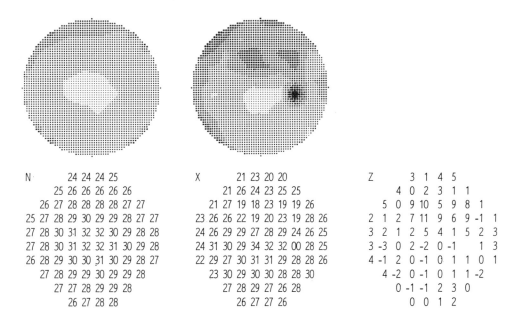

```
N    24 24 24 25              X    21 23 20 20              Z     3 1 4 5
    25 26 26 26 26 26             21 26 24 23 25 25            4 0 2 3 1 1
   26 27 28 28 28 28 27 27        21 27 19 18 23 19 19 26      5 0 9 10 5 9 8 1
 25 27 28 29 30 29 29 28 27 27    23 26 26 22 19 20 23 19 28 26  2 1 2 7 11 9 6 9 -1 1
 27 28 30 31 32 32 30 29 28 28    24 26 29 29 27 28 29 24 26 25  3 2 1 2 5 4 1 5 2 3
 27 28 30 31 32 32 31 30 29 28    24 31 30 29 34 32 32 00 28 25  3 -3 0 2 -2 0 -1   1 3
 26 28 29 30 30 31 30 29 28 27    22 29 27 30 31 31 29 28 28 26  4 -1 2 0 -1 0 1 1 0 1
   27 28 29 29 30 29 29 28        23 30 29 30 30 28 28 30       4 -2 0 -1 0 1 1 -2
    27 27 28 29 29 28             27 28 29 27 26 28             0 -1 -1 2 3 0
    26 27 28 28                   26 27 27 26                  0 0 1 2
```

Fig. 14-2. Visual field status: evaluating the significance of defects. N: normal visual field of a given age group (numerical values are in decibels, see Fig. 14-1). X: individual field. Z: difference N − X (local defect depths). 30-degree-field OD. The grayscales represent the same data (N,X). Statistical tests for normality are based on table Z (see text). Octopus examination program 32.

location is represented in mathematical formulas as $n(i)$. The symbol x is used to represent the actual measured value in the field test, with $x(i)$ being the value at the particular location i. After an examination the data involved in the evaluation thus include a set of actual results [$x(1)$, $x(2)$, $x(3)$, etc.] and the normal values [$n(1)$, $n(2)$, $n(3)$, etc.], together with a more complete statistical description of the normal visual field of the patient's age group (Fig. 14-2). The difference between actual and normal sensitivities at each point is calculated by the formula $z(i) = n(i) - x(i)$.

(With the Octopus system, the table of the $z(i)$ is available with the so-called CO-printmode).

When it comes to deciding whether or not a visual field change has taken place between two examinations A and B data involved are the results $x(i,A)$ and $x(i,B)$, normal values are less important. The change of measured threshold from one time to another is symbolized as y and the set of local changes $y(i) = x(i,B) - x(i,A)$ constitute the "difference table" (Fig. 14-3). (With the Octopus system, the difference table $y(i)$ is available with program Delta).

```
X(A)    17 19 16 16           X(B)    18 16 19 12          Y     1 -3 3 -4
       17 22 20 19 21 21             19 20 15 18 15 19           2 -2 -5 -1 -6 -2
      17 23 15 14 19 15 15 22        16 24 11 12 19 09 15 18    -1 1 -4 -2 0 -6 0 -4
    19 22 22 18 15 16 19 15 24 22    17 20 22 17 12 13 20 16 26 21  -2 -2 0 -1 -3 -3 1 1 2 -1
    20 22 25 25 23 24 25    22 21    19 23 20 21 23 22 29    24 20  -1 1 -5 -4 0 -2 4    2 -1
    20 27 26 25 30 28 28    24 21    17 25 29 22 31 25 32    24 23  -3 -2 3 -3 1 -3 4    0 2
    18 25 23 26 27 27 25 24 24 22    20 20 19 22 22 26 22 24 25 15  2 -5 -4 -4 -5 -1 -3 0 1 -7
      19 26 25 26 26 24 24 26        20 26 30 27 26 25 29 23    1 0 5 1 0 1 5 -3
       23 24 25 23 22 24             27 27 22 17 20 24          4 3 -3 -6 -2 0
       22 23 23 22                   22 19 22 22               0 -4 -1 0

EXAMINATION A :  MEAN = 22.0    EXAMINATION B :  MEAN = 21.0    CHANGE :  MEAN = -1.0
                                                               DISTRIBUTION = -1.0 +-2.8
```

Fig. 14-3. Visual field change with time. X(A), X(B): same patient, examinations 6 mo apart. Y: table of local change (in decibels). Statistical tests for change of mean sensitivity or local changes are based on table Y (see text). 30-degree-field OD. Octopus, program 32.

IS THERE A VISUAL FIELD CHANGE WITH TIME?

This section is devoted to the problem of detecting changes of contrast sensitivity with time. In order not to obscure the basic ideas, and to show typical orders of magnitudes, the presentation refers to a numerical example; in a typical situation, two examinations have been performed, possibly weeks or months apart. An example of the data involved is illustrated in Fig. 14-3. We assume that the patient's short-term fluctuation, as determined from double determination of thresholds within the same examination (as is standard with many examination programs of the Octopus system) is $S_1 = 2$ dB, a commonly met value when dealing with pathologic visual fields.

Local Change

Let us first inspect the difference table between two examinations for marked local changes (Fig. 14-3, right insert). Whereas most differences $y(i)$ are of the order of ± 1 to ± 4 dB, there is one extraordinary change (it amounts to 7 dB). In view of the fact that this change exceeds the short-term fluctuation (which is the accuracy of single results) by more than a factor of 3, one might be tempted to take it as significant. However, this is not the case as may be shown with the following estimate of the probability that such a difference would occur accidentally due to short-term fluctuations. Suppose there is no actual difference between the threshold at any point between the examination, but that there is variability of measurement due to a 2-dB short-term fluctuation. It is not likely that the same value will be obtained at very many locations but there will usually be some difference between the two measurements. The standard deviation of the difference (S_2) will be the square root of two times the short-term fluctuation of the measurements, or about 3 dB in our example with a short-term fluctuation of 2 dB. Assuming then an approximate normal distribution of the local differences, 5 percent of the values are expected to exceed two times the standard deviation or 6 dB, even if it is assumed that no true change has taken place at all. In a typical examination covering about 70 test locations, this corresponds to about 3 to 4 points. Therefore, it is by no means astonishing to encounter one local change of 7 dB. In the terminology of statistics the observed change is not significant at a level of 5 percent.

We may draw several conclusions from this simple example. First, for medical practice one must recognize that single values in the difference table have much less significance than is generally assumed. For instruments not reaching the precision of threshold determination, as assumed above, the situation is even worse. Second, inspecting single differences may not constitute a very sensitive test; no attempt is made to attenuate the short-term fluctuations.

Intuitively, it is unlikely that two points that show a 7-dB change would happen by chance to be neighbors, and even less likely that three should be in a cluster. In an early version of the Octopus Delta program a cluster analysis was implemented, searching for correlated change in up to nine adjacent test locations. However, this version has not been widely distributed due to possible problems related to reliable interpretation.

Overall Sensitivity and Overall Change of Sensitivity: Reducing the Effect of Short-term Fluctuation

If a group of locations is considered together, the randomness of short-term fluctuations will cause some threshold values to be too high and others too low. These errors will tend to cancel each other out if the values are averaged over a region or over the whole field, thus suppressing the effect of short-term fluctuation. It can be calculated by routine statistical formulae that by averaging over the results of 70 test locations, for example, the measurement error is attenuated by a factor of about 8 (the square root of 70). Thus if short-term fluctuation produced an error of about 1.5 dB (1 SD) at any one point, averaging the results over 70 points reduces the error of the average to about $S_3 = 0.2$ dB (1 SD).

Such averaging techniques also reduce the error of the difference between the mean sensitivity of two examinations which assumes an accuracy of $S_4 = S_3 \sqrt{2}$ (1 SD), which amounts to about 0.3 dB for the present example. An observed change of mean sensitivities exceeding two times S_4 (0.6 dB in the present example) is then significant at a level of 5 percent. In the example displayed in Fig. 14-3 the mean change exceeds 0.6 dB and therefore is significant. An overall change of the threshold is much easier to detect than changes at single test locations; this is illustrated in Fig. 14-3. Whereas individual local changes are not significant in the present example, our simple estimate has established with a reasonable probability that the mean sensitivity was in fact not the same at the times of the two examinations.

Test for Change of Overall Sensitivity

The analysis as outlined in the above paragraph by means of a numerical example actually corresponds roughly to the t test well known in applied statistics. In more general terms, the essentials may be summarized. As in any statistical test, there is a null hypothesis; in our case, the hypothesis that there is no true change of mean sensitivity, but only independent, random local differences $y(i)$, which are due to shortcomings of the measurement procedure, i.e., lack of reproducibility of the response of the visual system. If the null hypothesis were true then the change of mean sensitivity (if solely

```
CONFIDENCE INTERVAL FOR MEAN DIFFERENCE / T-TEST
 (1) PATHOL. AREA      - 0.8 +- 1.2  (T-TEST: DATA DO NOT PROVE ALTERATION)
 (2) WHOLE FIELD       - 1.6 +- 0.8  (T:TEST: ALTERATION IS INDICATED)
```

Fig. 14-4. Octopus program Delta. Resident evaluation program. Section relating to *t* test for significance of change of mean sensitivity.

due to the short-term fluctuations) would be normally distributed (at least to a good approximation). With a probability of 95 percent the difference between the mean thresholds on two occasions should be within an interval from −R to +R, where the confidence limit R is to be estimated from

$$R = t \times S_2/\sqrt{I}$$

Here, S_2 again denotes the standard deviation of the set of local differences y(i), I is the number of test locations, and t is taken from the table of the t-distribution for I-1 degrees of freedom and 0.05 probability level (for I > 30, t amounts to about 2.0).

The magnitude of the actually observed change (C) of mean sensitivity may now be checked against the limit R, giving rise to one or the other of the two possible outcomes of the test. If C is within the range, then data do not disprove the null hypothesis, in other words, there is not enough evidence to conclude that there is a true overall change (at the chosen level of significance of 5 percent).

If C happens to be outside this range, then it may be assumed that the mean light sensitivities were in fact different (at the level of significance of 5 percent). Note that this will occur with a probability of 5 percent in cases that in fact did not have a true change.

Carrying out such calculations in the individual case is quite tedious without a computer. With the Octopus system this task can be taken care of by the Delta program.[11–13] Technically, its handling is very easy: the operator calls the Delta program and denotes the two examinations (or two groups of examinations) to be compared; corresponding examination results are then retrieved from the diskette where they are permanently stored. The program carries out the t test, together with other data reductions (like the table of local changes, mean sensitivities, etc.), and displays the result (see Fig. 14-4). Probably, the Delta program of the Octopus system was the first attempt to provide reduced data and an appropriate analysis of the results of perimetric examinations by means of a resident program on an automated perimeter.

What Does a Statistically Significant Change of Mean Sensitivity Signify?

As estimated, a typical value for the limit R of the 95 percent confidence interval of mean change is 0.6 dB in normal fields. In an empirical study with glaucoma-tous visual fields,[11] R was a bit larger, 0.8 dB on the average. This means that the t test applied to two examinations (having the presumed qualities) is able to assert that a statistically significant change at a level of significance of 5 percent has taken place, even if the mean change is as low as about 1 dB (depending on the given data).

What does it mean now in practice when a change is claimed to be statistically significant? For example, there may be a change of mean sensitivity of 1, 2, or 3 dB encountered from one examination of a glaucoma-tous field to the next, perhaps weeks or months later. On one hand, we can be reasonably sure that the overall sensitivity was not the same on the two occasions. However, the analysis is not complete without taking into account the homogeneous component of long-term fluctuations, which, for glaucomatous fields, are known to be of the order of 1 dB (1 SD). The meaning of the homogeneous component of long-term fluctuations is illustrated in Fig. 14-5.: the mean differential threshold actually fluctuates up and down from one examination to the next and it may be a statistically significant amount. Therefore, a statistically significant change of 1 to 2 dB (or even more) picked up by the t test may be real but nothing other than a physiologic reversible variation in sensitivity. Under these circumstances, data provided by two examinations (like A and B in Fig. 14-3) are not sufficient to allow for reliable conclusions about the trend of the underlying pathological processes. Progressive deterioration of the field can be documented only if there is a continuous downward trend, or if the deterioration is too great to be attributed to these up and down variations (long-term fluctuations) in the fields.

This is an intrinsic problem of highly sensitive techniques of modern computerized static perimetry. The problem cannot be overcome by any instrument or any computer methods. The problem is that there is an actual slight change in everyones visual sensitivity from one time to another and this is the meaning of the term long-term fluctuation. At the present time, as far as glaucomatous fields are concerned, we are not aware of any other way to assess a trend reliably except to perform a series of examinations over extended periods of time.

The remarks in this section point to the extraordinary difficulties that one encounters in the reliable evaluation of perimetric data when the pathologic changes are small. The complex mathematic consider-

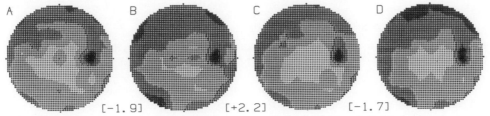

Fig. 14-5. Four examinations of the same pathological visual field. Interval: 2 mo. Though change of mean sensitivity (as given in brackets) was significant from each examination to the next, trend cannot be derived from one pair of examinations. This is due to long-term fluctuations (see text). 30-degree-field, Octopus examination program 31.

ations seem difficult to apply in individual cases. On the other hand, this strict analysis permits us to get closer to the actual behavior of visual fields and it also helps us avoid misinterpretations.

IS THE VISUAL FIELD NORMAL?

The purpose of the first examination of a visual field is primarily to decide whether it is normal or not and should there be any obvious defects, to classify them according to some scheme. As will be seen, both tasks have much in common, especially if they are approached by means of mathematical procedures.

Unless there are obvious defects decisions may be difficult[14] for two basic reasons; the measurements are necessarily subject to inaccuracies (as discussed above)

but additionally there is overlap of normal and pathologic fields.

Inaccuracy applies to apparently normal results as well as to disturbed ones. In static perimetry its magnitude is expressed by the patient's short-term fluctuation, which can be measured by double determinations within the same examination (this is done routinely in many examination procedures of the Octopus system) and expressed as the RMS of the variability. Again, it will turn out that knowledge of this quantity is essential in order to be able to discuss the significance of disturbed results and the detectability of minor deviations from normal.

"Overlap" of normal with pathological fields is illustrated in Fig. 14-6: though this visual field does not exactly look like an average normal field, it may be termed normal in the sense that it is perfectly stable, has never changed, and no disease has been detected. However, if it should have evolved, for example, within one year from a field looking like the normal field in Fig. 14-2, then it is most probably pathologic. Evidently, momentary pictures of intrinsically normal fields may look the same as visual fields that have already undergone pathologic change. This problem, of course well known in practice, will also find its counterpart in the statistical description of normal and pathological visual fields. Within the framework of a one-time examination the ambiguity can not be solved, not even by attenuating short-term fluctuations by means of averaging over repetitions of the examination. It is only when the examinations are repeated over extended periods of time that definitive information may become available. We shall mainly concentrate next on the detectability of early minor defects and on more advanced techniques of separating normal from pathologic results. Again, the computer is relatively unimportant as far as the basic issues are concerned. Computer methods help only by permitting statistical analysis of large amounts of data that might otherwise be impossible to handle.[15] This has led to considerable insight into the behavior of visual fields; and as a result, appropriate data reduction techniques are just now approaching application in individual cases[16]: they

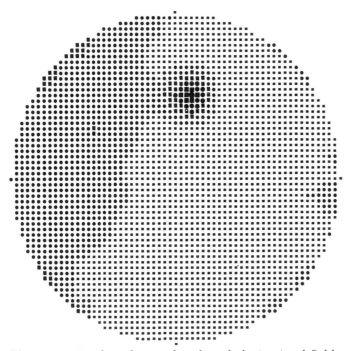

Fig. 14-6. Overlap of normal with pathologic visual fields. Though the result was perfectly reproducible, on the basis of a one time examination it cannot be decided whether the field is normal or abnormal. Individual normal fields may look the same as fields already having undergone pathological change.

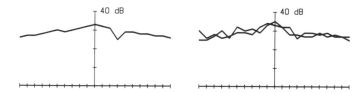

Fig. 14-7. Detection of marginal local defects. Left, individual true visual field profile as determined by averaging over many measurements (21 test locations, 30-degree field); one local defect, 5 dB deep. Right, same visual field; one measurement per test location (about five stimuli, accuracy 1.5 dB, 1 SD), two typical outcomes. The defect may be buried in noise, and pseudoscotoma may show up. Vertical scale: same as in Fig. 14-1.

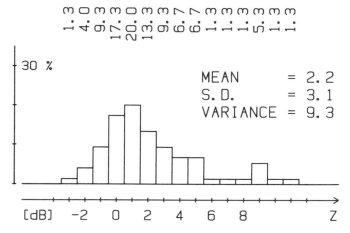

Fig. 14-8. Individual field, one examination; thresholds determined at about 70 test locations. Distribution of local defect depths z (same data as in Fig. 14-2, right insert). Main features of this distribution may be described in terms of a few indices (like MD, variance, skewness and others; see text) aimed at characterizing the individual field. Statistical tests based on these indices are outlined in text.

may soon be assisting the user of sophisticated computerized perimeters.

Detectability of Local Deviations from Normal

To begin with, let us again consider a specific example, symbolized in Fig. 14-7 (left). Assume that numerical results are available at 70 test locations, and that the patient's short-term fluctuation is 1.5 dB (i.e., the deviation of the measurement from the unknown true thresholds has a standard deviation of 1.5 dB; the error may be assumed to be approximately normally distributed). Let us further assume that the field looks normal and smooth, with the exception of one test location where the result deviates by 5 dB from the mean of adjacent values (Fig. 14-7, left). (Note that the point in question is not being compared with the normal value of that point but with surrounding points; in other words, one is looking for a scotoma).

At first sight, an event exceeding 3 SD seems to be highly significant. In the present context, however, it is not: in a normal distribution events outside 3 SD occur with a probability of 0.3 percent. If 70 points are examined and tested in one exam, 350 points will have been tested after five patients are examined. It would be expected that among the 350 points examined, 1 of them (i.e., 0.3 percent of 350) will deviate more than 3 SD. In other words, every fifth examination may display such a pseudoscotoma and accordingly its significance is low, occurring once a day if five patients are tested each day. (Even worse, the tails of the distribution may be more pronounced than expected from a normal distribution.)

It is important to note that the situation (Fig. 14-7, left) has been depicted too ideally. In fact, not even the true threshold profiles (obtained from averaging over many measurements) are so smooth and furthermore, short-term fluctuations are superimposed. A more realistic display of typical results is shown in Fig. 14-7, right panel. Now, decisions are even more difficult to make and looking for marked local defects may be the wrong approach. Why not assume that early defects

would affect several test locations? Why not analyze the entirety of tiny local depressions in order to find out whether it is significantly indicative of a departure from normal? In static perimetry this idea has recently been formulated most clearly by J. Flammer and colleagues,[15] using the terminology of statistical analysis.

The Basis of Visual Field Indices and Related Statistical Tests

We shall now consider the set of all results x(i) as a whole, instead of focusing on single test locations. More precisely, we are considering all local differences (also to be termed defects) z(i) = n(i) − x(i) between the measured results x(i) and the respective normal values n(i), assuming that the latter are known for the patient's age group.

In the terminology of statistics the set of the differences z(i) forms a distribution (see Fig. 14-8). It is well known that the essential properties of a distribution are contained in relatively few parameters, for example, the mean, and some measure of dispersion such as the standard deviation. Such standard measures of applied statistics can represent the local differences ("defect depths") z(i) for all the points that were measured in the visual field and compared to the normal threshold. The statistical measures to be introduced are listed in Table 14-1; a detailed account of their properties will be given.

These statistical measures possess remarkable properties and potential applications, among which their use in statistical tests for normality may be the most promising. First, they depend on not just some but all the measured thresholds of an examination, by means of an averaging procedure. They are not very

Table 14-1
Summary of Visual Field Indices

	Symbol	Type of early defect to which the index is sensitive
Mean defect	MD	All kinds of defects, especially those affecting a large fraction of the test locations; diffuse defects; uniform loss
Loss variance	LV	Any local irregularities of the visual field; nonuniform defects; medium or large number of marginal defects
Corrected loss variance	CLV	
Third central moment	M3	Low number of defective test locations (scotomas)
Skewness	Q	
Spatial correlation	SC	Clusters of defective test locations

dependent on an accidentally erroneous measurement at one spot but do detect a shallow defect covering a large area. Second we may hope that small threshold reductions covering several test locations produce a cumulative effect, even when no single local value of a dramatic nature can be spotted. Third, each of these indices has its characteristic dependence on the type and depth of defects; thus, each may pick up a different type of defect and the type of field loss may be classified in terms of a few well defined parameters. Finally, once their distribution is known for normal visual fields they may be used in the construction of statistical tests aimed at separating pathologic from normal behavior. This is the essential idea. Let us now turn to a detailed account of definition, properties, and our present knowledge of these visual field indices.

Standard Visual Field Indices

Mean Defect

The easiest way to think of the index mean defect (MD) is to consider it as the difference between the mean sensitivity actually measured and the average normal mean sensitivity for the points tested. It is actually calculated through the mathematically equivalent procedure of subtracting actual measured threshold of the individual from the "normal threshold" for that persons age at all points. These values represent the defects at each point and are averaged.[11] The word defect as it is used here does not mean abnormality but simply a deviation from the average normal value. In fact, there is a range of normal around the so-called

Table 14-2
Percentiles of the Interindividual Distribution of Visual Field Indices, as Obtained from Normal Visual Field Studies

	M		LV		CLV		M3		Q		
Study	A	B	A	B	A	B	A	B	A	B	C
50%	−0.1	−0.2	2.5	3.1	0.8	0.8	1	0	0.4	0.0	
84%	1.2	1.0	4.5	4.1	1.6	1.5	6	2	1.4	0.4	
90%	1.8	1.5	5.5	4.8	2.2	2.0	11	3	1.7	0.7	0.8
95%	2.4	2.0									
IX(50-90)	2.0		3		1.4		10	(?)			

(Example: For 90% of normal visual fields, CLV is smaller than 2.2). See Table 14-3 for the characteristics of studies A, B, and C. IX denotes the increase from the 50th to the 90th percentile used in estimating the sensitivity curves as displayed in Fig. 14-9.

normal threshold and so also a range of normal for the index MD. The mathematical formula for MD is:

$$MD = \frac{1}{I} \sum_{i=1}^{I} z(i); \qquad z(i) = n(i) - x(i)$$

Where n(i) denotes the normal sensitivity at test location i for the patient's age group, and x(i) is the set of measured results. (MD may also be interpreted as the difference of the mean measured sensitivity from the mean normal sensitivity for the arrangement of test locations used.)

An average normal individual whose threshold values are in the middle of the normal range will have an MD of zero. In the normal population some individuals have sensitivity somewhat above or below average so that the standard deviation of MD is ± 1.2 dB, which means that 95 percent of the population is within the range ± 2.4 dB. The studies showing that are summarized in Table 14-2 (n was defined by linear regression with respect to age, slope 0.6 dB per ten years of age). Within the 95 percent interval the normal distribution constitutes a fairly good description with a standard deviation amounting to 1.2 dB. Up to age 70, the width of the distribution was not significantly dependent on age. The numerical values given in Table 14-2 will be made use of in related statistical tests.

MD is obviously affected within the limit of 2.4 dB (2 SD) by normal variation in retinal sensitivity. However, its usefulness is that it is also affected by all kinds of visual field defects, especially by overall depression, as well as by irregular diffuse defects spreading over large parts of the field examined. To give a concrete example, another slight uniform depression of 2.5 dB (or of 5 dB at half of the test locations) yields an MD of 2.5 dB, which is abnormal at the 5 percent level of significance (see Table 14-2). More advanced field defects will give an MD value that is clearly beyond the normal range. An obvious disadvantage of MD as a test

Table 14-3
Characteristics of Normal Visual Field Studies Used to
Derive the Distributions of Visual Field Indices
(see Table 14-2)

Study	A	B	C
Number of eyes	164	40	112
Number of subjects	130	40	62
Number of examinations	164	104	112
Age	20–70	20–45	
Instrument (Octopus)	201	2000	201
Examination program	JO	31	32
Test locations per exam (CA)	50	70	70
Threshold determination/exam/test location	2	1	1
Number of exams used to derive			
one value of MD, LV, M3, Q	0.5(*)	1	1
one value of CLV	1	2	
First examination used	Yes	No	No

A: from J. Flammer's normal field pool (preliminary data).
B: author's data. C: From W. Whalen and R. Brechner (1984).
(*) Octopus examination program JO consists of two independent phases, each carrying out threshold determinations at all test locations. Indices MD, LV M3, and Q were derived from each phase separately.

statistic for subtle defects lies in the fact that its determination relies on an accurate knowledge of the mean normal values n(i) for the patient's age group, or at least the mean normal sensitivity for the respective grid of test locations must be known for each age group. The efforts necessary to make MD a reliable test statistic therefore should not be underestimated. As far as the Octopus system is concerned relevant data are available, at least within the 30-degree field; however, for safe application in any individual case it will be wise to wait for the results of a normal value study being undertaken cooperatively by several users of Octopus systems in North America.

Loss Variance

The index MD gives the average loss over the entire region tested, for example, the central 30 degrees. Such a loss could be due to a uniform generalized depression due to glaucoma, diffuse retinal disease, media opacity, or (if the MD is small enough) simply a normal variation in sensitivity. An abnormal MD could also result from a defect in which one part of the field is severely affected and other parts are less affected or are perhaps normal. The index LV (loss variance) indicates to what degree the field is unevenly affected. Its potential usefulness is that when MD is only small and perhaps even in the normal range, the LV may be abnormal. This shows that there are localized field defects, perhaps slight enough to have had little effect on MD. In the case of a large MD, the LV could distinguish a generalized depression that could be due to several

causes from localized defects that are more specific for glaucoma.

To calculate the LV, the normal threshold value at each point is adjusted by the amount of the MD calculated for that patient. This is equivalent to assuming just for the moment that either the loss is just a variation from normal or that it is due to a uniform generalized depression of sensitivity. Then for each point the actually measured value is subtracted from the adjusted normal threshold. If the hill of vision is of a smooth contour and of normal shape, as momentarily assumed, these calculated differences will not be large but will simply reflect the usual slight inaccuracies of threshold measurement (short-term fluctuation). However, if there are marked irregularities in the hill of vision, such as scotomas, or grooves resulting from nerve fiber bundle defects, some of the differences will be large.

The calculation of LV involves squaring each calculated difference (to get rid of negative values), adding them up and, as is standard in statistical analysis, dividing by one less than the number of points involved. In statistical jargon this "loss variance" is defined as the intraindividual variance[15] of the distribution of the measured defect depths z(i):

$$LV = \frac{1}{I-1} \sum_{i=1}^{I} [z(i) - MD]^2$$

This index measures the dissimilarity of the local deviations z(i) from normal, irrespective of the arrangement of the defects. Again, the interindividual distribution, as obtained from normal visual field studies is given in Table 14-2.

As mentioned LV is by nature sensitive to nonuniform defects, to scotomas and to any irregularities of the results. In Fig. 14-9, an attempt has been made to characterize the different types of defects to which the two indices MD and LV are sensitive. To give an example, defects 4 dB deep affecting 25 percent of test locations are just sufficient to increase LV by 3 dB, i.e., to shift it from its interindividual average value (3 dB) out to the 10 percent level of significance (see Table 14-2). Note that the same model of defects affects the mean sensitivity by only 1 dB, not enough to be statistically significant at the same level. In other words, in the present example LV would constitute a more sensitive indicator than MD at the same level of significance (10 percent). Thus MD is sensitive to uniform generalized loss, whereas LV is more sensitive for localized defects and nonuniform generalized defects. A noticeable advantage of LV is that it does not depend on having absolutely accurate normal values because they are adjusted in any case by the MD for that patient. However, the values used for normal must be correct relative to one another (i.e., the slope of the hill of vision must be correct).

On the other hand, LV suffers from the obvious disadvantage that some irregularity is always present in

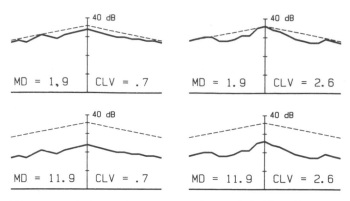

Fig. 14-9. Information content of visual field indices MD and LV (or CLV). Four different visual field profiles. From left to right: increasing loss variance. From top to bottom: increasing mean defect. Loss variance measures dissimilarity of local defects. (See text.)

the measured hill of vision because of variable responses or short-term fluctuation (or more exactly LV is affected by the square of the short-term fluctuation). In more general mathematical terms the mean square of the short-term fluctuations always contributes to LV. As a consequence if a particular patient responds more inconsistently than usual, he will have a larger value of LV, even though there were no intrinsic irregularities of the visual field. The way out of this problem by correcting for that person's own variability of threshold measurements is presented in the following section.[15]

Corrected Loss Variance

Simply stated CLV (corrected loss variance) is simply the LV from which is subtracted the square of the patients own short-term fluctuation (S_1) as estimated from double determinations of thresholds within the same examination. The formula estimating CLV is:

$$CLV = LV - S_1{}^2$$

The theoretical basis for CLV came about when it was realized[15] that intrinsic loss variance (or "corrected loss variance," CLV) defined by the variance of the true local defects $z_0(i)$ (as obtained, in principle from intraindividual local averaging over many repeated threshold determinations) would not depend on the patient's short-term fluctuations. In fact, the above formula may be converted to the following:

$$CLV = \frac{1}{I} \sum_{i=1}^{I} [z_0(i) - MD]^2$$

Both CLV and LV carry about the same type of information on visual field irregularities and their sensitivities to given true changes are similar. CLV is superior in that it does not depend on the individual short-term fluctuation but at the cost that more measurements have to be made. It is important that the measurement of the individuals short-term fluctuations, S_1 be accu-

rate. The accuracy of any parameter relates to the square root of the number of points measured. MD and LV are reasonably accurate, being based on measurements of 70 points (MD is about eight times ($\sqrt{70}$) more accurate than the measurement of any one point). The estimate of short-term fluctuation is based on only 10 points in routine Octopus programs and this may be sufficient for most purposes, but more independent threshold determinations at more than 10 locations (say, up to 30 locations) may be carried out depending on the accuracy of CLV desired.

As in the case of mean sensitivity or MD, the disturbing short-term fluctuations are thus eliminated, at least to a good approximation provided the number of test locations is not too small. The remaining inaccuracy of CLV may be estimated by standard methods of statistics. For normal visual fields the distribution of CLV is given in Table 14-2. The sensitivity of CLV to models of defects is indicated in Fig. 14-10. Note that neither LV nor CLV reveals where the defects are located.

Third Central Moment M3 and Skewness Q

As compared to mean defect MD, the corrected loss variance CLV (as well as LV) exhibits an enhanced sensitivity to scotomas or disturbances affecting the visual field nonuniformly. This is due to talking the squares of the z(i) in the computation of CLV or LV, whereas MD involves z(i) only linearly. Recently, it has been suggested[17] that we go one step further and consider the third central moment M3 of the distribution of the z(i) or similarly, its skewness Q:

$$M3 = \frac{1}{I} \sum_{i=1}^{I} [z(i) - MD]^3; \qquad Q = \frac{M3}{(LV)^{3/2}}$$

Theoretically, these indices are expected to be even more sensitive than MD, LV, and CLV to defects restricted to a very low number of test locations. However M3 and Q will be less sensitive to diffuse defects than the lower moments (MD, LV, CLV). Data on the distribution of skewness in normal fields are given in Table 14-2. The expected sensitivity of M3 to standard defect models is discussed in Fig. 14-10 but until further clinical validation is conducted it is premature to consider these potentially useful indices in more detail.

Spatial Correlation

Visual field indices introduced so far (MD, LV or CLV, M3 and skewness) do not account for the location of the defects. It may be useful to have indices not only aimed at detecting the presence of abnormalities but also to classify the type of pathologic visual fields. Such an index would not behave the same way when the abnormal points of a certain depth are arranged at independent locations (at random) as when they are arranged so as to form clusters.

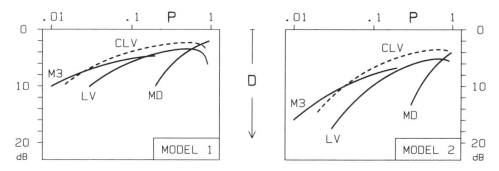

Fig. 14-10. Sensitivity of different tests for normality, based on visual field indices MD, LV, CLV, and M3. Model calculations. P: fraction of test locations assumed to be affected by defects. D (from top down): minimum defect depth necessary to increase various indices from 50th to 90th percentile of their interindividual distribution as derived from normal visual field studies (see Table 14-2). Higher moments (like M3, or skewness) of distribution of local defect depths are most sensitive for small number of defective test locations, whereas mean defect (MD) is most sensitive for large number of defective test locations. Models 1 (left) and 2 (right) are defined in text.

The index SC might be defined as the average of the value obtained when the corrected loss at each point is multiplied by the loss at each of its adjacent points. This value will be largest when two adjacent points have a large defect but will be lessened when a point with a large loss is multiplied by the value of an adjacent point with a small loss. The mathematical formula for such a standard measure of the density of correlated defects is given by:

$$SC = \frac{1}{N} \sum_{(i,\,j)} [z(i) - MD] \times [z(j) - MD]$$

where the summation extends, for example, over all pairs (i,j) of adjacent test locations; n is the number of terms summed up. SC tends to be very small if a small number of apparent scotomas are distributed at random or more generally, if defect depths at adjacent test locations are independent of each other. SC will increase if defects are clustered.

Further refinements of this concept are possible. For example, spatial correlation could be defined by extending the summation in the above formula over all values of i and j independently, but introducing a weight factor W(i,j) to be defined as some function decreasing with increasing distance of i and j.

Realistically, however, not much experience with the notion of spatial correlation is available and further mathematical refinement is out of place at the present stage. More urgently, we need to know in statistical terms to what extent early glaucomatous defects, for example, do cluster or if early defects often start as more widely scattered abnormal points. In any case, spatial correlation is certainly interesting enough to be studied, leaving open the question of applicability to the detection of early defects at least for the time being.

Statistical Test for Normality

This section is devoted to the application of standard visual field indices as introduced earlier, to statistical test procedures aimed at deciding whether the individual field is normal or abnormal. Considering only one specific measure, for example, mean defect depth MD, the way that a corresponding statistical test is set up is as follows: for normal fields the distribution of the test statistic MD is known (see Table 14-2); in particular MD is usually less than a cut-off critical value MD' of 2 to 2.5 dB, this magnitude is only exceeded by 5 percent of normal fields (1 percent exceeding a somewhat higher critical value). If in an actual case, MD turns out to be less than the critical value MD', then it is said in the terminology of statistical tests that "data do not disprove normality at the 5 percent level of significance." On the other hand, if MD exceeds MD', that "MD is not normal at a 5 percent level of significance." The generalization to other levels (i.e., 1 percent significance level) or to other indices (LV, CLV, M3, Q, SC) is straightforward.

In view of practical application it is of utmost importance to understand what such assertions do and do not mean. The first thing to be clear about is that the test will return about five erroneous decisions should it be applied to 100 normal fields. Obviously this percentage, the so-called level of significance, can be controlled; it may be lowered by choosing a larger critical value of MD but then of course sensitivity for detecting small true defects is diminished. While the behavior of the test in its application to normal fields can thus be known, the meaning of the level of significance in practical applications to mixed populations containing both normals and abnormals (and we do not know which person is which; that is why we do the test) is much more difficult to judge with confidence.

To make matter concrete let us assume, for illustration purposes that 90 percent of the visual fields tested in a given clinical environment are in actual fact normal and 10 percent are pathological. If a 95 percent level of significance is used then about 5 percent of normals will have a false positive test. Of 100 examinations about 15 thus would produce a "positive" result interpreted as pathological by the test. Ten of these are in fact pathological, but another 5 are due to false positive tests in normal individuals. Evidently, within the figures assumed in this illustration one third of the fields declared defective are incorrectly classified. This demonstrates clearly that the rigidity of the test should not be overestimated; nicely sounding assertions, like "5 percent level of significance" are often misinterpreted. It is important to keep in mind the lesson taught by this example: a 5 percent level of significance does not indicate that if a pathological result is obtained there is only a 5 percent risk that the test gave false positive or that there is only a 5 percent chance that the visual field is actually normal. Rather, the probability for this occurrence may be higher and was 33 percent in our example here. This will be one of the difficulties once statistical test procedures are made widely available in automated perimetry. This important point deserves to be made over and over again (see Chapters 5 and 10).

Available Programmed Assistance

The Delta program, which has been available and used on the Octopus since 1982 is able to process individual visual field results obtained with this perimeter. It has two modes of operation, series and change, which are aimed at different tasks. In the series mode it performs general data reduction, computing data like mean sensitivity (averaged over test locations; over the entire field, quadrant wise and for different ranges of eccentricity), mean, and total loss, and fluctuations. Up to six examinations may be included in the same run. The change mode aids in the evaluation of temporal changes (from one examination to the next or between two groups of examinations); the t test for the changes of the mean sensitivity, which is also a component of the Delta program, has been mentioned (see Fig. 14-4). The reader is referred to the Delta manual for details.[11]

As to the tests for normality, commercial programs are not yet available that perform at the level envisaged in this chapter. Nevertheless, for the Octopus perimeter an examination program is being developed[16] that calculates at least some of the indices discussed here immediately following the measurement. They are then printed out along with the test results. This "new glaucoma program" (now designated as G1) measures the thresholds at around 60 test locations in the central 30-degree region, either once or twice, as the operator chooses. If twice, then the necessary information is available for calculating the CLV index. If only one measurement per test locations is done, only indices such as MD, LV, M3, and/or Q can be made available. Moreover, these are less accurate due to the more limited information (i.e., only one threshold determination per test location). Much empirical experience must yet be gathered before one can consider using this test procedure routinely and unthinkingly. It is hoped that the recipients of this new type of program will share in its evaluation.

Judging the Sensitivity of Visual Field Evaluations

The reader must be warned that proposing some measure (for example MD, CLV, Q, or any other function of threshold results and normal values) on intuitive grounds is certainly nothing but a first step. So far, the sensitivity and practical usefulness of a particular statistical test relies solely on belief. Also, demonstrating that a certain index reacts in a seemingly impressive manner when applied to clearly abnormal fields does not yet prove anything. Rather, one has to attempt to clarify the sensitivity of the procedure at a given level of significane of the test and to compare it with the sensitivity of other indices by actual clinical trials. This task may be accomplished as follows.

First, the distribution of the proposed measure has to be determined carefully for normal visual fields of disease-free eyes. This will automatically account for inherent fluctuations. As a result, the critical limits will be known for given levels of significance (see Table 14-2); in other words, the probability that the test would produce a false positive answer when applied to a normal field can be controlled. This is important, especially if the efficiency of different measures is to be compared.

Assessing the sensitivity of the test is more difficult to achieve. While so far only normal visual fields were involved it is now the marginally pathological fields that are important. The goal may be approached along two entirely different ways or preferably along both of them. One is by means of empirical studies involving actual patients with early stages of pathologic fields. The other, purely theoretically, is by superimposing parametrized model defects onto normal results and studying the influence on the measures to be compared, taking into account, again, the critical limits for a given level of significance. In the next paragraphs these two methods are discussed in more detail.

Sensitivity of Statistical Tests: Empirical Studies

At first sight, a reliable approach seems to be barred by the problem of defining and selecting slightly disturbed visual fields. However, for the sake of comparing the efficiency and usefulness of different visual field indices in a realistic environment, it is actually sufficient and appropriate to define a population that may be assumed to contain a considerable fraction of slightly disturbed fields together with some normal fields and with more advanced stages of visual field disturbance. The distributions of the indices may then be determined for this mixed population and compared with the ones obtained earlier for fields that are known to be normal. In particular, the number of fields declared abnormal when a specific test is applied to the mixed population will emerge and these figures may be compared for the different measures. False-positive test results originating from the normal fields among the population under test, tend to drop out in the differential discussion by virtue of equal levels of significance; similarly, the cases with very definite defects may be assumed to be identified by any of the measures.

This outline is modeled on an excellent analysis,[15] in which the practical usefulness of the measures MD and CLV are discussed for a population of eyes with elevated intraocular pressure. Interestingly enough, it turned out that most of the defective fields are already identified by MD alone. Though one cannot exclude the possibility that the conclusions mentioned in this investigation are dominated by the relatively large number of clearly disturbed visual fields. It is possible that the importance of CLV for early defects is higher than that assumed here. In any case, CLV should be considered as a supplementary index still able to detect a minority of nonuniformly defective fields for which MD is not sufficiently sensitive.

Defect Models

As a preliminary and indeed as a supplement for actual clinical testing, much insight into the limits of detectability and into the sensitivity of different measures can be gained by theoretical mathematical modeling. This is done by computing the change of an index when assumed model defects are superimposed onto normal visual field results. Subsequently, we shall consider two models that have in common that the thresholds are left unchanged in a fraction (1-P) of the test locations. The assumptions concerning the defects in the remaining fraction P of test locations are given: model 1, defect depths are all the same, their magnitude being denoted by D; model 2, defect depths at the disturbed test locations are assumed to be independent random numbers with an even distribution ranging from zero to a maximum depth (D).

In both models defects are characterized by two parameters, P and D. Due to the simplicity of the assumed pattern of defects, induced changes of indices may be easily calculated; for example, the increase ILV of LV is given by:

$$ILV = D^2 \times P \times (1 - P), \quad \text{(model 1)}$$
$$ILV = D^2 \times P \times (\tfrac{1}{3} - \tfrac{1}{4}P), \quad \text{(model 2)}$$

From Table 14-2 (bottom row), the changes necessary to increase the medians of our indices to their critical values corresponding to the 10 percent level of significance amount to IMD = 2, ILV = 3, ICLV = 1.4 and IM3 = 10 (note that the estimate of IM3 is rather uncertain; fortunately, for the estimate of the critical depth of defect this is relatively unimportant since it is only the third root of IM3 which enters the formula for the critical D). Inserting these estimates into the formulas the corresponding critical defect depths can be figured out for any fraction P of defect test locations. The results are depicted in Fig. 14-10 for both models defined above.

As to be expected, MD is most sensitive to diffuse defects (i.e., P approaching 1) whereas M3 is most useful in cases where the number of defects is very small. Note that the results given in Fig. 14-10 also shed some light on the density a defect must have in order to be recognized as being significant. Again, requirements are considerably higher than what is often expected on intuitive grounds. It should also be remembered that the situation is certainly worse with examination procedures not reaching the level of accuracy as assumed here. Note that the sensitivity curve given for CLV in Fig. 14-10 relies on the assumption that two independent measurements are carried out at all test locations whereas one measurement per test location is sufficient for MD, LV, M3 (and Q).

CONCLUDING REMARKS

Possible difficulties with programmed analysis of visual field data are discussed as tests for change with time and as tests for normality. Some advantages however, are obvious:

1. Stability and clear definition of criteria for normality and for progression based on careful scientific study of the normal limits of visual fields and the nature of early defects.
2. Rapid computerized statistical analysis available even to users untrained in statistical test procedures.
3. Systematic use of all available data.
4. Avoidance of overestimating observed changes, if they are recognized by the program to be explainable by the short-term fluctuations.
5. Knowledge and control of the percentage of cases in which the test will erroneously be positive even though there is no overall change in actual fact. This percentage (i.e., the level of significance of the test) was chosen earlier to be 5 percent. Evidently, lowering this percentage means reducing the probability that an exceptional configuration of random errors

would make us believe a true change has occured. At the same time however, the sensitivity of detecting true changes is decreased.

On the other hand, we saw previously that statistical test procedures may constitute a misleading tool when their results are not interpreted carefully. The existence of these difficulties, however, does not mean that statistical tests are useless. It is at this point that we should devote a little thought to the choice of the level of significance and to the interpretation of the statistical results. Problems as mentioned above could of course be easily avoided by operating the test at a very strict level of significance (1 percent or less), at the cost of reduced sensitivity. In practice, this may not be the most useful approach. It may be preferable to proceed at a level of significance of 5 to 10 percent but to devote immediately one or two supplementary examinations to the cases failing the test for normality, especially when there is reason to assume that the results are marginal or doubtful in some way. The point of view adopted in this approach then is to use the test as a guide for proceeding according to well-defined schemes rather than using it as a tool for immediate and dogmatic decisions concerning the state of the visual field. In many cases, an immediate and reliable separation will not be possible for reasons which have been explained. Any contention that claims that a certain measurement or data processing procedure is able to establish a strict separation between normal and pathological fields should not be believed.

We have indicated the structure of the problems involved in a careful evaluation either of the normality of a visual field or the temporal progression. As far as one is concerned with formulating conclusions from data subject to error and judging their significance, one is actually involved with a standard problem in statistical evaluation methodology. Designing statistical tests requires excellent empirical knowledge of the statistics of normal visual fields (to establish significance). Further, one must also possess better knowledge of the statistics of typical pathological early changes than what we have at the moment (this in view of evaluating the sensitivity of various conceivable tests). Such working programs are however being developed and one can hope that they will be advanced with a systematic adequate amount of material and an even greater concern for methodology than has been possible.

REFERENCES

1. Frisén M: Evaluation of perimetric procedures: a statistical approach. Doc Ophthalmol Proc Ser 19:427–431, 1979
2. Niesel P: Zur Bedeutung der planimetrischen Evaluation der kinetischen Perimetrie mit dem Goldmann-Perimeter. Klin Monatsbl Augenheilkd 180:17–19, 1982
3. Frisén L, Frisén M: Objective recognition of abnormal isopters. Acta Ophthalmol 53:378–392, 1975
4. Susanna R, Drance SM: Use of discriminant analysis. I. Prediction of visual field defects from features of the glaucoma disc. Arch Ophthalmol 96:1568–1570, 1978
5. Drance SM, Schulzer M, Douglas GR, et al: Use of discriminant analysis. II. Identification of persons with glaucomatous visual field defects. Arch Ophthalmol 96:1571–1573, 1978
6. Krakau CET: On time series analysis of visual acuity; a statistical model. Acta Ophthalmol 47:660–666, 1969
7. Wirtschafter JD, Becker WL, Howe JB, et al: Glaucoma visual field analysis by computed profile of nerve fiber function in optic disc sectors. Ophthalmology 89:255–267, 1982
8. Bebie H, Fankhauser F, Spahr J: Static Perimetry: accuracy and fluctuations. Acta Ophthalmol 54:339–348, 1976
9. Flammer J, Drance SM, Schulzer M: The estimation and testing of the components of long-term fluctuation of the differential light threshold. Doc Ophthalmol Proc Ser 35:383–389, 1983
10. Flammer J, Drance SM, Schulzer M: Covariates of the long-term fluctuation of the differential light threshold. Arch Ophthalmol 102:880–882, 1982
11. Bebie H, Fankhauser F: DELTA manual. INTERZEAG AG, CH-8952 Schlieren, Switzerland, 1982
12. Bebie H, Fankhauser F: Statistical program for the analysis of perimetric data. Doc Ophthalmol Proc Ser 26: 9–10, 1981
13. Gloor B, Schmied U, Fässler A: Changes of glaucomatous field defects; analysis of OCTOPUS fields with programme Delta. Doc Ophthalmol Proc Ser 26:11–15, 1981
14. Fankhauser F, Bebie H: Threshold fluctuations, interpolations and spatial resolution in perimetry. Doc Ophthalmol Proc Ser 19:295–309, 1979
15. Flammer J, Drance SM, Augustiny L, et al: Quantification of glaucomatous visual field defects with automated perimetry. Invest Ophthalmol Vis Sci 26:176–181, 1985
16. Flammer J: A glaucoma program with characteristic visual field indices. Octopus Users' Society Meeting, Denver, Colorado, March 1984
17. Whalen W, Brechner R: Creation of the transformed "Q" statistic probability distribution to aid in the detection of abnormal OCTOPUS visual fields. Octopus Users' Society Meeting, Denver, Colorado, March 1984

15

Fluctuations in the Visual Field

Josef Flammer

When the visual threshold is measured several times at a location, the result is not always identical. The variability of the threshold value obtained has been termed "fluctuation," and is divided into a short-term and a smaller long-term component.

Short-term fluctuation is the variability of repeated measurements on one occasion. It depends in large part on the zone of uncertain responses for stimuli near threshold, which is described by the frequency-of-seeing curve. The amount of fluctuation is influenced by the visual sensitivity at the location, by whether or not the location is normal or defective, by the frequency of the patient's false positive and false negative responses in catch trials, and by the exact strategy used by the machine to determine threshold. In glaucoma patients the pupil size also influences the scatter, but age and reaction time of the patient does not. The short-term fluctuation is estimated in Octopus perimetry as the "root mean square" of differences between duplicate measurements at selected locations.

Long-term fluctuation is an additional component of the variability of sensitivity values obtained when the field test is done on a different day. This occurs because the actual physiologic state of the visual system (and the threshold at each location) undergoes an actual change up and down from one day to another. The level of sensitivity may be influenced by the systemic physiologic state but also by intraocular pressure and drugs on a given day. The long-term fluctuation is divided into a "homogeneous" component in which all locations undergo a change in threshold in unison (the entire hill of vision rises or falls) and a smaller "heterogeneous" component that accounts for the fact that the various locations do not change by the exact same amount.

The clinical relevance of the short-term fluctuation is that it limits the accuracy of threshold determination during field testing, and it must be taken into account when considering the clinical significance of one point at which the threshold is out of line. Statistical analysis may some day be able to make diagnostic use of the fact that the scatter is greatest in abnormal regions of the field. When interpreting a change in the field from one time to another, one must consider whether the change is simply a result of the long-term fluctuation or is a genuine pathological progression of the field defect.

The usual magnitude of the standard deviation of the short-term fluctuation is estimated to be 1.5 dB, of the homogeneous component of the long term fluctuation to be 1.1 dB, and of the heterogeneous component of the long term fluctuation to be 0.9 dB.

During quantitative static perimetry a threshold is measured for the differential light sensitivity at a selected retinal location for a defined background luminance, spot size, and exposure duration. The results of repeated thresholding at the same test location of the same eye are not identical, in fact they exhibit a scatter. This variability of thresholds of the differential light sensitivity is the topic of this review. This chapter deals with the origin and size of this scatter as well as with factors influencing it. The theoretical background as well as a summary experimental studies is discussed. Finally the theoretical and practical implications are discussed.

Before beginning to analyze this scatter, let us look more closely at the nature of the threshold that is being measured.

AUTOMATIC PERIMETRY IN GLAUCOMA
ISBN 0–8089–1705–6

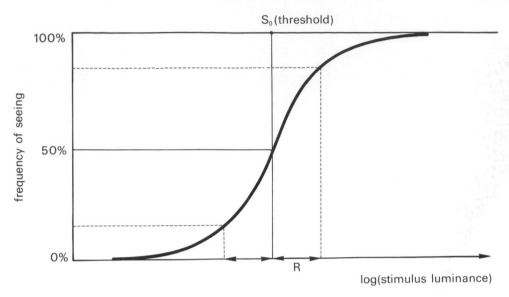

Fig. 15-1. Illustration of a psychometric function. The threshold So is defined as the stimulus luminance intensity with a 50% probability of being detected. R is the standard deviation of the cumulative frequency curve.

CHARACTERISTICS OF THE THRESHOLD OF THE DIFFERENTIAL LIGHT SENSITIVITY

Initially, our consideration will be given to just one test location of one eye. This retinal location has a threshold, which we would like to measure or better estimate. The measurement is a psychophysical test in which the patient can only respond "yes" (seen) or "no" (not seen). Barring inattention or false responses by the patient, for very dim stimuli the stimulus is never seen, and very intense stimuli are always seen. In between there is a range of marginally visible stimuli to which sometimes the patient fails to respond and sometimes he does respond. If we would like to have an accurate measurement of the "threshold," we have to present a large number of stimuli of differing intensity in this marginal zone and to plot a frequency of seeing curve (Fig. 15-1). This would allow us to know the threshold So, defined as the stimulus luminance intensity with a 50 percent probability of being detected. To measure the threshold of a test location in this way

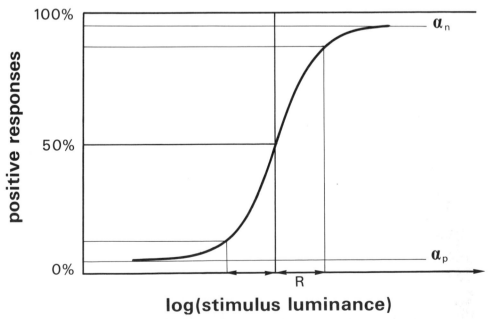

Fig. 15-2. Patients have a certain rate of false positive responses ($\alpha\rho$) and false negative responses ($\alpha\eta$). The probability for positive responses approaches but never reaches zero or one.

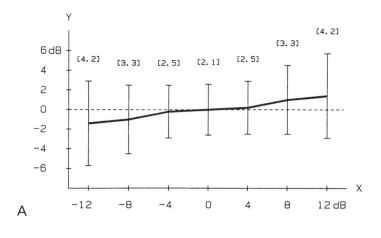

A

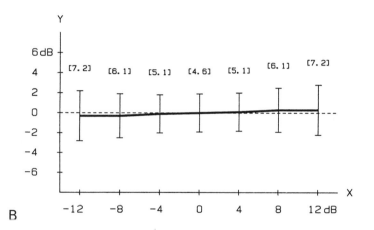

B

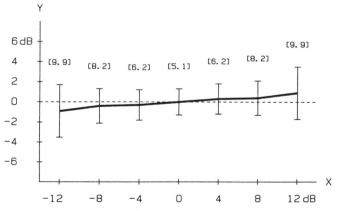

C

Fig. 15-3. Relationship between X (difference between first stimulus intensity and threshold) and Y (difference between measured threshold and real threshold). Plotted are mean ± SD calculated by means of computer simulations [R = 2 dB; α = 0.05]. The numbers in brackets indicate the number of stimuli needed to measure the threshold. (A) Method of limits. Step size 4 .., (2), (B) Up and down bracketing procedure. Step size 4 .., 2 .., (1), (C) Up and down bracketing procedure. Step size 2 .., 1 .., (1/2).

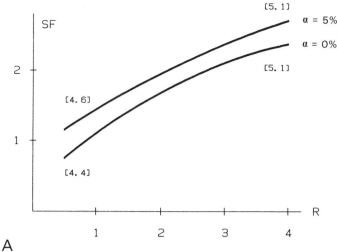

A

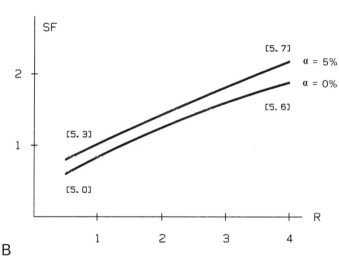

B

Fig. 15-4. Relationship between R and SF, calculated by computer simulation. X was assumed to be 0 ± 3 dB (normally distributed). (A) Step size 4 .., 2 .., (1), (B) Step size 2 .., 1 .., (1/2).

with a large number of stimuli is too time consuming for practical use. We are forced rather to estimate the threshold of a retinal test location by presenting only a few stimuli. The patient may happen to see a stimulus that he sees only 30 percent of the time and our measurement of his threshold (Sx) may differ from the actual strictly defined threshold (So) by some amount. These threshold estimations, Sx, scatter somehow around the real threshold So with a standard deviation sigma, σ.

This σ shall be our main topic. The size of σ depends on the actual threshold So and on the breadth of the transition zone around the actual threshold (see Fig. 15-1). The scatter σ also depends on the rate of false responses by the patient and the strategy applied to measure threshold.[1] Although the concepts necessary

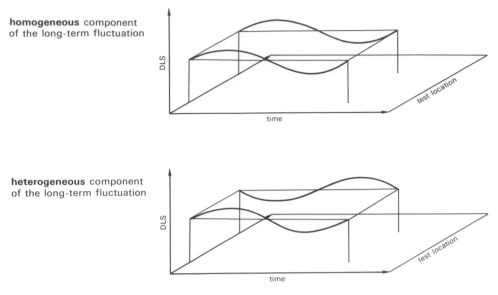

Fig. 15-5. Schematic drawing of two test locations showing an LF(HO) (in the upper half) and an LF(HE) (in the lower half).

for the clinician may be understood intuitively, the careful study and analysis of these fluctuations requires that they be expressed mathematically, which can be done as follows.

The breadth of the transitional zone around the threshold is expressed in the standard deviation R of the frequency of seeing curve. If we assume that this plotted probability curve can be approximated by a cumulative normal distribution,[2] the probability P(S) for a positive response as a function of the stimulus intensity S can be expressed as:

$$P(s) = \int_{-\infty}^{s} ds' \, \frac{1}{R\sqrt{2\pi}} \, e^{-(S-So)^2/2R^2}$$

Most patients, however, are not absolutely ideal observers since they have a certain rate of false positive and negative responses that are estimated on the Octopus perimetry by catch trials.[3] The probability for a positive response never quite reaches zero or one (Fig. 15-2). For the sake of simplicity, we shall assume that the rate of false positive responses $\alpha \rho$, is on the average equal to the rate of false negative responses, $\alpha \eta$ and this rate will be called α.

$$[\alpha = \alpha\rho = \alpha\eta]$$

The probability function is then modified in the following way:

$$P(s) = \alpha + (1 - 2\alpha) \int_{-\infty}^{s} ds' \, \frac{1}{R\sqrt{2\pi}} \, e^{-(S-So)^2/2R^2}$$

INFLUENCE OF THE STRATEGY

The real threshold will be called S_o, the outcome of our measurement S_x, the first stimulus intensity of the measurement S_1; $x = S_1 - S_{o'}$ and $y = S_x - S_o$.

An ideal strategy to measure the threshold would have the following properties: $y = 0$, implying no systematic error; $y \neq f(x)$, which means that the outcome of the measurement does not depend on the starting point, in other words, on our preknowledge of the threshold; The time needed to estimate S_o should be short, in other words the number of stimuli needed should be small; $\sigma \neq f(x)$, in the same way as for y, σ should not depend on the preknowledge; σ should be small, implying good reproducibility.

The optimal solution that approaches this goal is the "up and down method" used for example in the Octopus automated perimeter.[4] In this context we are especially interested in points 4 and 5. The superiority of the up and down method over the method of limits is illustrated in Fig. 15-3 with the aid of computer simulations.

We shall, therefore, confine the subsequent considerations of the scatter σ observed when using the method of the up and down procedure. Our experimental results are based upon data collected with program JO on the Octopus perimeter.[5,6] In program JO the so-called Octopus normal strategy is used, but the step sizes are half that of the other Octopus programs. Reducing the step size by a factor 2 reduces σ by about 20 percent.[1] Keeping the strategy used constant, σ is just a function of R and α, in other words of the character of the threshold to be measured and the ability of the patient to cooperate, a relationship represented in Fig. 15-4.

DEVIATIONS IN THE MIDPERIPHERY

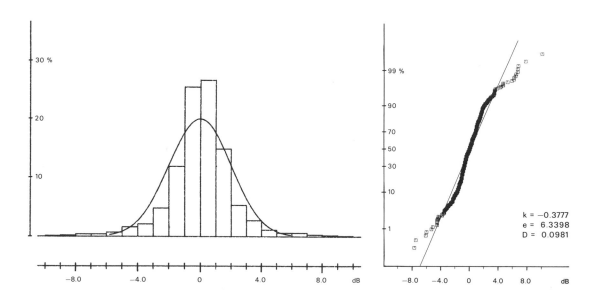

STANDARDIZED DEVIATIONS IN THE MIDPERIPHERY

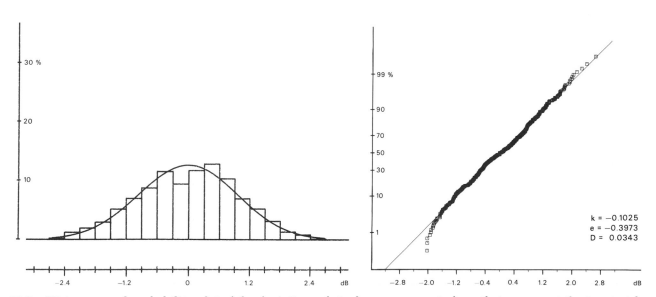

Fig. 15-6. Histogram and probability plot of the deviations of single measurements from their means at the two test locations tested ten times in each session using the Octopus program JO. Superimposed are calculated normal distributions with the same mean and SD. k = skewness, e = kurtosis, D = maximal deviation by Kolmogoroff-Smirnoff. (A) Midperipheral test location (x = −15° / y = +15°) (B) Central test location (x = 0° / y = 0°). [*From J. Flammer and M. Zulauf, Doc Ophthalmol Proc Ser.*]

DEVIATIONS IN THE CENTER

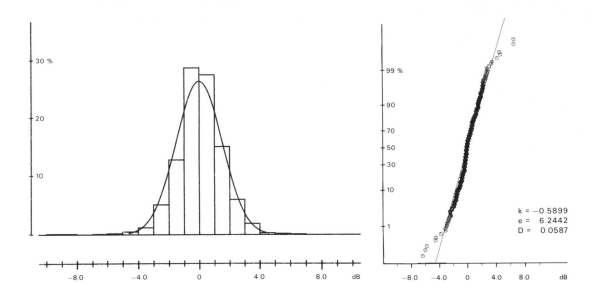

STANDARDIZED DEVIATIONS IN THE CENTER

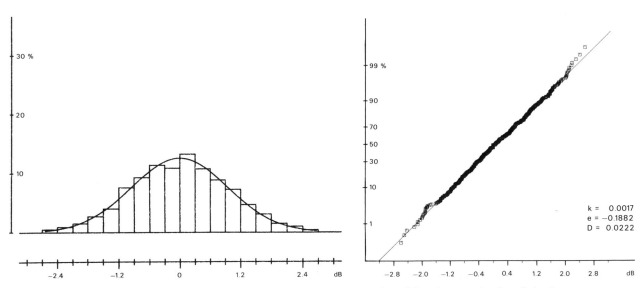

Fig. 15-7. As in Fig.15-6, but the deviations are replaced by the standardized deviations. These distributions are very close to normal. [*From J. Flammer and M. Zulauf, Doc Ophthalmol Proc Ser.*

THE COMPONENTS OF FLUCTUATION

At present our consideration remains limited to just one test location of one eye. The outcome of a repeated threshold measurement scatters with a standard deviation σ. The total variance (σ_τ^2) can be split up into several components of variance, the main components being the short-term fluctuation, SF(σ_s^2), and the long-term fluctuation, LF (σ_L^2). $[\sigma_\tau^2 = \sigma_s^2 + \sigma_L^2]$.[7,8] Using this relationship, we define the component of variance of the long-term fluctuation as the variation in the reading over time when the variation due to replicated measurements at a given time has been removed.

To calculate the component of variance, we can use the following model of analysis of variance[8]:

$$y_{lk} = \mu + V_1 + E_{lk}$$

y_{lk} is the individual threshold estimation of the chosen test location in the visual field test 1 on phase (or replication) k, is the overall mean value. V (visual field) is the effect of the individual field examination. This component is the LF. E is the experimental error evaluated on the basis of replications during each visual field test. This component is the SF.

Consideration can now be given to several test locations of a visual field simultaneously. Since the various retinal locations tested can show a homogeneous (uniform) change in the sensitivity as well as a heterogeneous change (different changes at different test locations), the LF has two components (Fig. 15-5).

Table 15-1
Correlation Coefficients Between The Components Of Variance (N = 31)

	LF (HE)	Test location	SF
LF (HO)	0.5590 (P = 0.001)	0.2170 (P = 0.121)	0.3146 (P 0.042)
LF (HE)		0.6605 (P = 0.000)	0.1600 (P = 0.195)
Test location			0.4086 (P = 0.011)

The first is the homogeneous component, LF(HO), and the second is the heterogeneous component, LF(HE). To calculate these components the following model of analysis of variance can be used:

$$y_{ilk} = \mu + L_i + V_l + LV_{ik} + E_{ilk}$$

y_{ilk} is the outcome of the threshold measurement on test location i in visual field test l on phase k. μ is the overall mean value. L (test location) is the effect of the test location. V is the effect of the individual field examination. The component of the factor V represents the LF(HO). L*V is the interation between L and V. The component of L*V represents the LF(HE). E is the experimental error. The component of E is the SF. The SF is estimated in the Octopus routine programs by replications at ten test locations and calculated as root mean square, RMS.

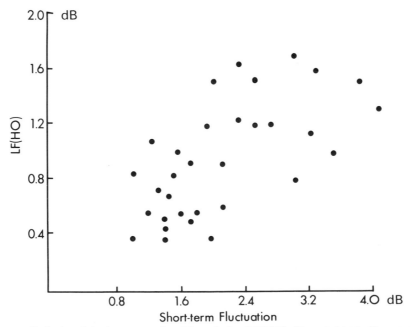

Fig 15-8. Relationship between the SF and the LF(HO) (R = 0.3146, P = 0.042). It appears that the long-term fluctuation is about half the short-term fluctuation. [*From J. Flammer, S.M. Drance et al., Arch Ophthalmol.*]

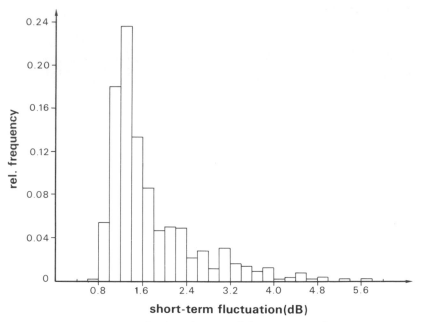

Fig. 15-9. Histogram showing the distribution of the mean SF of 265 eyes (86 normals, 110 glaucoma suspects, and 69 glaucomas). [*From J. Flammer, S.M. Drance et al., Arch Ophthalmol.*]

Based upon four visual fields per patient measured with Octopus program JO, we found in 6 healthy subjects, 15 glaucoma suspects and 9 glaucomas the following mean components of variance[8]:

$$LF(HO) = 1.2 \ (dB)^2$$
$$LF(HE) = 0.8 \ (dB)^2$$
$$SF = 2.1 \ (dB)^2$$

THE SHAPE OF THE FREQUENCY DISTRIBUTION OF THE DEVIATIONS OF THE SINGLE THRESHOLD MEASUREMENTS FROM THEIR MEANS

So far the scatter of the individual measurement of the threshold measurements was quantified with the standard deviation assuming a normal distribution. This hypothesis was tested on a large pool of visual fields and a distribution that is very close to normal was found.[3] If absolute scotomas are excluded the distribution is symmetric (no relevant skewness) (Fig. 15-6). By pooling heterogeneous material we may observe a positive or negative kurtesis. This can be avoided by taking standardized deviations (Fig. 15-7). There is no substantial difference between the points tested in the midperiphery and the center of the visual field. The deviations in normal areas are not only smaller but their distribution is also closer to normal than in relative scotomas.[2]

CORRELATIONS BETWEEN THE DIFFERENT COMPONENTS OF VARIANCE

One of the main concerns of the clinician is the recognition of a change of the visual field over time. This is made difficult by the LF. Comparing two visual fields, one does not know whether a real change or a reversible change due to the LF has occurred. This fluctuation can be observed in normals and is larger in glaucomas and glaucoma suspects. Comparing visual fields quantitatively by applying data reduction such as the calculation of the overall mean reduces the influence of the short-term fluctuation as well as of the heterogeneous component of the LF. The influence of the homogeneous component of the LF(HO) however remains unchanged. It would therefore be of special interest to be able to predict the LF(HO).

The different components of variance were correlated and without exception they showed positive correlations (Table 15-1).[9] Of greatest interest was the correlation between the SF and the LF(HO) (Fig. 15-8). Although there is a significant correlation between LF(HO) and SF (R = 0.3146; P = 0.042) it is too weak to allow prediction of the LF(HO) in an individual patient with sufficient accuracy. The LF(HO) is on the average about half as large as the SF (Fig. 15-8).

FACTORS INFLUENCING THE SHORT-TERM FLUCTUATION

Although the results of static perimetry always have scatter, there are a number of factors influencing the extent of this scatter. The influence of the strategy on scatter was already discussed. Other parameters will now be examined more closely.

In a first step,[10] the interindividual variation of the SF of 265 eyes of 180 individuals, normals, individuals with glaucoma, and glaucoma suspects was examined in a joint frequency distribution (Fig. 15-9). The SF was calculated for each visual field as the RMS of the local standard deviation. The average SF of each test location for normals, glaucoma suspects, and glaucomas was then calculated. The topography of the different sizes of the SF is shown semiquantitatively by a grayscale in Fig. 15-10. Up to the eccentricity of 27° measured by program JO on the Octopus, we found on the average no larger influence of the test locations or the eccentricity on the SF in normals and glaucoma suspects. The glaucomas, however, showed a more heterogeneous distribution of the average scatter in the upper half of the field (Fig. 15-10c), where defects are also more frequently found.[11]

A multiple regression analysis was used to test for other possible factors, taking the SF, averaged over a visual field, as the dependent variable (Table 15-2).[10] The main factor related to the SF appears to be the level of the differential light sensitivity; the higher the sensitivity, the lower the scatter. This is not only valid for the relation between the mean sensitivity and the mean SF of the total visual field but also between the local mean sensitivity and the local SF (Fig. 15-11). The scattergram shows further that the SF can amount to up to several decibels in relative scotomas. As shown before in a theoretical model (Fig. 15-4), the SF is also empirically related to the rate of false positive and false negative responses estimated by the catch trials (Table

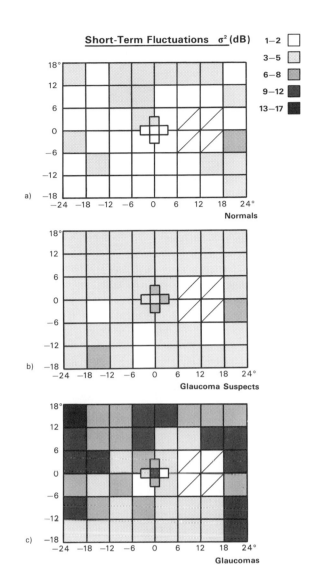

Fig. 15-10. Average local SF in each of the 49 locations tested with program JO. The SF seems not to be dependent on the location in normals and glaucoma suspects. There is, however, a slight tendency in glaucoma patients for a larger SF in the upper half of the visual field. [*From J. Flammer, S.M. Drance et al., Arch Ophthalmol.*]

Table 15-2
Multiple Regression Analysis with the Short-Term Fluctuation as the Dependent Variable

Variable	Normals		Glaucoma suspects		Glaucoma patients	
	Regression coefficient	F-value	Regression coefficient	F-value	Regression coefficient	F-value
Constant	1.562		1.478		1.313	
Overall mean sensitivity	−0.0180	36.72*	−0.0153	91.44*	−0.008	84.75†
False positive responses in catch trials	0.2495	21.14*	0.2140	19.91*	0.1621	6.43†
False negative responses in catch trials	0.2429	8.30*	0.0444	1.23	0.1322	7.40*
Age	−0.004	1.67	−0.006	3.32	−0.001	0.096
Pupil size	0.0060	2.97	0.0044	2.35	−0.0068	4.135†
Mean reaction time	0.0273	0.66	−0.0196	0.13	−0.20229	0.4153

* $P < 0.01$.
† $P < 0.01$.

Table 15-3
Analysis of Cavariance of the LF (HO)

Source variation	Sum of squares	DF	Mean squares	F	Significance of F
Main effect: patients	995.347	15	66.356	93.248	0.000
Covariates: reaction time	8.435	1	8.435	11.853	0.001
SF	17.051	1	17.051	23.961	0.000
IOP	2.790	1	2.790	3.919	0.051
Residual	54.794	77	0.712		

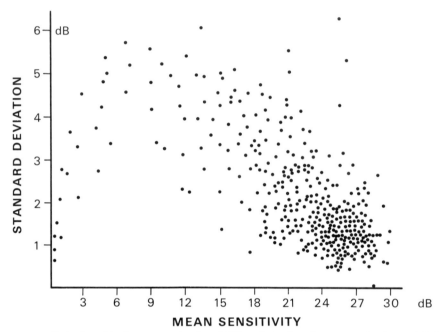

Fig. 15-11. Relationship between the local SF and the local mean retinal sensitivity at a midperipheral test location (−15° / +15°). [*From J. Flammer, S.M. Drance et al., Arch Ophthalmol.*]

Table 15-4
Square Root of the Means of the Variance Components in Three Groups

Component of variance of:	Normals	Glaucoma suspects	Glaucoma patients	Kruskall-Wallis test (P value)
	N = 43	N = 43	N = 43	
SF	1.6	2.4*	2.6*,†	0.000
LF (HO)	0.5	0.9*	1.2*	0.000
LF (HE)	0.2	0.4	0.5*,†	0.008
Test locations	2.1	2.5	5.7*,†	0.000

* Significantly different from normals
† Significantly different from glaucoma suspects } 3 $P < 0.005$ (Mann-Whitney Test)

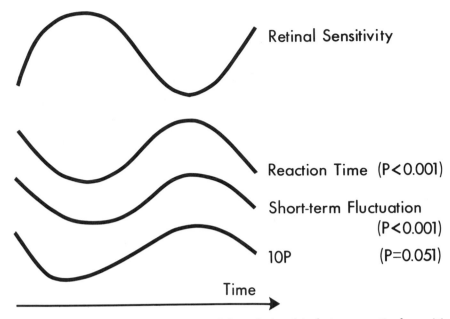

Fig. 15-12. Qualitative representation of the relationship between retinal sensitivity, reaction time, SF, and IOP. [*From J. Flammer, S.M. Drance et al., Arch Ophthalmol.*]

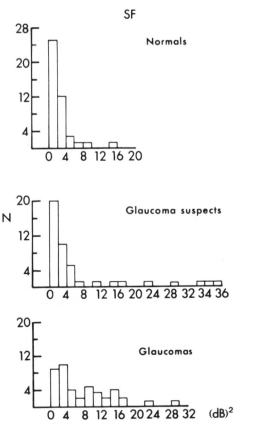

Fig. 15-13. SF variance component distribution across normals, glaucoma suspects and glaucomas. [*From J. Flammer, S.M. Drance et al., Arch Ophthalmol.*]

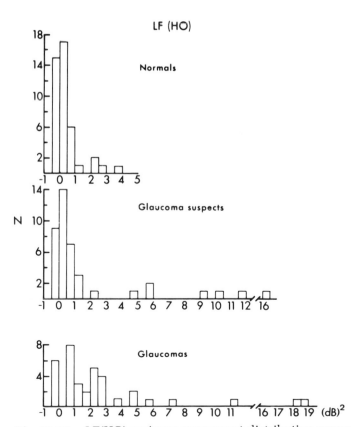

Fig. 15-14. LF(HO) variance component distribution across normals, glaucoma suspects and glaucomas. [*From J. Flammer, S.M. Drance et al., Arch Ophthalmol.*]

15-2). The higher the rate of false responses, the larger the SF.

The pupil size was significantly related to the SF only in the glaucoma group. The smaller the pupil, the larger the SF. Age as well as the mean reaction time of the patient were not significantly related.

COVARIATES OF THE LF

The short-term fluctuation was explained by the character of the threshold to be measured and the strategy applied. The causes for the LF are not yet established.

As a first approach to explain the LF, the relationship of the spontaneous homogeneous fluctuation of the retinal sensitivity to the spontaneous fluctuation of other parameters[9] was tested. The following model of variance and covariance was applied:

$$y_{ij} = \mu + P_j + (RT_{ij} - RT_i) + (SF_{ij} - SF_i)$$
$$+ (10P_{ij} - 10P_i) + \cdots E_{ij}$$

y_{ij} is the overall mean differential light sensitivity of the patient i on the visual field test j.

The mean differential light sensitivity of the whole group is μ, P the patient effect. The patient's mean adjusted values of the reaction time (RT), intraocular pressure (IOP), short-term fluctuation (SF), blood pressure, pulse rate, false positive and false negative responses, were studied as covariates. E is the experimental error.

There was a highly significant relationship statistically (Table 15-3) between LF(HO) and the variation of the SF so that when the retinal sensitivity was higher the SF was lower (Fig. 15-12). The relationship between the variation in reaction time and the variation in retinal sensitivity was also highly significant. At the time when the sensitivity was higher, the reaction time was usually shorter.

The LF of the retinal sensitivity was also related to the variation in IOP, although this relationship reached only borderline statistical significance. At the time when the IOP was higher, the retinal sensitivity was on the average lower.

THE SF AND LF IN GLAUCOMA PATIENTS AND GLAUCOMA SUSPECTS

So far the behavior of retinal differential light sensitivity largely independently of the diagnosis was analysed. We compared in a further step the components of variance of glaucomas and glaucoma suspects with age-matched normals.[12]

All the components of fluctuation showed a tendency to increase in size from normals through the

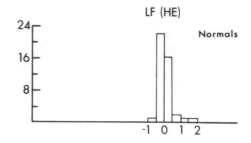
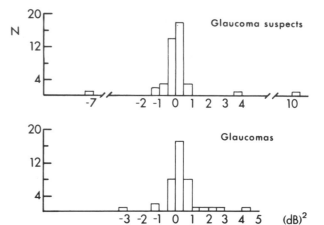

Fig. 15-15. LF(HE) variance component distribution across normals, glaucoma suspects and glaucomas. [*From J. Flammer, S.M. Drance et al., Arch Ophthalmol.*]

glaucoma suspects to the glaucoma patients (Table 15-4). The group of glaucoma suspects appears in this respect to lie between the two other groups. The frequency distribution of the components (Figs. 15-13, 15-14, and 15-15) reveals that the difference in the mean values between glaucoma suspects and normal individuals is produced by a few glaucoma suspects having large components, whereas the majority exhibited normal behavior.

The increase of the LF(HO) is of special interest. This indicates that the total island of vision can in some cases of glaucoma patients or glaucoma suspects move up and down quite remarkably, which has obviously practical implications for quantitative perimetry.

CLINICAL RELEVANCE OF THE FLUCTUATION

SF and LF are basic characteristics of the differential light sensitivity. The components of fluctuation are additionally increased in disturbed visual fields. These components however are also increased in patients with increased IOP and otherwise still normal visual fields. It seems therefore in some cases that an increased fluctuation can be a precursor of the glaucomatous visual field defects.[13–15] An increased scatter might therefore, on the one hand, be a helpful indication of early glaucomatous damage; but, on the other hand, it handicaps the recognition of a trend towards improvement or deterioration of visual fields. One needs therefore several visual fields to be able to recognize progression or improvement with sufficient accuracy.[16] This limited reproducibility should also be kept in mind when comparing different types of perimeters. Whatever reference field is taken, neither a very high sensitivity nor specificity is possible, especially regarding relative scotomas.

It can also be concluded that in glaucomatous fields one should not overinterpret the result of a measurement at a single test location but one should consider the results from all examined test locations by resorting to various forms of data reduction such as calculating global indices.[17]

ACKNOWLEDGMENT

The author would like to express his appreciation to L. Augustiny, H. Bebie, and A. Funkhouser for all their assistance.

REFERENCES

1. Bebie H, Fankhauser F, Spahr J: Static perimetry: strategies. Acta Ophthalmol 54:325–338, 1976
2. Flammer J, Zulauf M: The frequency distribution of the deviations in static perimetry. Doc Ophthalmol Proc Ser (in press)
3. Fankhauser F: Problems related to the design of automated perimeters. Doc Ophthalmol 47:89–138, 1979
4. Spahr J: Optimization of the presentation pattern in automated static perimetry. Vision Res 15:1275–1281, 1975
5. Jenni A, Flammer J, Funkhouser A, et al: Special Octopus software for clinical investigation. Doc Ophthalmol Proc Ser 35:351–356, 1983
6. Flammer J, Drance SM, Jenni A, et al: JO and STATJO: programs for investigating the visual field with the Octopus perimeter. Can J Ophthalmol 18:115–117, 1983
7. Bebie H, Fankhauser F, Spahr J: Static perimetry: accuracy and fluctuations. Acta Ophthalmol 54:339–348, 1976
8. Flammer J, Drance SM, Schulzer M: The estimation and testing of the components of long-term fluctuation of the differential light threshold. Doc Ophthalmol Proc Ser 35:383–389, 1983
9. Flammer J, Drance SM, Schulzer M: Covariates of the long-term fluctuation of the differential light threshold. Arch Ophthalmol 102:880–882, 1984
10. Flammer J, Drance SM, Fankhauser F, et al: Differential light threshold in automated static perimetry; factors influencing short-term fluctuation. Arch Ophthalmol 102:876–879, 1984
11. Nicholas SP, Werner EB: Location of early glaucomatous visual field defects. Can J Ophthalmol 15:131–133, 1980
12. Flammer J, Drance SM, Zulauf M: Differential light threshold; short- and long-term fluctuation in patients with glaucoma, normal controls, and patients with suspected glaucoma. Arch Ophthalmol 102:704–706, 1984
13. Werner EB, Drance SM: Early visual field disturbances in glaucoma. Arch Ophthalmol 95:1173–1175, 1977
14. Stürmer J, Gloor B, Tobler HJ: Wie sehen Glaukomgesichtsfelder, wirklich Aus? Klin Monatsbl Augenheilkd 184:390–393, 1984
15. Gloor B, Stürmer J, Vökt B: Was hat die automatisierte Perimetrie mit dem Octopus für neue Kenntnisse über glaukomatöse Gesichtsfeldveränderungen gebracht? Klin Monatsbl Augenheilkd 184:249–253, 1984
16. Holmin C, Krakau CET: Automatic perimetry in the control of glaucoma. Glaucoma 3:154–159, 1981
17. Flammer J, Drance SM, Augustiny L, et al: Quantification of glaucomatous visual field defects with automated perimetry. Invest Ophthalmol Vis Sci 26:176–181, 1985

16

Choosing an Automatic Perimeter

Charles D. Phelps

An ophthalmologist looking for an automated perimeter for the office may find the variety of choices bewildering. The purpose of this chapter is to provide the would-be purchaser with some guidelines to use when evaluating the various instruments. Listed first are some of the possible features that might be incorporated in the design of an ideal automatic perimeter. The features available in each of the presently available instruments are also briefly described.

The reader should keep in mind that no automatic perimeter will be perfect for every use or situation. The ophthalmologist shopping for a perimeter must determine those features that are important for his practice and select the instrument that most closely fulfills his needs.

It should be obvious to the reader that this list of requirements for an "ideal perimeter" reflects the author's biases and prejudices. Many of the features listed will seem unimportant to a practitioner who has a limited number of tasks that the machine should do. In addition, since low cost is one feature of my ideal perimeter, no instrument will ever have all the features listed. The greater the number of features, the greater the instrument's cost will be. Finally, the list of ideal features is not all encompassing; the ingenuity of instrument designers will soon invent features not yet imagined.

FEATURES OF AN IDEAL AUTOMATED PERIMETER

The Instrument Should be Fully Automated

Some instruments, such as the Baylor Visual Field Programmer (WCO/HOV, Inc., Bradston, Fl) and the Friedmann Visual Field Analyser (Clement Clarke International Ltd., Essex, England), are not really automatic. They do not present the stimulus without the assistance of a technician. Instead, they are mechanical devices that indicate to the technician where the stimulus should be manually presented in order to accomplish a predetermined test strategy. Although these semiautomated instruments control some of the technician variability that plagues conventional manual perimetry, they do not eliminate it. Only an instrument in which the stimulus presentation is totally controlled by a microprocessor removes technician variability from the test and can be classified as an automatic visual field testing device.

The Instrument Should be a Perimeter, not a Tangent Screen

Some instruments, such as the Automatic Tangent Screen (The Computation Company, San Diego, CA) and the Digilab 300 version of the Heijl-Krakau Competer, are tangent screens rather than perimeters. Although automated, they suffer from the same three defects that always made a tangent screen less desirable than a perimeter, even for manual visual field examinations.

First, with a tangent screen it is impossible to have the background illumination even and calibrated. Instead, the screen has "hot spots" and dark areas. In contrast, the spherical screen of a bowl perimeter can be uniformly illuminated by a single light source. This illumination can be easily calibrated with a light meter. (The calibration, of course, should be done automatically in an automated instrument!) Since perception of a stimulus depends on the difference between target and background illumination, an even and known illumination throughout the field is critical. Otherwise,

AUTOMATIC PERIMETRY IN GLAUCOMA
ISBN 0–8089–1705–6

the value of the stimulus will vary in an unknown manner from point to point throughout the field.

Secondly, with a tangent screen as the target moves away from the point of fixation it becomes further from the patient's eye. This causes it to subtend a smaller visual angle and to appear less bright. On the other hand, with the spherical screen of a bowl perimeter, if the patient's eye is located at the center of the bowl the target distance is always the same. Thus, the target subtends the same visual angle and has the same brightness wherever in the bowl it is presented.

Finally, with a tangent screen it is possible to test only the central field of vision. With a perimeter it is possible to test out to the absolute limits of the patient's field of vision. A few eye diseases impair vision only in the periphery of the visual field and can be evaluated only with a perimeter, not with a tangent screen.

The target size, intensities, and position should be variable

All of the automatic instruments use a stimulus light as a test target. The stimulus light is presented by one of three mechanisms: illumination of one of a fixed array of fiberoptic cables that insert into the perimetric screen, illumination of one of a fixed array of light-emitting diodes (LEDs) that are embedded in the perimetric screen, or projection of a light onto the screen. The latter is the most expensive to construct, because quick and accurate movement of a projected stimulus requires a very precise and rapid system of servomotores, but it is by far the most versatile mechanism for varying the stimulus.

A projected stimulus can be presented almost anywhere on the screen. The resolution on the Octopus 201 Perimeter, for example, is 0.1 degrees. This means that with appropriate programming the Octopus can be made to present stimuli as close together as 0.1 degrees anywhere in the bowl. The size, intensity, and color of a projected stimulus can be easily changed simply by inserting an appropriate field stop or filter in the path of the stimulus light.

In contrast, a fiberoptics system has little flexibility. The stimuli are of a fixed size and are placed in a limited number of locations. Although the stimuli can be presented individually, their brightness cannot be individually altered, and a typical testing program is run at the same level of luminance for all stimuli presented. If another luminance is desired, the entire program must be run again. Thus, fiberoptics instruments are more suited for constant-level suprathreshold screening than for threshold measurements.

An LED system offers more flexibility than a fiberoptics system because the brightness of the LEDs can easily be individually altered. However, the LEDs are still fixed in position and size.

It is fair to state that the fixed stimulus position of the fiberoptic and LED instruments is not a great limitation if the density of positions is sufficient and if the stimuli are optimally located for detection and description of the most common types of visual field defects. Some of the available devices have between 200 and 400 lights within 30 degrees of the fixation target; this density exceeds the requirements of most test strategies.

The Fixation Monitor Should be Automatic and Continuous

Accurate fixation is a fundamental requirement for accurate perimetry. Exactly how accurately we should expect the patient to fixate is uncertain, because little research has been done about the effect on perimetric accuracy of tiny shifts in fixation. We know that fixation is never absolutely steady, even for the most conscientious and well-trained subject, and some tolerance for small drifts is necessary. However, patient responses must be discarded if fixation has shifted more than three or four degrees from the center.

Current instruments use one of several methods to monitor fixation. The simplest method, although one that is not automatic, is to have a technician view the patient's eye through a telescope or on a television monitor. Some television systems also have an automatic monitor that is triggered when the patient's eye moves a certain amount. All Synemed instruments incorporate a patented mosaic eye movement detector that quite accurately detects small movements; the detector's tolerance can be preset, and the instrument will reject all patient responses if fixation drift exceeds the preset tolerances. This device appears to be the most accurate of currently available automatic fixation monitors.

Many instruments use a "blind spot method" to monitor fixation. A stimulus is presented in the blind spot at intervals and, if the patient sees the stimulus, it is an indication of poor fixation. What is done with this information varies from instrument to instrument. Some perimeters simply record the absence of fixation as an index of the patient's unreliability, while others discard the last few patient responses, warn the patient, and renew the testing sequence. The blind spot method has two disadvantages. First, it is not continuous and may fail to detect large movements of the patient's eye if they take place between the blind spot presentations. Second, the tolerance of the system is uncertain; it depends on where in the blind spot the fixation test stimulus is presented and the direction in which the patient's fixation moves.

An ideal method, although one which is not yet available, would be a projection system that keys the coordinates of the projected test stimulus to the patient's eye position. With a very accurate monitoring system and a rapid servomotor system, the stimulus could always be projected at a known location in the patient's visual field, no matter where the patient might be looking. Although this sounds like science fiction, it is not. A similar eye-monitoring system has been used by the Air Force to aim the guns of a fighter plane simply by having the pilot look at the target!

A Sufficient Variety of Stimulus Presentation Software Programs Should be Available

No one program is adequate for every purpose. Instead, a number of test strategies must be available, so that the ophthalmologist can select the program or programs that are required for a particular patient.

For example, for rapid mass screening, one might select a program that presents a suprathreshold target at a limited number of test loci selected because of their frequent involvement in common visual field defects. To detect glaucomatous visual field loss, one might choose a program that uses threshold-related suprathreshold perimetry with a dense grid of target presentations in the paracentral visual field to detect paracentral scotomas, a number of presentations above and below the nasal horizontal meridian out to 60 degrees to detect nasal steps, and a few presentations temporal to the blind spot to detect temporal sector-shaped defects. To search for visual loss from a neurologic lesion, one might select a program that compares thresholds on either side of the vertical meridian.

It is desirable, but not possible with most automated perimeters, to have programs that are "intelligent." These programs, after detecting a defect with a suprathreshold screening strategy, automatically switch to a description strategy: they blanket the defective area with a denser grid of threshold determinations. This allows the perimeter to do automatically what every well-trained perimetrist does: after detecting a defect with a screening strategy, the perimetrist uses quantitative threshold perimetry (either static or kinetic) to describe the size, shape, slope, and depth of the defect as a basis for future comparisons.

The Perimeter Should Permit Both Static and Kinetic Perimetry

Currently available instruments use only static perimetry. No compelling case can be made at present for the use of automated kinetic perimetry, but the subject is worthy of future investigation. Software programs utilizing kinetic perimetry can be written for projection perimeters, but not for LED or fiberoptic perimeters.

The Test Strategies Should Have Built Into Them Methods for Estimating Threshold Fluctuation and Patient Reliability

The brightness threshold measured in perimetry has an inherent variability. If measured several times, the threshold at a given point will differ slightly each time. The inherent fluctuation varies from patient to patient, from normal to abnormal areas of the field, and from examination to examination. It is the background noise against which abnormality or change must be determined. By repeat testing at a number of locations, one can estimate the short-term threshold fluctuation. This information is necessary in order to judge if a field defect has changed on subsequent examinations.

The reliability of a patient's performance depends on the patient's attentiveness, cooperation, and understanding. Reliability can best be determined by a number of catch trials in which either no stimulus or a markedly suprathreshold stimulus is presented.

The Computer Should Have Stored in its Memory Age-Standardized Data from a Large Number of Normal Subjects

The determination of whether a slight elevation of threshold is normal or abnormal depends on a knowledge of the average normal threshold and its variance in normal subjects tested on the same instrument, under the same conditions, at the same test locus.

The User Should be Able to Write Software Programs

This feature is likely to be of more interest to the researcher than to the clinician, as long as the standard programs provided with the perimeter are sufficiently varied and well written. Most clinicians have neither the time nor the expertise to write their own software. However, it is crucial that researchers be able to write their own test programs. New knowledge about perimetry will come only from the exploration of new testing strategies, and it is short-sighted for a company to sell a perimeter run by a computer that can be accessed only by the company's programs.

It Should be Possible to Store the Data and Retrieve it at a Later Data

This is necessary to prevent loss of data if hard copies are lost or destroyed. It is required if a computer is to compare fields tested on different days. It is also necessary if, for purposes of research or record keeping, one wishes to transfer information from the perimeter computer to a larger computer.

It is difficult to understand why some manufacturers have chosen to use microprocessors to control their perimeters but have not provided data storage.

The Printout of the Data should be Permanent and Easily Interpreted

Some thermal printers provide a printout that fades with time. If the data are not stored in the computer's memory, the record may be lost.

The method of data display varies from instrument to instrument, and most physicians find some displays more revealing than others. The printouts of some instruments appear to be cluttered and nearly incomprehensible to the author. Almost all displays take some getting used to, especially for the physician who is accustomed to looking at isopters plotted during manual kinetic perimetry. Graphic or grayscale printouts provide a quick overview, but a printout of the actual thresholds is necessary for a complete understanding of the test results.

Programs Should be Available that Permit
the Statistical Comparison of Data from
Two Different Tests

Currently, the Octopus Delta program permits this, to a limited extent. In the future, software programs will be written that allow the physician to calculate the probability that an observed change in threshold is disease-related and not just due to spontaneous variation. For instance, some programs will analyze a series of fields for trends, and others will compare the change in clusters of test loci, such as a group of points arranged along a nerve fiber pathway,[1] with the change in the field as a whole. The latter will be especially valuable if compared to the average threshold change in the remainder of the field.

The instrument should be inexpensive,
sturdy, and easy to run

Perimetry must be affordable. The Octopus 201 perimeter that is used in the author's hospital costs about $90,000. If about six patients per day are tested, each patient must be charged $55 to $60 for the hospital to break even. About one third of this amount goes to pay for the cost of the instrument, and the other two thirds goes to pay for upkeep, repairs, overhead, and a technician. If our perimeter had cost $15,000, the hospital would break even at about $40 per patient.

Equipment breakdowns are likely with any perimeter. A prospective buyer of any instrument would do well to obtain the names of other ophthalmologists who have purchased the instrument and find out from them how frequently the instrument has needed repairs, how quickly these were accomplished, and how expensive they were.

FEATURES OF PRESENTLY AVAILABLE INSTRUMENTS

In table 16-1, some features of currently available instruments are listed. This information was up-to-date in January, 1984.

The author was limited in preparation of this table by lack of firsthand experience with several of the instruments. To overcome this obstacle, information was solicited from all manufacturers regarding their instruments, many salesmen and company representatives were questioned, instruments exhibited at scientific meetings were examined, and the excellent consumer guide prepared by Keltner and Johnson was consulted.[2] Nevertheless, hands-on experience with all of the instruments would have been preferred before an attempt to critically compare their features.

A final caveat is that the field of automatic perimetry is changing rapidly, and new instruments and new features are added to product lines almost monthly. Much of the information presented here about specific features of specific instruments thus may be outdated by the time it is published.

CONCLUSION

One final word to the ophthalmologist who is for the first time entering the world of automatic perimetry. Whatever instruments you select, it is likely to be superior in some respects to whatever manual method you now use. It will eliminate the vagaries of the technician, because the tests will always be done in exactly the same way. The random stimulus presentation that is used by all of the instruments eliminates much of the impetus for the patient to shift fixation and, thus, improves the accuracy of the test. The speed of the automatic bracketing strategies allows the instrument to obtain far more information in a given amount of time than can be obtained by any manual method.

On the other hand, there may always remain some patients with wandering fixation, slow responses, or other traits that make it difficult to comply with the automated test requirements. A skilled technician with friendly persuasion and other methods (e.g., noting only those responses that occur while fixation is straight ahead) can obtain diagnostically useful information that is superior to that obtained by an automatic instrument.

Moreover, there is one thing that automatic perimetry will not do. It will not replace the brain of the clinician. If anything, the ophthalmologist will have to be even more aware of the pitfalls of perimetry with automatic perimetry than with manual perimetry. The patient will still be sitting behind the perimeter, with inconstant attention, inaccurate fixation, and variable threshold. The physician will still have to select the right strategy for the purpose at hand. When interpreting the initial field of a patient, the physician will have to consider the expected normal values, whether the patient's refraction was correct, whether the defects

Table 16-1

A Comparison of Semi-automatic and Automatic Perimeters—1984

Instrument	Company	Price	Stimulus loci			Test Modes			Data display	Stores data	Programmable (by Owner)
			Total	Within 30	Fixation Monitor	Supra-threshold (const.)	Supra-threshold (Threshold related)	Threshold			
Semi-automatic											
Friedmann VF analyzer	Clement Clarke	3,000	97	97	No	×			Grid (manual)	No	No
Baylor VF programmer	WCO	3,995+ Goldmann perimeter	Kinetic in periphery	69	Telescope		×	Kinetic	Goldmann VF chart (manual)	No	No
Tangent screens (all LED)											
ATS 1	Computation	2,750	114	114	Blind spot	×			Grid of marked misses (manual)	No	No
ATS 2000	Computation	4,195	172	148	Blind spot	×			Grid of marked misses (automatic)	No	No
Digilab 300 (American modification of Competer)	Digilab	7,290		164	Blind spot			×	Numerical grid, loss of sensitivity	No	No
Fiberoptics perimeters											
Tubinger automatic perimeters	Oculus	14,500	249	191			×		Grid of missed points	No	No
Fieldmaster 101PR	Synemed	10,900	99	62	Eye movement detector	×			Grid of missed points	No	No
Fieldmaster 200	Synemed	16,000	113	82	Eye movement detector	×			Grid of missed points	No	No
Fieldmaster 255	Synemed	22,500	149	99	Eye movement detector	×	×	Meridional	Grid of missed points and profiles	No	Yes

(continued)

Table 16-1 (continued)

	Manufacturer	Price			Fixation			Output	Grid of missed points (grey grid) (Compaction of peripheral visual field)	?
LED Perimeters										
Peritest	Rodenstock	22,000	206	151	Blind spot	X			No	?
Dicon 2000	Cooper Vision	9,000–15,000	372	239	Blind spot and telescope	X	X	Grayscale, numeric	Yes	No
Dicon 3000	Cooper Vision	25,000	512	379	Television	X	X	Grayscale, numeric, profiles	Yes	Yes (Zeta)
Fieldmaster 50	Synemed	8,000–17,500	362	252	Blind spot, telescope, and eye movement detector	X	X	Grayscale, numeric, profiles	No	Yes
Projection Perimeters										
Humphrey field analyzer	Humphrey	14,000	Indefinite	Indefinite	Blind spot and telescope	X	X	Grayscale, numeric, profiles	Yes	?
Octopus 500	Interzeag (Clico)	15,000–20,000	Indefinite	Indefinite	Telescope (TV optional)	X	X	Grayscale, numeric	No	No
Octopus 2000	Interzeag (Cilco)	37,500	Indefinite	Indefinite	TV	X	X	Grayscale, numeric, gray grid, profiles	Yes	No
Octopus 201	Interzeag (Cilco)	89,500	Indefinite	Indefinite	TV	X	X	Grayscale, numeric, gray grid, profiles	Yes	Yes (Sargon)
Squid	Synemed	97,500	Indefinite	Indefinite	TV and eye movement detector	X	X	Grayscale, numeric, profiles	Yes	Yes

correlate with the ophthalmoscopic findings, and whether the test strategy chosen was sufficiently sensitive or overly sensitive. When comparing subsequent fields with the original, the physician will have to keep in mind the confounding effects of changes in pupil size, refraction, and media opacity, and the inherent short- and long-term fluctuations of thresholds. None of this will be done automatically!

REFERENCES

1. Wirtschafter JD, Becker WL, Howe JB, et al: Glaucoma visual field analysis by computed profile of nerve fiber function in optic disc sectors. Ophthalmology 89:255–267, 1982
2. Keltner JL, Johnson CA: Comparative material on automated and semiautomated perimeters—1983. Ophthalmology 90(9S):1–35, 1983

Index